DEMOCRACY AND ISLAM IN INDONESIA

Religion, Culture, and Public Life

RELIGION, CULTURE, AND PUBLIC LIFE
Series Editors: Alfred Stepan and Mark C. Taylor

The resurgence of religion calls for careful analysis and constructive criticism of new forms of intolerance as well as new approaches to tolerance, respect, mutual understanding, and accommodation. In order to promote serious scholarship and informed debate, the Institute for Religion, Culture, and Public Life and Columbia University Press are sponsoring a book series devoted to the investigation of the role of religion in society and culture today. This series includes works by scholars in religious studies, political science, history, cultural anthropology, economics, social psychology, and other allied fields whose work sustains multidisciplinary and comparative as well as transnational analyses of historical and contemporary issues. The series focuses on issues related to questions of difference, identity, and practice within local, national, and international contexts. Special attention is paid to the ways in which religious traditions encourage conflict, violence, and intolerance and also support human rights, ecumenical values, and mutual understanding. By mediating alternative methodologies and different religious, social, and cultural traditions, books published in this series will open channels of communication that facilitate critical analysis.

Democracy and Islam in Indonesia

Edited by

Mirjam Künkler and Alfred Stepan

COLUMBIA UNIVERSITY PRESS   NEW YORK

COLUMBIA UNIVERSITY PRESS

Publishers Since 1893

NEW YORK   CHICHESTER, WEST SUSSEX

cup.columbia.edu

Library of Congress Cataloging-in-Publication Data

Democracy and Islam in Asia / edited by Mirjam Künkler and Alfred Stepan.

     pages.   cm. — (Religion, culture, and public life)

    Includes bibliographical references and index.

    ISBN 978-0-231-16190-9 (cloth : alk. paper) — ISBN 978-0-231-16191-6 (pbk. : alk. paper) — ISBN 978-231-53505-2 (ebook)

   1. Islam and politics—Indonesia. 2. Democracy—Indonesia. 3. Indonesia—Politics and government—1998– I. Künkler, Mirjam, 1977– editor of compilation. II. Stepan, Alfred C., editor of compilation. III. Series: Religion, culture, and public life.

    BP63.I5D457   2013

    320.9598—dc23

2013000949

COVER DESIGN: Alejandro Largo

COVER IMAGES: Top: © Bay Ismoyo/Getty; Bottom: © iStockphoto

References to websites (URLs) were accurate at the time of writing. Neither the author nor Columbia University Press is responsible for URLs that may have expired or changed since the manuscript was prepared.

CONTENTS

ACKNOWLEDGMENTS

We are thankful to the Institute for Religion, Culture, and Public Life and the Center for the Study of Democracy, Toleration, and Religion at Columbia University as well as to the Henry R. Luce Initiative on Religion and International Affairs for funding research and conferences on democracy in Muslim majority countries such as Indonesia. Thanks also go to Melissa Van and Emily Brennan for their organizational assistance. The chapters of this book were improved greatly by the intellectually rich contributions by several other conference participants and colleagues to whom we want to give special thanks: Dodi Ambardi, Azyumardi Azra, Michael Buehler, Greg Fealy, Colm Fox, Robert Hefner, Nadirsyah Hosen, Jeremy Menchik, and Musdah Mulia.

BIN   Badan Intelijen Negara (National Intelligence Agency)
DPR   Dewan Perwakilan Rakyat (People's Representative Council)
FPI   Front Pembela Islam (Islamic Defenders' Front)
GAM   Gerakan Aceh Merdeka (Free Aceh Movement)
GDP   gross domestic product
Golkar   Golongan Karya (Functional Groups)
HMI   Himpunan Mahasiswa Indonesia (Islamic Students Association)
HTI   Hizbut Tahrir Indonesia (Indonesian Party of Liberation)
IAIN   Institut Agama *Islam* Negeri (State Islamic Institute)
JAT   Jamaah Ansharut Tauhid (Group for the Oneness of God Partisans)
JI   Jemaah Islamiyah (Islamic Community)
KOMPAK   Mujahidin Komite Aksi Penanggulangan Akibat Krisis (Mujahideen Crisis Management/Prevention Committee)
KPPSI   Komite Persiapan dan Penegakan Syariat Islam (Committee for the Preparation and Creation of Islamic Sharia)
LeIP   Lembaga Kajian dan Advokasi untuk Independensi Peradilan (Indonesian Institute for an Independent Judiciary)
LSI   Lembaga Survei Indonesia (Indonesian Survey Institute)

Masyumi	Majelis Syuro Muslimin Indonesia (Council of Indonesian Muslim Associations)
MMI	Majelis Mujahidin Indonesia (Indonesian Jihad Fighters Council)
MPR	Majelis Permusyawaratan Rakyat (People's Consultative Assembly)
MPU	Majelis Permusyawaratan Ulama (Ulama Deliberative Council)
MUI	Majelis Ulama Indonesia (Indonesian Ulama Council)
NGO	nongovernmental organization
NU	Nahdlatul Ulama (Rise of the Ulama)
Parmusi	Partai Muslimin *Indonesia* (Muslim Party of Indonesia)
PDI	Partai Demokrasi Indonesia (Indonesian Democracy Party)
PDIP	Partai Demokrasi Indonesia Perjuangan (Indonesian Democracy Party/Struggle)
PK	Partai Keadilan (Justice Party)
PKI	Partai Komunis Indonesia (Indonesian Communist Party)
PKS	Partai Keadilan Sejahtera (Prosperous Justice Party)
PNI	Partai Nasional Indonesia (Indonesian Nationalist Party)
PPP	Partai Pesatuan Pembangunan (Development and Unity Party)
TNI	Tentara Nasional Indonesia (Indonesian National Military)
WH	Wilayatul Hisbah (Sharia Police)

1602 Dutch East India Company established in Java.

1800 Dutch East India Company dissolved; Netherlands establishes Dutch East Indies (originally Java and parts of Sumatra) as a nationalized colony.

1870–1910 The Netherlands expands its authority to include much of what is now considered Indonesia (Celebes, the Moluccas, western New Guinea, Aceh, and Borneo come under Dutch control).

1908 The first nationalist movement, Budi Utomo (Prime Philosophy), established.

1912 Islamic grassroots organization Muhammadiyah (Followers of Muhammad) founded in Yogyakarta by K. H. Ahmad Dahlan.

1912 First mass-based nationalist party, Sarekat Islam (Islamic League), established.

1914 Founding of the Partai Komunis Indonesia (Indonesian Communist Party), known as the Indies Social Democratic Association until 1924.

1918 The advisory Volksraad (People's Council) convenes for the first time. Budi Utomo and Sarekat Islam accept representation in the council. Of thirty-eight members, half are appointed, half elected by local councils.

1925 The Volksraad gains some legislative powers: may sponsor laws, must approve budget.

1926 Nahdlatul Ulama (Rise of the Ulama) founded in Surabaya by a group of ulama (religious scholars) as a traditionalist response to the growth of modernist Islamic organizations.

1926–27 Indonesian Communist Party launches a revolt against Dutch colonial government in Java in late 1926 and in western Sumatra in early 1927. Both revolts are quickly crushed.

1927 Partai Nasional Indonesia (Indonesian Nationalist Party) is formed under the leadership of Sukarno.

October 28, 1928 A number of representatives of youth organizations issue the Sumpah Pemuda (Youth Pledge), vowing to recognize one Indonesian motherland, people, and language.

September 18–21 1937 The Islamic federation al-Madjlisoel-Islamil-Alaa Indonesia (Great Islamic Council of Indonesia) is created to unite Islamic organizations.

February 1942–August 1945 Japan invades and occupies the Dutch East Indies.

November 1943 The Japanese administration transforms the Great Islamic Council into a political party, Masyumi.

August 17, 1945 Sukarno and Hatta proclaim Indonesian independence. Japanese troops withdraw from the archipelago.

August 18, 1945 The 1945 Constitution takes effect. Pancasila is adopted as the national ideology.

August 1945 Sukarno is made president of the republic (1945–1967) and Hatta vice president (1945–1956).

September 1945–August 1949 Indonesian military fights war of independence against Dutch troops that seek to reoccupy the country. By 1947, the Dutch reclaim nearly all former territory except for parts of Java.

1948–1962 The Darul Islam (House of Islam) movement emerges to promote the Islamic State of Indonesia. Beginning in West Java, the movement expands to include movements in Aceh and South Sulawesi. The movement is not defeated by the Republican army until 1962.

August 1949 In response to international diplomatic pressure, the Netherlands agree to transfer sovereignty to an independent federal United States of Indonesia.

August 1950 Indonesia returns to the unitary 1945 Constitution. A seven-year period of liberal democracy begins.

1952 Nahdlatul Ulama splits off from Masyumi and becomes an independent political party.

April 1955 The first Asia–Africa Conference is held in Bandung, and the Nonaligned Movement is established.

September 1955 Indonesia's first free elections for a parliament and for a constitutional assembly are held. Nahdlatul Ulama Party, Masyumi, Sukarno's Nationalist Party, and the Communist Party each receives between 16 and 22 percent of the vote.

1956–1959 The Konstituante (Constitutional Assembly) deliberates over a new constitution; the Pancasila state model and the Islamic state model fail to garner a two-thirds majority.

1957 Sukarno establishes election-free "Guided Democracy" with support from a coalition cabinet of nationalists, religious parties, and Communists. With the declaration of martial law, the army begins to expand its role into economic and administrative areas.

1958–1960 Military leaders and Sukarno exile or imprison leaders of Masyumi. The party is formally banned in August 1960.

July 5, 1959 President Sukarno dissolves the unstable Constitutional Assembly and reactivates the 1945 Constitution by presidential decree.

1963 Indonesian military finally exerts full control over entire territory and crushes the last bastions of secessionism in Sulawesi and Kalimantan.

January 27, 1965 Sukarno signs Presidential Order No. 1 on the Prevention of the Abuse and/or Desecration of Religion. The order formalizes the Ministry of Religion's privileging of orthodox religions over syncretic and animist faiths.

March 1965 Sukarno holds the second Asia–Africa Conference in Bandung under the banner of Islamic unity.

September 30, 1965 Six generals are murdered in a failed coup attempt allegedly committed by Communists. The military leads a retaliatory pogrom, coordinated closely with Nahdlatul Ulama branches across the country. Killings total more than half a million. General Suharto starts to consolidate power and is eventually recognized as chief of staff of the army.

August 1966 The military commits itself to *dwifungsi*, the "dual function" of defense as well as political and economic stabilization.

March 1967 Indonesian legislature recognizes Suharto as acting president.

March 1968 Suharto formally assumes the presidency, marking the beginning of the "New Order."

1967 The Association of Southeast Asian Nations is formed.

1973 "Simplification of the Party System": parties are forced to merge into two proto-opposition parties—the four Muslim parties into the Partai

Persatuan Pembangunan (Development and Unity Party); the Christian and nationalist parties into the Partai Demokrasi Indonesia (Indonesian Democratic Party). Pancasila is reasserted as the national ideology.

1975–1976 Indonesia invades East Timor, a Portuguese colony since an 1860 treaty with the Netherlands, and establishes it as an Indonesian province despite significant local resistance.

1985 All organizations are ordered to adopt Pancasila as their sole ideological foundation (*asas tunggal*).

1990 Dr. B. J. Habibie establishes the Ikatan Cendekiawan Muslim se-Indonesia (All-Indonesia Union of Muslim Intellectuals) with Suharto's approval. The creation of the union was seen as the onset of a period of reconciliation between modernist Muslim intellectuals and Suharto.

1997 The Asian financial crisis devastates the Indonesian economy, forcing Suharto to seek assistance from the International Monetary Fund.

May 21, 1998 Suharto resigns from the presidency; Vice President B. J. Habibie is sworn in as president.

June 7, 1999 The first free and fair elections since 1955 are held. No party receives a majority.

September 1999 Referendum in East Timor results in secession from Indonesia amid much bloodshed. Full independence is achieved in 2002.

October 20, 1999 Abdurrahman Wahid is elected president by the Majelis Permusyawaratan Rakyat (People's Consultative Assembly).

October 30, 1999 Law on Decentralization permits regencies (at the sub-province level, approximately five hundred units) to pass their own laws in areas other than foreign policy, defense and security, monetary policy, the legal system, and religious affairs.

July 23, 2001 Wahid is impeached by a coalition organized by Amien Rais; Megawati Sukarnoputri is elected president by the People's Consultative Assembly.

October 12, 2002 A bombing in Bali's nightclub district kills 202 people; Jemaah Islamiyah (Islamic Community) is blamed for the attack.

August 5, 2003 A car bomb is detonated in front of the Marriott Hotel in Jakarta, killing 12 people and injuring 150.

October 2004 First-ever direct presidential elections are held; Susilo Bambang Yudhoyono is elected.

July 2005 The conservative Majelis Ulama Indonesia (Indonesian Ulama Council) issues a series of controversial legal opinions (fatwas) against liberalism, secularism, pluralism, interfaith prayer, interfaith marriage, and the heterodox Islamic Ahmadiyya (Followers of Ahmad).

August 15, 2005 Free Aceh Movement separatists sign a peace agreement with central government (Helsinki Memorandum of Understanding) providing for disarmament and national government troop removal from the province, ending a thirty-year conflict.

June 2008 A Joint Decree of the minister of religious affairs, the attorney general, and the minister of the interior calls for an end to the deviant religious practices of the Ahmadiyya and warns the public not to engage in vigilantism.

October 2008 Antipornography bill passed.

July 2009 Yudhoyono is reelected president.

April 12, 2010 The Constitutional Court upholds the 1965 law used to limit state recognition to six orthodox faiths: Islam, Hinduism, Confucianism, Catholicism, Protestantism, and Buddhism.

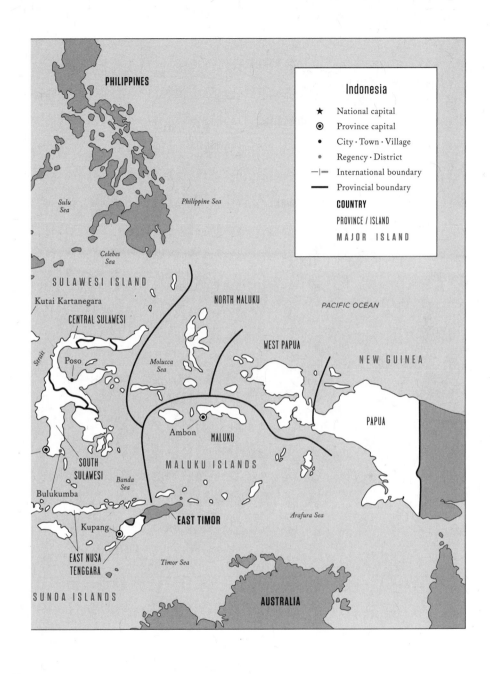

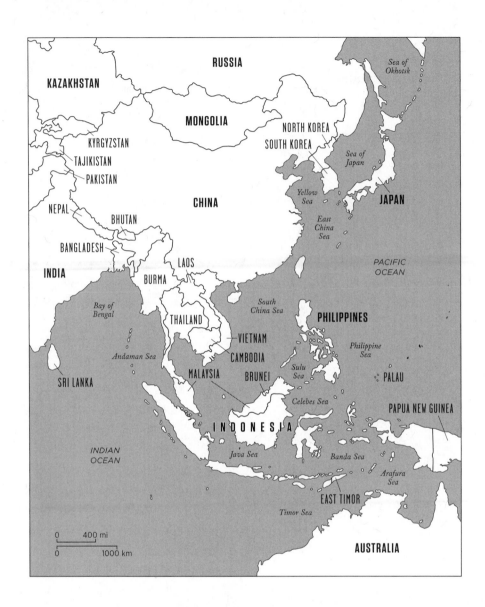

DEMOCRACY AND ISLAM IN INDONESIA

Part I
Introduction

Indonesian Democratization in Theoretical Perspective

Mirjam Künkler and Alfred Stepan

The democratization literature in political science does not have a widely used, full-scale volume devoted to democratic transition and possible consolidation in an Islamic country. Thus, our understanding of varieties of possible democratizations, especially how democracy can be crafted in Muslim-majority countries, remains impoverished.[1] This volume is an attempt to fill these lacunae.

Indonesia, the world's most populous Muslim-majority country, began a transition to democracy with the overthrow of Suharto in 1998 and now strikes most observers as a democratization miracle.

Indonesia declared its independence in 1945, but its "stateness" has often been challenged: by Dutch reoccupation of its major cities until 1949 and by secessionist movements in areas such as Sulawesi until 1967 and Aceh until 2005. The sheer size and diversity of its polity, scattered over seventeen thousand islands, speaking more than seven hundred living languages, and stretching across five time zones, have at times made Indonesia seem ungovernable.[2] Moreover, though the country is rich in oil, gas, tin, and copper resources, wealth has been unevenly distributed, and Indonesia's per capita gross domestic product (GDP, purchasing power parity) in 1998 was $2,266, with half of the population living under the two-dollar-a-day poverty line.[3]

From independence until recently, Indonesia had a history of weak parliamentary institutions and was ruled continuously by the military from 1965 until 1998. Moreover, at the beginning of the democratic transition in 1998, the country found itself in the midst of its worst economic crisis since independence, with –14.3 percent growth; indeed, Indonesia's per capita GDP did not consistently return to 1997 levels until the fifth year of the transition, in 2003.[4]

For all these reasons and the fact that Indonesia had a Muslim majority with what appeared to be growing violent militants, at the end of the 1990s the country seemed to many analysts an extremely unlikely candidate for a successful democratic transition, much less one to be talked about in terms of democratic consolidation.

But where does the country stand today? Surprisingly, in Freedom House's world rankings of "political rights," India, the longest-enduring democracy in the developing world, and Indonesia have since 2006 had an identical ranking, a 2, the second-highest possible score on the Freedom House seven-point democracy scale. Furthermore, Indonesia receives a score of +8 in Polity IV's twenty-one-point ranking of all countries in the world, where +10 is the most democratic and –10 the most autocratic.[5] Indonesia's combined democratic ranking by Freedom House and Polity IV has been better since 2006 than any of the nine other Association of Southeast Asian Nations countries, including Catholic Philippines, Confucian Singapore, and Muslim Malaysia.

In the context of its new political stability, Indonesia for the period 2005–2010 joined China, India, and Brazil as one of the world's fastest-growing economies. Furthermore, the Economist Intelligence Unit estimates that Indonesia's real GDP growth from 2011 to 2030 should continue at more than 5 percent per year. If so, the acronym used to designate the world's major emerging economies, BRIC (Brazil, Russia, India, and China) might have to change to include Indonesia.[6]

How did Indonesia go from thirty-three years of continuous military rule to civilian rule accompanied by dangerously heightened religious and secessionist conflicts and economic disarray from 1998 to 2002, then to completing its democratic transition by 2005, and ultimately to being a possible candidate for democratic consolidation in 2011?

The present volume brings together eleven leading political scientists, legal analysts, scholars of religion, and anthropologists to explore these questions. All the chapters are bound together by reflection on the issues of democratic transition and consolidation. In this chapter, we attempt to put Indonesia's challenges and achievements and the volume's structure in theoretical perspective.

Chapter 2, by R. William Liddle, often called the doyen of Indonesian studies in the United States, and Saiful Mujani, Indonesia's leading survey analyst, offer a conceptual and empirical overview of the end of authoritarianism in Indonesia, the beginning of the democratic transition, and the possibilities of democratic consolidation. In "Indonesian Democracy: From Transition to Consolidation," Liddle and Mujani address Indonesia's post-1998 political performance through the lens of Juan J. Linz and Alfred Stepan's conceptual approach to democratic transitions and consolidations.[7] The transition, Liddle and Mujani argue, was completed as early as 2004: the outgoing Parliament in November 1998 set a date for the country's first free elections since 1955; free and fair elections were held in 1999; the newly elected Parliament then democratized the Constitution in four rounds of constitutional amendments (1999–2001);[8] and, finally, the military's undemocratic participation in the legislature and the election of the president was eliminated in 2004.

Linz and Stepan outline in their framework three dimensions of democratic consolidation, and Liddle and Mujani analyze these three dimensions for Indonesia: the *attitudinal* dimension toward democracy both before and after the transition; the *behavioral* dimension, particularly of the key groups that have the capacity to possibly overthrow the democratic regime or fragment the state; and the *constitutional* dimension, whereby the new regime establishes not only a democratic constitution, but a series of horizontal and vertical checks, particularly on the state apparatus itself, so that the democratic regime itself is law bounded, transparent, responsive, and not solely majoritarian.

Although there is, of course, some overlap between attitudinal, behavioral, and constitutional dimensions, we have divided the volume into three additional parts based on these dimensions. Part II is devoted to citizens' attitudes, in particular Muslim and non-Muslim religious actors' attitudes toward democracy. Part III explores the behavioral dimension of three groups who could have overthrown the new democracy or fragmented Indonesia's precarious territorial integrity: the military, violent Islamists, and territorial secessionists. Part IV explores constitutional dimensions and the rule of law, especially the question of Indonesia's growing "legal pluralism," to examine whether there is indeed a sufficient degree of legal hierarchy for democratic consolidation.

Part II. Attitudes: The Development of a Democratic Consensus by Religious and Political Actors

In the literatures on secularism, liberal democracy, and democratic consolidation, two major areas concerning religious actors' attitudes are frequently debated and are particularly relevant for this volume. The first concerns whether religious actors are a positive or negative force for democratization. There obviously are numerous examples throughout history where various religions have played a nondemocratic role. However, at times religion has been able to act as a positive force, and how this has come about has been underanalyzed in much of these literatures. The second major debate concerns attitudes toward secularism and whether religion, even if it is a positive force, should be an active participant at all in the public sphere of a democracy. Indeed, John Rawls, the most famous twentieth-century political philosopher in the English-speaking world, argued that religion must be "taken off" the political agenda in order to build the "overlapping consensus" he saw as necessary for liberal democracy.[9]

Is Rawls's influential injunction that religion should be taken off the public agenda democratically and philosophically reasonable? In our analysis of Islam and democracy in the modern world, we believe that the case for putting Islam and democracy "on" the public agenda is strong in general and particularly strong in four arenas where democratic attitudes can possibly be developed: (1) core scholarship within Islam about religion, the state, and democracy; (2) public intellectuals; (3) civil society; and (4) political society. Consider the following set of hypotheses.

Assume a political situation within a polity where arguments are fairly commonly disseminated in the public sphere by religious and scholarly actors who make the case that modern democracy is incompatible with one or more of the following requirements of a good Islamic society: the need for a worldwide Islamic caliphate (and thus the illegitimacy of any democracy located in only one state); the requirement that God (not citizens or electorates) governs and thus that God-given laws (sharia), not man-made laws, must be obligatory for all; or the content of a Muslim state is spelled out in binding (and democratically restrictive) detail in the Qur'an. If a situation like this exists—and it does in many polities—the chances that tolerance and democracy will become a consensual sentiment in that polity are much greater if excellent scholarship on Islam is carried out and incorporated into public arguments that confront these arguments and help citizens create what Charles Taylor would call an "imaginary" of committed Muslims living—indeed, in Taylor's sense, "flourishing"—in a democracy.[10]

We also hypothesize that the chances for democracy becoming a consensual value in the politics of the polity will become even greater if some of the intellectuals who are engaged in core scholarly or at least conceptual development of a beneficial relationship between Islam and democracy are also public intellectuals. Such public intellectuals' task is to challenge antidemocratic arguments supposedly based on Islam as soon as they are articulated and to offer in the public sphere credible and attractive democratic alternatives via the creative and constant use of popular and elite press, radio, and television.

We also assume that the chances for winning Gramscian "hegemony" in civil society for democratic values and practices and for protecting a possible democratic transition and consolidation with ideological and organizational "moats" will be vastly increased if some of these public intellectuals are also leaders of major civil society organizations that are active and influential in the public arena for various reasons.[11] Leaders of such organizations might have many followers. This state of affairs would raise the cost to the authoritarian regime of imprisoning, torturing, censoring, exiling, or assassinating major visible civil society leaders. Such leaders might also create massive member networks that are engaged in activities that can become increasingly supportive of a more inclusive democratic politics and even available for resistance to the authoritarian regime.

Finally, we assume that if some of these civil society leaders become active in political society, it might increase the impact of their ideas in public life, help legitimate the key institutions of democracy for their followers, and give their organizations incentives and opportunities for entering into pro-democratic alliances and coalitions with secular activists who share democratizing goals with them.

In our judgment, none of the activities by religious actors in these public arenas necessarily violates democratic practices and what Alfred Stepan calls the "twin tolerations" (toleration of democracy by religion and toleration of religion by democratic leaders); indeed, they can advance such activities.[12]

Indonesia has the two largest member-based Islamic civil society organizations in the world, both of which have taken strong positions against Indonesia as an Islamic state and the establishment of sharia as the *only* source of law. Both also were strongly supportive of the democratic transition in 1998. One association, Nahdlatul Ulama (NU, Rise of the Ulama) has an estimated

35 to 40 million followers, drawn from a largely tolerant, rural religious tradition built upon Islam, with some additions from animism, Buddhism, and Sufism. In a survey in 2002, 42 percent of Indonesian respondents identified themselves with the NU community, and another 17 percent said they felt close to NU, although they were not affiliated. NU arguments about the state, religion, and democracy are well disseminated among its followers and even reach a broader public. The other large Islamic civic association in Indonesia is Muhammadiyah (Followers of Muhammad), a more urban organization that has what it calls a rational direct engagement with the Qur'an as well as approximately 30 million members, thousands of schools, high-quality universities that offer doctorates on secular and religious topics, and hundreds of hospitals.

In chapter 3, "How Pluralist Democracy Became the Consensual Discourse Among Secular and Nonsecular Muslims in Indonesia," Mirjam Künkler addresses the crucial question of how democratic attitudes emerged within the major Muslim civil society groups, NU and Muhammadiyah. She documents in great detail how key religious actors and organizations put Islam and democracy on the public agenda and in the process contributed both to the erosion of the authoritarian regime and to the building of democracy by their actions in all of the four public arenas and, as hypothesized, actually had a positive effect on eroding the authoritarian regime and supporting a democratic transition.

If we compare Egypt and Tunisia with Indonesia, the fact that NU and Muhammadiyah arrived at a consensus supportive of democracy before the transition began contrasts sharply with the situation in Egypt. Egypt's Muslim Brotherhood has not undergone a comparable change. Indeed, three months after Hosni Mubarak was overthrown in 2011, a resolution was still on the Muslim Brotherhood's Web site announcing that no woman or Christian could be president of Egypt, thus eliminating 60 percent of the population from the presidency. Also on the site was a suggestion that Parliament have all of its laws reviewed by a court of Islamic judges, thus limiting parliamentary power.

Alfred Stepan has argued that in Tunisia the leaders of the Ennahdha Party, Tunisia's moderate Islamist party, had arrived at consensual support for democracy beginning in the early 1990s.[13] However, because most of Ennahdha leaders were either in exile in England or underground in Tunisia at the time to avoid arrest, they could not develop the routine civil society educational and organizational networks that help socialize followers into democratic beliefs and practices in any way comparable to what happened in Indonesia. In Tunisia, although much of the work to develop consensual discourse on democracy was accomplished in the two decades before the end of the dictatorship, connecting that work with civil society is only now beginning.

Indonesia stands in even sharper contrast to Iran. Künkler, whose work compares the failed democratization movement in Iran with Indonesia's democratization movement, does not think that any person in Iran in the past twenty years has been able to sustain activity in more than one or at the most two of the four arenas.[14] In Iran, of course, there were some outstanding scholars who wrote on the need for democracy in Islam, such as Abdolkarim Soroush,[15] but none have been able to be as active in civil or political society as Indonesians; rather, they have faced credible threats of imprisonment, torture, exile, and sometimes even death. Likewise, in Egypt to date no one we have interviewed or read has made a convincing case that any activist has been effective in all four arenas for a long period of time. In fact, many of the prominent religious activists for democracy in Egypt under Mubarak were rapidly silenced by censorship, co-optation, imprisonment, or exile.

The Indonesian transition thus cannot be comprehended without attention to the constructive role that the large Islamic organizations played in fostering the pro-democratic attitudes and movements that helped weaken the authoritarian regime, facilitate the transition, and bolster consolidation efforts. Künkler's chapter broadens our theoretical and historical understanding of this phenomenon, which was one of the most important events of our times, and clearly raises fundamental questions about the wisdom and necessity of Rawls's injunction that religion should be *off* the public agenda.

The official state ideology in Indonesia since 1945 has been to recognize five religions (Islam, Hinduism, Catholicism, Protestantism, and Buddhism). Since the democratic transition, Confucianism (which some see as more of a philosophy) has been added to this list. The recognition that Indonesia is composed of many different religions is an essential part of the state doctrine of Pancasila. This doctrine emerged less than forty-eight hours after the leader of Indonesian independence, Sukarno, agreed to make Indonesia an Islamic state in 1945. This decision immediately met objections from some members of the independence movement who were not Muslims, from Hindus in Bali, from many Muslims who did not want an Islamic state, and from some still-present Japanese naval officials who argued that many of the outer islands had strong Protestant or Catholic majorities and would probably secede if Indonesia became an Islamic state. Sukarno, after intensive negotiations, substituted the doctrine of Pancasila in place of the doctrine of an Islamic state. In the Konstituante (Constitutional Assembly) debates of 1955–1957 and in constitutional debates at the beginning of the democratic transition in 1999–2001, the question of making Indonesia an Islamic state reemerged as a central demand by some Islamic groups. However, the idea of the state imposing sharia on all of its citizens was ultimately rejected during each of these constitution-making moments, and the idea of Indonesia as a home for many religions has been embedded constitutionally and broadly accepted. As democratization advanced in Indonesia, the vote share of parties that explicitly campaigned for state-imposed sharia declined from 14 percent in 1999 to 11 percent in 2004 and then to 7 percent in 2009.[16]

Not only are major non-Muslim religions officially recognized, but there is a degree of "co-celebration" of minority religions in Indonesia not found even in western Europe.[17] For example, in Denmark, Norway, Sweden, Germany, Netherlands, and Switzerland, there are fifty-four total compulsory paid religious holidays for the majority Christian religions, but *zero* for minority religions. In sharp contrast, in Pancasila Indonesia there are six compulsory paid religious holidays for the majority Muslim religion and a combined total of seven for the minority religions.[18]

Given the importance of non-Islamic religions within Indonesia, we are very fortunate to have as chapter 4 Franz Magnis-Suseno's article "Christian and Muslim Minorities in Indonesia: State Policies and Majority Islamic Organizations." Magnis-Suseno is an important participant-observer of interreligious relations in Indonesia who comes from a minority religion, Catholicism. He is a German-born Jesuit who is now an Indonesian citizen and was a major Catholic participant in pro-democratic, interreligious movements such as the Forum Demokrasi (Democratic Forum) organized, as Künkler's article discusses, by Abdurrahman Wahid (also known as Gus Dur), the three-time NU president. Magnis-Suseno asserts that "the astonishing fact is that relations between Christians [the largest minority religion] and Muslims, although still far from being without problems, are developing well." He goes on to say that, "undetected by most of the public, the democratic period has seen five major developments that I consider positive . . . for the deepening development of an inclusive, pluralist democracy in Indonesia." The most important development in his judgment is that "the Pancasila national consensus—that Indonesia belongs to all Indonesians—still stands essentially unchallenged."

However, Magnis-Suseno strikes a cautionary note when he argues that Muslims' interreligious toleration of other religions is greater than the Muslim majority's intrareligious toleration of the Muslim minority group Ahmadiyya (Followers of Ahmad), which offends orthodox Muslims because it does not recognize Muhammad as the last prophet and is thus seen as an inner-Islamic heretical group. For Magnis-Suseno, the major problem is not majority opinion, but state policy. Violent mobs occasionally attempt to burn down Ahmadiyya mosques, and the democratic state has failed to act quickly and robustly to defend citizens' rights and to uphold the law.

Part III. Behaviors: Challenges to the Democratic Transition and State and Their Transcendence

Notwithstanding the fact there had been a broad attitudinal consensus in favor of democracy in Indonesia, some strategically placed groups were seen as having the potential power to derail democratization or fragment the state: the military could have imposed great limits on the state's authority or overthrown it; violent Islamic groups could have sparked religious conflict; and regional separatists, if successful, could have eroded the legitimacy of democratic incumbents and been a source of calls for the return of the military.

By 2004, through a series of creative measures, some of which were unprecedented in the history of democratization, the new Indonesian democracy managed to subdue all three of these potentially severe challenges. Part III of this volume examines this behavioral dimension, exploring how democracy increasingly became the "only game in town" even for many of the once democratic challengers.[19]

The Transformation of the Military

Not only had the Indonesian military continuously ruled Indonesia for the thirty-five years preceding the democratic transition, but at the start of the democratic transition it appeared to be able to count on great resources. The doctrine of the military's dual function (*dwifungsi*) was still on the books: it was assigned not only security functions, but also territorial-political functions that gave it administrative authority and physical presence down to the village level. In the Majelis Permusyawaratan Rakyat (People's Consultative Assembly), which until 2004 was responsible for the election of the president, the military held 20 percent of the seats. Moreover, 70 percent of military revenues came from off-budget sources. Thus, a key instrument of democratic civil control over the military—that is, control over the "purse strings"—was not available.

In chapter 5, "Veto Player No More? The Declining Political Influence of the Military in Postauthoritarian Indonesia," Marcus Mietzner, the author of the leading book on the Indonesian military in the democratic period (a book extensively praised by *The Economist*, which said that it and the Indonesian experience should be studied closely by would-be reformers in military-dominated countries such as Burma),[20] explores how most of these resources of relative political autonomy have now been reduced greatly.

Since the start of the transition to democracy, the portion of military "self-financing" has dropped from around 70 percent in 1988 to less than 30 percent in 2010. The government, without appearing to attack the military head on, subjected it to the same politywide market reforms that reduced many subsidies to state enterprises. In the process, many of the army's profitable businesses were purchased by the private sector, most of the unprofitable military businesses went bankrupt, and some of the more legally questionable military businesses, such as those providing "protection" services to mining interests, were increasingly deemed improper or even illegal.[21]

Mietzner also notes that although the military has preserved its dual-function territorial command structure, democratic governments have both decentralized Indonesia and opened up its entire territory to elections. This decentralization process has steadily produced civilian instead of military governors: in 1998, 50 percent of the governors were retired generals, but by 2005 the number had dropped to 27 percent and by 2009 to only 12 percent.

One of the most revisionist parts of Mietzner's analysis is his argument that as Suharto aged and his rule of the military became more personalistic, the *military as institution* became more distant from the *military as government* and that "through its veto against a last-minute crackdown and its tacit support for the regime change, the military made a larger contribution to the democratic transition than political scientists tend to admit." In fact, in the context of the growing mainline Muslim and secular demands for democratization that we have documented, some military regime "soft-liners," in classic democratization theory style, bargained with some opposition "soft-liners" to ensure a peaceful transition from military to civilian rule.

This mode of transition helps put Indonesia in sharper perspective. In comparative terms, Indonesia's democratic transition was a relatively fast one. The Brazilian transition started in 1974 and was only completed with the direct election of a president in 1989. It thus lasted more than twice as long as the Indonesian transition. In Portugal, the Salazar regime was overthrown in 1974 by junior officers, but it was not until 1982 that the revolutionary colonels lost their de facto veto power over all legislation passed by the Assembly of the Republic.

Furthermore, in many Latin American countries, even though the armed forces left office, they often retained sufficient power to insert many of their prerogatives and "reserved domains" into political practice or, indeed, into the Constitution. For example, in Chile, even though the democratic opposition defeated Augusto Pinochet's effort to be reelected in 1989, Pinochet was able to continue to serve as the extremely powerful commander-in-chief of the army until 1998. Just as important, the new democratic Parliament was highly constrained in its ability to reverse many of Pinochet's laws because nothing embedded in his 1980 Constitution could be altered without a two-thirds majority vote of the Senate. Before Pinochet left office, he appointed a number of the country's senators, so that major constitutional changes were much harder to implement.[22] In sharp contrast, within less than five years of the start of the democratic transition in Indonesia, surprisingly few such military prerogatives or "reserved domains" constrained democratically elected officials.[23]

By 2003, discussions and fears of a military reconquest, which had been quite high at the start of the transition, began to recede sharply. Indeed, Mietzner closes his revisionist analysis with the assertion that four years into the post-Suharto transition "the armed forces could not point to a single key element of the new polity that had been adopted because of their insistence."

The Post-transition Emergence and Decline of Violent Islamism

Various violent Islamist groups, both homegrown and transnational, rapidly came out of hiding or emerged in the early years of the democratic transition. They made their presence felt through terrorist and vigilante attacks on nightclubs, bookstores, and coffee shops and eventually in bloody interreligious conflicts on the outer islands.

We are very fortunate to have as the analyst of the rise and fall of religious violence Sidney Jones, who has written chapter 6, "Indonesian Government Approaches to Radical Islam Since 1998." The chief researcher of the International Crisis Group in Southeast Asia, Jones is renowned as one of the great specialists on violence, in particular religious violence. She has studied post-transition radicalism very carefully. The majority of the armed forces, as Mietzner shows, accepted the democratic transition, but some, possibly to maintain personal or institutional leverage in the new context, did not. Jones's research documents the high level of complicity of some military officers in prominent post-1998 religious armed conflicts, such as in Ambon in April 2000, where the Laskar Jihad (Warriors of Jihad or Jihad Militia) received valuable transportation and arms from the Indonesian army. Soaring interreligious violence made many observers doubt a possible democratic future for the country. However, since 2004 the violence has abated. Why? The Bali bombings and the terrorist attacks in the United States on September 11, 2001, made many people who were previously sympathetic to violent Islamist causes rethink their willingness to support violence. Also, once human rights groups and journalists documented a serious degree of military complicity with jihadist violence, such complicity became more costly for the military, both nationally and internationally. In the end, Jones argues, violence by Islamists strengthened state security institutions, but *civilian* ones rather than *military* ones. The state made significant inroads toward identifying, prosecuting, and putting on trial those engaged in militant activities. Under the rubric of creating a special branch of the state apparatus to fight terrorism, the police were removed from army control and reconstituted as a separate organization. Jones shows how police training was dramatically changed to include matters such as investigation procedures, the organization of prisons, and programs focused on sensitivity to local cultural and religious traditions. Working with state authorities, the new Indonesian police force also forged new mechanisms for coordinating regional intelligence services with their counterparts in Malaysia, the Philippines, and Australia.[24] In contrast, in Brazil, whose democratic transition began in 1989, most of the heavily armed police units are still under the command of the military authority more than twenty years later and have received relatively little state-of-the-art training in police investigation or international intelligence cooperation.

From the Threat of Disintegration to New Mechanisms of Democratic Participation and Territorial Integration

In a geopolitical and historical context where the Soviet Union and Yugoslavia had recently territorially disintegrated, there was great concern within the Indonesian military about the possible fragmentation of Indonesia. The

Yugoslav and Soviet examples in particular intensified the military's already deep dislike of federalism, which they saw as a state-weakening device and which they associated with the Dutch-initiated federal constitution of Indonesia in 1949.[25]

State officials, especially the security apparatus, applied coercion against independence movements in East Timor, Papua, and Aceh, reducing the attractiveness of the secessionist model in other provinces and helping to prevent it from spreading. Although this repression contributed to Indonesia's survival as a nation and therefore can arguably be seen as indirectly contributing to the country's successful democratic transition, it also seriously compromised the quality of that democracy. In East Timor, major crimes against humanity were committed by the security forces' attempts to preempt and then respond to the United Nations–supervised vote in favor of independence; similar state crimes also occurred in Aceh and to a lesser extent in Papua, along with a host of other abuses against civilians.

To his credit, the transition president, B. J. Habibie, responded to secessionist ambitions by quickly devolving political authority and fiscal resources. Indonesia underwent one of the most thorough-going and rapid decentralization processes ever recorded in the history of democratization. Within a period of two years, its highly centralized administration was transformed, as a World Bank publication suggested, into "one of the most decentralized . . . in the world. . . .[R]egional spending rose from an estimated 17 percent of all government spending in 2000, to over 30 percent in 2001; 2/3 of central civil servants were re-assigned; [and] over 16,000 public service facilities were handed over to the regions."[26]

This radical decentralization was accomplished while still retaining the integrity of the state, unlike the decentralization processes in the Soviet Union and Yugoslavia, which led to these two states' becoming at last count more than twenty-five independent states. How did Indonesia decentralize so much and so fast without disintegrating? Prize-winning author Edward Aspinall addresses this question in chapter 7 in this volume, "How Indonesia Survived: Comparative Perspectives on State Disintegration and Democratic Integration."

A cornerstone of the decentralization process was the devolution of finances and authority to the *subprovincial* level of 495 county-like districts and municipalities rather than to the thirty-four larger *provinces*. The intention was to avoid the revivification of provincial pro-autonomy sentiments such as those that had challenged the integrity of the Indonesian unitary state ever since independence.

This strategy has turned out to be quite successful in terms of quelling secession and increasing support for democracy. Not only were municipalities and regions given hitherto unprecedented amounts of money, much of it under their direct discretion, but the chief officials in charge of these subprovincial units were for the *first time ever* in Indonesian history *elected* by local constituencies instead of *appointed* by the central government. Through this process, the 495 elected incumbents and thousands of their would-be successors increasingly became invested in the continuation of elections as "the only game in town." We should note that some observers also call these units "495 corruption centers." But whatever we call them, at the very least they are a new source of political and financial power in Indonesia that is directly related to the democratization process. In many cases, this strategy put an end to separatist demands, while giving increased credence to the emerging democracy. One of the foremost historians of Indonesia, M. C. Ricklefs, also argues that the presence of pro-democracy activists in elected positions in all of the country's major cities inhibited the brutality of the central government security forces.[27]

In Aceh, decades of armed struggle for independence led by the Gerakan Aceh Merdeka (GAM, Free Aceh Movement) came to an end when the fighting parties reached a "mutually hurting stalemate." A new creative formula of autonomy that Alfred Stepan, Juan J. Linz, and Yogendra Yadav call a "federacy" was agreed upon.[28] In October 2005, this new "federacy" was accepted by the military and the elected president of Indonesia, General (retired) Susilo Bambang Yudhoyono because GAM agreed to remain within the unitary state of Indonesia according to the newly crafted autonomy arrangements. For its part, GAM accepted the status of a federacy because it gave the organization a whole series of federal-like prerogatives and a high degree of self-rule not available to any other unit of Indonesia.

Edward Aspinall's analysis of the Aceh peace process and Indonesia's creative pattern of radical decentralization concludes that "the Indonesian experience helps to demonstrate that state structures that accommodate ethnic and regional diversity may be a source of state fragility *during* democratization, but a source of democratic robustness *after* it" (emphasis in original).[29]

The successful reintegration of the Indonesian state and collaboratively respectful democratic "twin tolerations" relationship between state officials and religious organizations have helped strengthen the Indonesian state's general capacity, in particular its capacity to educate peacefully its citizens in secular and religious schools in all parts of the country. A striking indication of this capacity is that girls at age fifteen have the same extremely high literacy rate as boys, 99 percent.[30] In striking contrast, in Pakistan only 58 percent of the girls and 79 percent of boys are literate. Unlike the cooperative relationship between state and religion in Indonesia, in many parts of Pakistan there is often a hostile relationship. Cooperation between Pakistani state educational authorities and religious authorities is so tenuous in the Northwest Frontier Province that of the more than sixteen thousand madrasas in the region, only fourteen hundred are registered.[31] In fact, the provincial secretary for education in this Pakistani province stated that no one from his office had ever visited half of the unregistered madrasas. In this nearly "stateless" territory, fundamentalist money, armed insurgents, and teachers, many from outside Pakistan, fuel intolerant and antidemocratic sentiments in a way that is unconceivable in Indonesia, where religion has won the right to participate democratically in the public sphere.

Part IV. Constitutionalism: The Role of Law and Legal Pluralism

One of the most contentious issues of modern politics and modern social science is legal pluralism. From our perspective as scholars concerned with democratic theory, if a country has two conflicting bodies of law and no effective system of resolution, it is a major problem for democracy because the definition of democracy requires rule of law and thus a hierarchy of law. However, if legal pluralism means that some types of issues can be dealt with by different systems of law without violating this hierarchy, it might be argued that legal pluralism can enhance rights for some individual citizens but not erode rule of law for the democratic state.

Before turning to chapter 8, "Contours of Sharia in Indonesia," by John Bowen, one of the world's leading legal anthropologists who has written about the religious practices and legal regulations in Indonesia, France, and the United Kingdom, let us build on some of his current fieldwork on sharia councils in London to construct a hypothetical example of conditions whereby legal pluralism may enable rights without eroding rule of law. In London's Sharia Councils, Muslim women have access to an Islamic divorce in addition to the civil divorce that the British state grants. For some Muslim women, this access is rights enhancing. Imagine a twenty-eight-year-old Muslim female British citizen with children who has been battered then abandoned by her Muslim husband. If this woman ever wants to marry again in the Muslim community, she has a personal need for a divorce that is Islamically sanctioned because her community will not recognize a British civil divorce. Institutions such as the London Sharia Councils can provide such a "divorce." At the same time, if this young woman wants, as is her right and need, to have a divorce that is civilly recognized and have the state use its democratic coercive capacity to compel the former husband to pay alimony and child support, she also needs the existence of and access to a formal legal system. In this case, we are assuming that there is a hierarchy of law in that only the state can grant a legal divorce that has legal standing and that only the state can imperatively demand that the husband support the child and wife. Such a situation of legal pluralism, where a religious "divorce" granted by Islamic councils complements civil law, is rights enhancing for that young women in need, but not law eroding for the democratic state.

The situation is not dissimilar in the Jewish case, where women need to receive the "Get" from their husbands in order for the divorce to be recognized in the conservative and orthodox Jewish community. In Ontario, Canada, Jewish courts of arbitration (Beit Din) were set up as early as 1915 to establish a judicial structure beside public law and public courts to dissolve a marriage.[32] When a similar institution was set up for the Muslim community in 2004, the public protested vehemently against the establishment of Islamic arbitration councils, and the entire Ontario law that permitted arbitration according to religious principles was eventually abolished, thus also bringing to an end the nearly one-hundred-year-old institution of the Beit Din.[33]

Indonesia has arguably intensified its polycentric legal environment as a result of the decentralization that gave regions the power to pass their own laws. What are the consequences of this legal pluralism for the quality of democracy? Does it enhance rights, or does it restrict rights and erode rule of law?

John Bowen discusses in his chapter what the growing use of sharia law means and does not mean for Indonesia. As Bowen shows, pro-Islamic legislation and regulations narrow some personal freedoms. In about 10 percent of Indonesia's 495 regions, sharia-based laws have been introduced, some of which contradict national law. For example, some of the regional laws, as in South Sulawesi, require both male and female civil servants to wear Islamic dress and to be able to recite key passages of the Qur'an as a qualification to hold public employment; some municipalities oblige Muslim couples to recite from memory the first seven lines of the Qur'an before a marriage ceremony; and some local bodies impose a special Muslim tax, *zakat*, and keep the additional revenues for their own purposes.

Bowen illuminates the phenomenon of the sharia-based laws as a new sign of provincial or regional distinctiveness and authenticity. In his account, sharia is above all a loose collection of signs, differentiated by province, region, and city. These signs are deeply situated in the history of the struggle for independence against the Dutch, ensuing struggles for autonomy against Jakarta, and debates about the relative role of religion in the country's law and politics. In the post-1998 era of reform and decentralization, sharia, for Bowen, first and foremost signifies the resurgence of local capacities to define and exploit ideas of authenticity, autonomy, and morality—ideas that have strong political, cultural, and often religious dimensions. They are part of a larger story, but that story is of an Indonesia in the process of redefining and relegitimizing its institutions, not an Indonesia captured by a uniform, national religious frenzy.

As editors of a volume that relates to Islam and democracy and as political scientists interested in democracy, we are concerned by one aspect of the growth of regional religious laws. As Bowen shows, some of these cases clearly violate national laws and constitutionally embedded human rights and de facto reduce individual rights. How does the center's legal system deal with the region's Islamization of law?

Tim Lindsey and Simon Butt, two of Australia's leading legal theorists, are also specialists on Indonesian law. They argue in the volume's concluding chapter, "Unfinished Business: Law Reform, Governance, and the Courts in Post-Soeharto Indonesia," that the democratic political system in Indonesia, as a set of laws, is correctly spelled out constitutionally and that the power to define and shape the legal relationship between state and citizens is formally in the hands of the Mahkamah Konstitusi (Constitutional Court) and the Mahkamah Agung (Supreme Court). Regulating the substance of regional laws—what these authors call "cleaning up the legal debris"—is the mandate of the Supreme Court. However, the massive process of decentralization since 2001 has created numerous parallel institutions and overlaps of mandates that the central state and legal system have yet to master and regulate. For example, as Lindsey and Butt document, the central government's right to review many types of new laws lapses sixty days after the laws are passed. Many localities avoid review by not sending the laws to the center until the sixty days have almost expired. Even if the courts get notice of a law that is in violation of national law or of constitutionally guaranteed individual rights, they often do not act.

This state of affairs leads us to the historical and theoretical reminder that in many countries the erosion of democracy comes more from acts of omission by democratic incumbents than by acts of commission by powerful non-democratic opponents.[34] Most problematical, the democratic state has been dangerously slow or even reluctant to stop practices that are in fact a violation of the Constitution or other citizen's rights. The contributors to this volume, depending on the features of the political system they weigh most heavily, are somewhat divided as to whether we should consider democracy fully consolidated in Indonesia or not. However, we editors believe there is a strong case to be made that before democracy can be considered consolidated in Indonesia, the democratic state will have to use more robustly its constitutionally embedded legal prerogatives to help craft a hierarchy of law within Indonesia's legal pluralism.

There are three democratic legal mechanisms available to the state to bring regional laws in line with national legislation and constitutional rights standards. The most important is the Supreme Court's right to review regional laws and declare them unconstitutional. Second, the minister of home affairs has the authority to invalidate regional laws on administrative grounds. Third, a regional law, once passed, is constitutionally reversible by a statute or a governmental or presidential regulation. Most important, as Butt and Lindsey emphasize, a "hierarchy of laws" ("tata urutan peraturan perundang-undangan")[35] actually exists *formally*, but failure to insist on compliance of the law results in the frequent violation of the hierarchy. In terms of legal hierarchy, regional laws rank below the Constitution, parliamentary-passed national laws, and many presidential and government regulations. For Lindsey and Butt, therefore, local laws "will have legal force, at least formally, *only if*, when passed, they do not contradict" this hierarchy (emphasis added). Thus, regional laws that violate national laws or constitutionally embedded human rights standards are de jure invalid, even without review by the Supreme Court or Ministry of Home Affairs. However, local civil servants and legislators often do not govern and legislate according to the "hierarchy of laws," and rights-reducing regional laws remain on the books. The central government has not made a point of exercising vigorously any one of the three mechanisms it legally has to enforce legal hierarchy.

This absence of a de facto hierarchy of law, in comparative terms, weakens Indonesia's status as a democracy. Indeed, in the World Bank's (admittedly economically more than politically oriented) review of twelve East Asian countries concerning the rule of law, only Cambodia ranks worse, and some nondemocracies, such as Vietnam and China, rank better than Indonesia.[36]

Corruption, particularly of state officials, is also something that can fall within the potential control of the state as well as of civil society and should be an aspiration of a government that is attempting to deepen its democracy. In this respect, there is much to do. Transparency International ranks countries in the world by the perception of corruption. In 2011, Indonesia ranks 100 out of 182, better than Russia, Pakistan, and the Philippines, but worse than some nondemocracies, such as Malaysia.[37] President Yudhoyono, elected in 2004, owed his sweeping reelection in 2009 to his campaigns against corruption. His most effective and prominent corruption-fighting cabinet minister was Minister of Finance Sri Mulyani. Her anticorruption vigilance led to the dishonorable discharge of 150 personnel in her ministry and to the punishment of 2,000 more. *Euromoney* named her "finance minister of the year" in 2006, and *Forbes* listed her as one of the "100 most powerful women in the world" in 2009. But in May 2010 she resigned in the midst of what appears to have been a losing struggle against Aburizal Bakrie, the coordinating minister of the economy, whom she was investigating for his company's tax evasion and involvement in the unprotected drillings that contributed to the Sidoarjo mud flows in East Java that left at least fifteen thousand villagers homeless.[38]

Finally, a word on how state negligence has allowed the rise to prominence of a civil society veto actor capable of undermining liberal standards in lawmaking. The Majelis Ulama Indonesia (MUI, Indonesian Ulama Council) was created by the military regime in 1975 as a government-funded council that rubber-stamped as "Islamic" many of the New Order's developmental policies. The military also made MUI the national *halal* certification body (designating what is proper or permissible).

After Reformasi (the reform era following the fall of Suharto), the MUI has become the central public commentator on what is "Islamically legitimate" when it comes to national legislation on religious and moral issues. Because most lawmakers do not dare to ignore the MUI's position, the MUI has become a crucial voice in the process of legislation. It still draws most of its funding from the government and therefore might be significantly inhibited if the government were to decide to cut its funding. But the MUI also draws millions of rupiah from private companies that seek its *halal* stamp. If the government were to decide to set up its own *halal* certification body in the Ministry of Health and embark on a major media campaign to show that it is superfluous to endow mass-consumed goods such as water and rice with *halal* stamps (superfluous because these goods are by their very nature *halal*), the MUI would quickly lose most of its political and economic power. So far, however, there seems to be no political will in the government to curtail the council's influence.

In 2005, the MUI passed several important fatwas that seriously undermined interfaith and intra-Muslim tolerance. Among them were condemnations (declarations of being haram) of joint interreligious praying, intermarriages, pluralism, secularism, and liberalism. Another fatwa condemned the Ahmadiyya sect. As a consequence of these fatwas, numerous attacks took place across the country against the Ahmadiyya, whose mosques were burned and private houses were looted and who were physically attacked. Some Protestant evangelical churches were damaged and closed.[39] Because a fatwa declared liberal Islam haram, militant Islamists took it as an implicit authorization to attack the Jaringan Islam Liberal (Liberal Islam Network) and attempt its closure in Jakarta. The NU reacted against the attacks on the Liberal Islam Network by sending its own youth militia, the Banser, who put an end to the assault.

If Indonesia had a well-functioning system of law enforcement, if there were sufficient political will and courage to protect the constitutionally guaranteed freedom of religion (Art. 29)[40] and the rights to free speech and assembly, groups of thugs such as the Front Pembela Islam (Islamic Defenders Front) who attack liberal Muslim organizations and minorities such as the Ahmadiyya or evangelical churches would not be able to take matters into their own hands. If the country had a well-functioning system of law enforcement, organizations such as the NU would also not have to counter attacks on affiliate institutions by deploying their own militia, let alone to employ an informal militia in the first place.

All these challenges to democratic consolidation are in their roots, however, violations of state law and therefore primarily phenomena that the state needs to confront. Militant Islamism, creeping shariazation and the influence of the MUI are all sources of illiberalism that the government needs to tackle; it does not lack the capacity to do so, but it has not made such action a democratic priority so far.

In conclusion, we should not be unreservedly celebratory about the state of democracy in Indonesia. There is much to be done. However, given the problems that existed in 1998, the speed and depth of Indonesia's democratization are impressive. Both Indonesia's accomplishments and continued problems are worth greater attention in democratization studies, particularly by activists and analysts who want to learn how the world's most populous Islamic country crafted a political system that the overwhelming majority of its citizens see as appropriate for their society and that most theorists should see as an original but welcome addition to the world's repertoire of democracies.

2

Indonesian Democracy

From Transition to Consolidation

R. William Liddle and Saiful Mujani

In Problems of Democratic Transition and Consolidation, Juan Linz and Alfred Stepan describe democratization as a two-stage process. A completed transition has occurred when four requirements are met: there is sufficient agreement about procedures to hold a democratic election; a government has been directly elected in a free popular vote; government has authority to formulate policies; and there is no power sharing outside the executive, legislative, and judicial branches.[1]

A consolidated democracy, the second stage, has three characteristics: with respect to behavior, no significant political groups are attempting to overthrow the democratic regime by "turning to violence or foreign intervention to secede from the state"; with respect to attitude, "a strong majority of public opinion" believes that any further change should take place within the "parameters of democratic formulas," even in the face of severe economic and political crises; and with respect to a constitution, all "governmental and non-governmental forces" agree that political conflict will be resolved "within the specific laws, procedures and institutions" of the new democratic regime.[2]

Finally, a consolidated democracy is conceived as an interacting system of arenas, each with its own organizing principle: civil society (freedom of association and communication), political society (free and inclusive electoral contestation), rule of law (constitutionalism), state apparatus (rational-legal bureaucratic norms), and economic society (institutionalized market).

Does the Indonesian case meet these criteria? We argue that the democratic transition began in 1998 and was completed in 2004. Since that time, on balance, behavioral, attitudinal, and constitutional democratic consolidation has been achieved.

Consolidation has not been complete or unproblematic, however. Obstacles and weaknesses remain with regard to each characteristic and to the five interacting arenas: the impact of a low level and slow rate of economic growth; the policy successes of Islamist social movements; the uneven quality of local governance; the continuing force of separatism, especially in Papua; the link in the public mind between perceptions of economic well-being and support for democracy; uncertainty about electoral rules and the relationship between the executive and legislative branches of government; weak rule-of-law institutions; and the concentration of economic power in the hands of a small political elite.

The Transition

Indonesia's democratic transition began in May 1998, when President Suharto resigned his office in the face of a collapsed economy, mass demonstrations throughout the country, and finally abandonment by his own elite supporters. The first three of Linz and Stepan's requirements were met within a year, when Indonesia held its first democratic elections since 1955, and the fourth was met when Parliament convened after the second democratic elections in 2004.[3]

Suharto had held power since October 1965, when as an army major-general he assumed the leadership of an armed forces devastated by the murder of six of its most senior officers. He soon took over the presidency, pushing aside Indonesia's first president and national founding father, Sukarno. Over the next three decades, Suharto's Orde Baru (New Order) government was known for its rapid economic growth (averaging 7 percent per year from 1969 to 1996), but also for one of the highest levels of corruption in the developing world and for its willingness to repress domestic opponents.

To legitimize his power, both domestically and internationally, Suharto created the simulacra of a democratic political system. Closely managed elections for Parliament (the Dewan Perwakilan Rakyat [DPR, People's Representative Council]) and for regional legislatures were held every five years between 1971 and 1997. In each of those elections, Suharto's own political party, Golongan Karya (Golkar, Functional Groups), won an absolute majority of the votes. Golkar was backed by the state bureaucracy and the armed forces, which maintained (and still maintains) a nationwide command structure paralleling the civilian government and political party branch hierarchies.

In all but the 1971 election, Golkar competed with only two other political parties, the Partai Persatuan Pembangunan (PPP, Development and Unity Party) and the Partai Demokrasi Indonesia (PDI, Indonesian Democracy Party). Both were fusions imposed by the Suharto government, PPP of Islamic parties and PDI of secular nationalist and Christian parties, most of which had participated in Indonesia's first democratic election in 1955.

After each parliamentary election, Suharto was reelected president by the Majelis Permusyawaratan Rakyat (MPR, People's Consultative Assembly), a kind of superparliament consisting of all members of Parliament plus an equal number of delegates appointed to represent regions and other political and social groups. According to the 1945 Constitution (since amended), the MPR (not the Indonesian people) was the holder of sovereign power and thus the formal legitimator of Suharto's rule.

Suharto was replaced after sharp protests on May 21, 1998, by his constitutionally ordained successor, Vice President B. J. Habibie, who within weeks of his accession to power freed the press, ended the prohibition on new political parties, and called for democratic elections for Parliament and regional assemblies within a year. How are we to explain these decisions? In the conventional wisdom, Habibie acted out of necessity, not choice. He was widely regarded as one of Suharto's most loyal servants, not as an independent or potentially independent leader in a post-Suharto period. His decisions were therefore a product of the concatenation of forces acting upon him at the time.

In our view, Habibie, like all political actors, was constrained and enabled by many factors, distant and proximate, cultural and structural. Within those limits, however, he made real choices for which he deserves considerable credit because the outcome was a successful transition.[4]

At the global level, the zeitgeist surely was a major force constraining antidemocrats and enabling pro-democrats. During the Suharto presidency, the international Cold War ended, and many countries became democratic in Latin America and Africa as well as in eastern Europe, so that elite Indonesian actors had few attractive alternative models. Thirty years of steady economic development in Indonesia had laid the supportive foundation of a modern society, as in neighboring Taiwan, Korea, and Thailand, all of which had recently democratized (although Thailand has been unstable since a 2006 military coup). More proximate in time, the student and mass demonstrators who had persuaded Suharto to step down continued to constrain Habibie, who was pushed to resign in favor of a "presidium" or broadly based temporary executive council that would oversee democratization.

For the most prominent civilian elite actors outside Habibie's government, representative democracy was the preferred outcome. These actors included Megawati Sukarnoputri, representing the powerful force of secular nationalism; Abdurrahman Wahid, head of the huge traditionalist Muslim organization Nahdlatul Ulama (Awakening or Rise of the Ulama); and Amien Rais, head of Muhammadiyah (Followers of Muhammad), the largest organization representing modernist Islam.

None of these civilian opposition leaders wanted a continuation of military rule, which, though not an immediate threat, was certainly a real possibility if the civilians failed to cooperate with each other. Armed forces commander General Wiranto, recently appointed by Suharto, had declared his personal and institutional loyalty to the Constitution of 1945 and therefore to the process by which Vice President Habibie had become President Habibie. This position was not unpopular within the armed forces, the army in particular. After thirty years of Suharto's New Order, many officers believed that the army's reputation had suffered from its involvement in and identification with the state party Golkar, perceived both as corrupt and as an instrument of Suharto's favoritism toward cronies and family members. By recognizing Habibie's constitutional legitimacy, General Wiranto also hoped to extend his own tenure as armed forces commander.

Each of the civilian leaders recognized that she or he could not govern independently, particularly as a dictator repressing the others in the style of Megawati's father, Sukarno, at the height of his power from 1959 to 1965. Moreover, no other political force threatened their dominance, as the Indonesian Communist Party had done to its predecessors in the 1950s and early 1960s. At the other end of the ideological spectrum, Wahid and Rais as well as the Muslim social and political organizations they represented had long since declared their opposition to an Islamic state, significantly reducing the anxiety once felt by tens of millions of moderate Muslims, Christians, Hindus, and others.

The availability and familiarity of Suharto-era electoral laws were also enabling factors. National elections had been conducted regularly throughout the New Order as part of Suharto's strategy to legitimize his rule. With a few changes, the most important being the opening of the party system and the freeing of the press, the old laws could serve well as the infrastructure for democratic elections. All three civilian opposition leaders and most of their followers thus readily acquiesced when Habibie declared—only one week after Suharto's resignation—that he would hold a democratic election within a year. They had much to gain and little to lose.

Although all of these factors must be included in a full explanation of the decision to democratize, the fact that it was B. J. Habibie who made the decision also matters in at least two senses. First, the pattern of constraining and enabling factors impacting Habibie, as described earlier, would have been different had a different individual occupied the presidential office at that time. As it happens, Habibie had replaced General Try Sutrisno, a former armed forces commander, as vice president just weeks before Suharto resigned the presidency.

As president, Try Sutrisno would have been institutionally much more dependent on the armed forces. He was also known, perhaps to a greater degree than other officers, for his contempt for civilian politicians, his fear of political Islam, and his belief that communism was still a powerful if latent force in Indonesia. As a career army officer, he was strongly committed to the defense of the integration of East Timor into the Indonesian republic. President Habibie, it will be remembered, called for and presided over a referendum on independence in East Timor. In doing so, he arguably helped Indonesia excise a rapidly growing cancer that might well have permanently damaged relations between the center and other provinces.

Second, as a conscious human being with the capacity to make reasoned judgments, Habibie might have chosen a course of action other than the paths preordained for him by the conventional wisdom, including stepping down in favor of a presidium and calling for elections he knew he was likely to lose. For example, he might have attempted to remain in office until the next scheduled elections in 2002 (the last New Order elections were in 1997) by cementing his personal alliance with General Wiranto (who was certainly interested in staying in his armed forces position and in becoming president after he retired from the military) and through Wiranto his institutional alliance with the armed forces (many of whose officers were certainly fearful of what would happen to them in a civilianized Indonesian polity).

In any event, Habibie became the president, and he decided to hold democratic elections on June 7, 1999. By agreement with the other major civilian players, the elections were conducted within the framework of Suharto's New Order electoral system, itself rooted in the 1955 democratic elections. Voters chose among closed party lists with provinces as the multimember electoral districts. After brief debate between defenders of this system and advocates of a single-member district plurality system (an idea the democrats frequently proposed during the New Order, but Suharto always rejected), most actors accepted the decision by a majority of members of Parliament to postpone serious discussion of reform until the next election.

The 1999 election was contested by forty-eight parties, twenty-one of which won at least one of the 462 contested seats of a total of 500 (the remaining 38 seats were occupied by the armed forces, whose members did not vote in the general election). Eighty percent of the vote was divided among five large- and medium-size parties. On October 20, Abdurrahman Wahid, leader of the fourth largest party, was chosen president by a majority vote in the MPR.

The 1999 assembly consisted of the 462 elected and 38 unelected members of Parliament plus 200 additional unelected members representing the armed forces, political parties in proportion to their percentage of votes in the parliamentary election, and other groups in society. To most observers, these events fulfilled the first three of Linz and Stepan's requirements for a transition (procedural agreement, free election, authoritative government), though admittedly imperfectly because of the large number of appointees, especially in the assembly, which was charged with electing the president. An end to power sharing with the armed forces, the fourth requirement, finally occurred in 2004, when all members of Parliament were elected, the president and vice president were directly elected for the first time in Indonesian history, the MPR was reduced to largely symbolic functions, and, finally, power sharing on security issues was greatly diminished with the military's acceptance of the presidential agreement on Aceh in 2005.

Few observers today would contest the claim that the transition to democracy was completed by the 2004 elections. Has it since been consolidated?

Democratic Consolidation I: Behavioral

No significant political group currently threatens to overthrow democracy or to separate from the Indonesian nation-state. Perhaps the largest potential danger comes from the Islamist movement, followed by a much smaller threat from antidemocratic secular nationalists in alliance with antidemocratic army officers. The separatist conflict in Aceh appears to be resolved in favor of a reestablishment of Indonesian identity. The conflict in Papua, although unresolved, appears to be a long-term rather than short-term problem. More fundamental, there is little separatism in Indonesia because Indonesian national identity has deep roots and is probably on balance being further strengthened by the process of decentralization that has accompanied democratization.

This situation compares favorably with Indonesia's first democracy (1950–1957), which was initially threatened by Islamists and Communists. It was overthrown by President Sukarno and the central army hierarchy headed by General Abdul Haris Nasution, leaders of the civilian, and military secular nationalists, respectively.

Islamism

Today's Islamist movement consists of pro-Islamic state (sharia) parties that work within the democratic process and social movement organizations that mobilize and act politically in part outside it. Although not an immediate threat to democratic consolidation, recent cooperation between these two types of organization has reduced religious freedom and women's freedom of movement. Islamists have also enjoyed the cooperation of officials in the Ministry of Religion, the Attorney General's Office, and the quasi-governmental Majelis Ulama Indonesia (MUI, Indonesian Ulama Council).

The oldest self-declared Islamist party is PPP, which won 7 percent of the 2009 vote (a decline from 8 percent in 2004 and 11 percent in 1999). Few observers see PPP as a genuine threat to democracy, however. Its leaders are widely believed to be more interested in the material than the spiritual benefits of political power. The party was created in 1973 by President Suharto, who fused existing Islamic parties into one and forced them to accept the non-Islamic name PPP and the state ideology of Pancasila as their basic doctrine. Pancasila is the pan-religious national credo first introduced in 1945 by President Sukarno, a secular nationalist, and imposed on all parties and social organizations by Suharto's authoritarian New Order. After democratization, PPP jettisoned Pancasila and adopted Islam as its doctrinal foundation. As late as 2002, PPP members of Parliament proposed amending the Constitution to restore the so-called Piagam Jakarta (Jakarta Charter) requiring all Muslims to follow Islamic law.[5]

The proposal received little support from other parties and was withdrawn without a vote.

To most observers, the Partai Keadilan Sejahtera (PKS, Prosperous Justice Party) is a greater threat to democratic consolidation than PPP. PKS is a cadre party founded in 1998 (as Partai Keadilan [PK, Justice Party]) by veterans of a widely supported university campus–based Islamist movement inspired by the Egypt-centered Muslim Brotherhood. Many of its cadres are well educated in domestic and foreign secular universities. PK won less than 2 percent of the 1999 vote, but PKS (the party was obliged to change its name under Indonesia's unusual threshold law)[6] surged to 7 percent in 2004, raising the hopes of many Islamists and the fears of many democrats.

PKS's own intentions, however, are more ambiguous (or perhaps ambivalent, the product in part of internal party differences). Although a self-declared dakwah (call, proselytizing for, and preaching within Islam) party, PKS campaigned in 2004 not on Islamism, but on the claim to be a "clean" (bersih) and "caring" (peduli) party. Party leaders fully recognize that most of their 2004 support came not from fellow Islamists, but from voters who bought the party's secular good-governance promise. In the hundreds of regional executive elections (provincial and district/municipality) held between 2005 and 2008, PKS formed coalitions of convenience with a wide range of parties, including the Christian Partai Damai Sejahtera (Prosperous Peace Party). In 2009, the party added "professional" as a new campaign theme, but only increased its parliamentary vote by 1 percent to 8 percent. It no longer appears as threatening to democracy (or as promising to clean-government reformers) as it did in 2004.

Though PKS's basic doctrine, like PPP's, is Islam, its leaders explicitly opposed the 2002 constitutional amendment championed by PPP and other Islamist parties requiring all Muslims to follow Islamic law. They claimed instead to support the Medina Charter, a reference to a historic agreement between the Prophet Muhammad and various non-Muslim groups, including Jews, that established the first Islamic polity. Critics, especially Indonesian Christians, argue that there is no substantive difference between an Indonesian state governed under the Jakarta Charter or one governed under the Medina Charter. The point may be moot because voter support for Islamist parties has waned.[7]

The main Islamist social movement organizations, in order of their popular recognition as reflected in national opinion polls, are Jemaah Islamiyah (JI, Islamic Group or Community), Front Pembela Islam (FPI,

Islamic Defenders Front), Majelis Mujahidin Indonesia (MMI, Indonesian Jihad Fighters Council), and Hizbut Tahrir Indonesia (HTI, Indonesian Party of Liberation).

JI is a shadowy terrorist conspiracy founded in Malaysia around 1992 by Abdullah Sungkar, Abu Bakar Ba'asyir, and other Indonesian Islamists in hiding from Suharto's New Order government.[8] Its roots are in the late 1940s Darul Islam (House of Islam) movement that first waged war on the secular Indonesian state. The leaders of FPI, founded in 1998, are self-proclaimed protectors of Islamic morality who conduct violent raids of nightclubs and bars, especially during the Islamic fasting month. MMI is a Surakarta-based organization of Islamists once headed by Abu Bakar Ba'asyir and regarded at that time as a front for JI. HTI, founded in Jerusalem in 1953, is an international mass-based Islamist organization that has been growing rapidly in Indonesia since the 1990s.[9] Like PKS, its appeal has been mainly to the educated middle class.

These and like-minded movements oppose democracy, and some, most notably HTI, oppose the nation-state as well. None is large enough to threaten democratic consolidation at the ballot box, and, indeed, none plans to contest elections. The danger instead lies in their growing ability to frame political issues in ways that advance their pro-sharia agenda. In particular, they have become skilled at persuading otherwise moderate Muslims that the Islamist position on a given issue is one that all Muslims must accept as Islamic.

Decentralization provided an early opportunity for pro-sharia Islamists. More than twenty-five districts (in a total of more than 450) quickly passed regulations either directly or indirectly reflecting Islamist norms, such as the requirement that women civil servants wear head scarves, bans on the sale of alcohol, antiprostitution ordinances, and so on. That part of the movement now appears to have lost steam, however. At the national level, two prominent 2008 examples of successful framing are the passage of an antipornography bill by Parliament and a campaign to ban Ahmadiyya (Followers of Ahmad), an Islamic sect whose founder, Mirza Ghulam Ahmad, is venerated by some sect members as a prophet after Muhammad.

In the case of the antipornography bill, social movement Islamists worked closely with Islamist members of Parliament to persuade moderate Muslim and other legislators to vote for a poorly worded bill that, if enforced, is likely to restrict the rights of women.[10] In the case of Ahmadiyya, Islamists took advantage of a fatwa from the quasi-governmental MUI (one of whose members is a prominent HTI leader) to mount a violent campaign to ban the organization. Several Ahmadiyya communities were attacked and mosques destroyed. The campaign ended with a joint ministerial decree "freezing" Ahmadiyya and presidential acquiescence to the decree despite clear violation of the constitutional right to freedom of religion. There have been no attacks on Ahmadiyya communities since the decree. The conflict has not been resolved, however, because Islamists still demand that Ahmadiyya declare itself non-Muslim or disband.[11]

Secular Nationalism

A small group of civilian and military secular nationalists appears to oppose democratization. During MPR debates between 1999 and 2002, they rejected the four packages of amendments to the 1945 Constitution that established today's presidential democracy.[12] These amendments specifically stipulated that members of Parliament and regional legislatures be directly elected; created a new and directly elected Dewan Pemerintahan Daerah (Regional Representative Council); provided for direct election of the president and vice president separately from Parliament; limited future presidents to 2 five-year terms; inserted several articles guaranteeing human and political rights; and established the Mahkamah Konstitusi (Constitutional Court) to review laws that conflict with the constitution.

The civilian opposition to the amendments was and is concentrated in a conservative or "Sukarnoist" faction of the Partai Demokrasi Indonesia Perjuangan (PDIP, Indonesian Democracy Party of Struggle), the largest political party in 1999 (33 percent of seats in Parliament), the second largest in 2004 (20 percent), and the third largest in 2009 (17 percent).[13] PDIP's roots are in the Partai Nasional Indonesia (PNI, Indonesian Nationalist Party), founded by Sukarno and other secular nationalist politicians in the 1920s. No longer led by but still associated in the public mind with President Sukarno, PNI won the most votes (22 percent) in the first democratic national elections in 1955.

During the New Order, PNI was forcibly incorporated into PDI. In the early 1990s, under the leadership of Megawati Sukarnoputri, Sukarno's daughter, PDI mounted the first serious political challenge to Suharto's New Order. As PDIP, the Struggle faction of the Suharto-era PDI, it is still led by Megawati, who succeeded Abdurrahman Wahid as Indonesia's president in 2001 and served until 2004.

Within PDIP, opposition to the four amendments was justified as support for a return to party founder Sukarno's original conception of the Constitution. Proponents of this return have not spelled out what it would mean in practice. In its original form, the Constitution leaves out such basics as how the members of Parliament and the MPR are to be chosen. The implication, however, is a desire to return to Sukarno-style authoritarianism or Demokrasi Terpimpin (Guided Democracy), the Sukarno–army coalition that ruled Indonesia from 1959 to 1965. Since 2002, conservative secular nationalist ideas have had little resonance in the polity, but it is not difficult to imagine their resurgence should separatist movements grow, the economy decline, or presidential leadership vis-à-vis Parliament weaken.

An undetermined number of active and retired armed forces (especially army—by far the largest, most powerful, and historically most politicized service) officers are also believed to reject the democratic idea on ideological and interest grounds. With respect to ideology, army officers have long claimed to be a self-created force—that is, a pro-independence army not established by the civilian rulers of the new Indonesian state.[14] It was founded instead by Dutch colonial–era and Japanese occupation–era officers acting on their own initiative shortly after the August 17, 1945, declaration of independence. Moreover, many officers continue to believe that it is they, not the civilian politicians, who wrested sovereignty from the Dutch and who repeatedly saved the country from separatist, Islamist, and Communist threats between 1949 and 1965.

In 1999, armed forces leaders formally abandoned their "twin functions" doctrine (claimed responsibilities both to defend the country against foreign and domestic enemies as well as to participate actively in government). It is not clear, however, whether they now genuinely accept the standard international democratic norm of civilian supremacy. Indeed, officers often negatively interpret the latter term as a civilian claim to superior knowledge and competence, not formal authority of elected officials over the armed forces.

For more than three decades of Suharto's New Order, preceded by several years of Sukarno's Guided Democracy, active and retired armed forces officers enjoyed privileged status and material benefits. Under Sukarno, they ran many of the plantations and other businesses seized from the Dutch in the late 1950s and began to penetrate the legislative arena. Under Suharto, they held many executive, legislative, and judicial positions in national and local government. They first dominated and later were influential in Golkar, the

New Order's state party, and their businesses monopolized many sectors of the economy.

Many of these privileges are now gone or greatly reduced. The government of President Susilo Bambang Yudhoyono (familiarly called "SBY"), himself a retired army general, has made an initial effort to rationalize and reduce the influence of the military-backed businesses, many of them protection rackets, that have long provided officers with substantial extra income. According to Human Rights Watch, however, little progress had been achieved by the end of Yudhoyono's first term.[15] The president has also explicitly warned active-duty military officers not to engage in politics. In response, there have been periodic outbursts of discontent, as in the early 2009 rumors of an "anybody but Yudhoyono" movement in the army.[16] None of these factors are to be taken seriously, however, as indicators of significant opposition to democracy. In chapter 5 in this volume, Marcus Mietzner makes a strong case that the military since 2005 has no longer been a veto power in Indonesian politics.

Separatism and Decentralization

The most powerful separatist movements in Indonesia have been in the northwesternmost province, Aceh, the former Portuguese colony of East Timor, and the southeasternmost province, Papua. Both Aceh and Papua remain potentially volatile, although Indonesian national identity is much stronger in the former than in the latter. For Indonesia as a whole, however, the most important center–region relations story has to do with the extraordinary decentralization process that has accompanied democratization.

In 1945, Acehnese leaders joined the Indonesian independence movement on the same terms as nationalists in other regions, laying the foundation for a supraethnic conception of national identity. Those same leaders first rebelled against the central government in 1953 on grounds of a betrayed promise of provincial autonomy. This act laid the foundation for two competing conceptions of identity, one of an ethnic group within the Indonesian nation but repeatedly betrayed and the other, more extreme, of an Acehnese nation that had struggled throughout history to maintain its independence.[17]

For decades, the contest in Aceh has been between the two latter identities. Few Acehnese now identify straightforwardly, as do most Indonesians elsewhere, with the Indonesian nation and state. The Gerakan Aceh Merdeka (GAM, Free Aceh Movement) attempted to persuade fellow Acehnese,

Indonesians, and the world that Aceh was an ancient nation entitled to statehood. Its rebellion against the Indonesian state began in 1976 and ended in 2005, when the province was given a unique autonomous status after long and brutal warfare followed by protracted negotiations under international auspices.

Acehnese have since directly elected a governor (himself a former GAM rebel) and members of a provincial legislature (in conjunction with the national parliamentary election in April 2009). Aceh's special relationship with the Indonesian state includes the right, not enjoyed in any other province, to form local political parties. In the April 2009 election, the Partai Aceh (Aceh Party) won thirty-three out of sixty-nine seats in the regional legislature, followed by SBY's Partai Demokrat (Democrat Party) with ten seats. Five other local parties contested, but none won seats.[18] The other twenty-six seats were for politywide parties. Despite fears, the election was conducted without significant violence. Given Aceh's history within Indonesia, future conflict is certainly possible. It is nonetheless realistic to conclude that the Acehnese have taken a major step toward renewing or accepting once again their Indonesian national identity. Indeed, in chapter 7 in this volume, Edward Aspinall makes a strong case that the Helsinki Agreement of 2005 will hold.

East Timor was forcibly incorporated into Indonesia in 1975. Few East Timorese accepted Indonesian nationality, however, then or later. After decades of occupation and civil war, the territory was finally allowed to secede in 2000. Relations between the two independent countries are now normal, and there is no movement on either side to restore Indonesian sovereignty.

Papua, though originally part of Netherlands India, to which Indonesia is the internationally recognized successor state, was not governed from Jakarta until 1963, after a U.S.-brokered withdrawal of Dutch forces and administration. Between 1950 and 1962, the Dutch educated an elite and supported their aspirations for independence separate from Indonesia. This elite was brutally suppressed by the Indonesian government and armed forces starting in 1963.

To many observers today, the region seems like an occupied territory still. Most Papuans appear to reject Indonesian nationality, although it is difficult to be sure because of Indonesian government restrictions on travel to and reporting from the region. A desultory separatist movement, the Organisasi Papua Merdeka (Free Papua Organization), has existed for decades.

Although by all accounts widely supported, it is poorly organized, even fragmented, resource poor, and not likely to mount a serious challenge to the Indonesian government for years, if not decades. Nonetheless, compared to Aceh, the greater ultimate separatist threat is in Papua.

Beyond Aceh and Papua, there is no significant separatist threat in Indonesia and little likelihood of one emerging. One reason for this lack of threat is how deeprooted Indonesian nationalism and national identity are from the colonial and revolutionary periods. Nationalism as an idea binding this very diverse society has prevailed despite the depredations of both Sukarno's and Suharto's excessively centralized and authoritarian governments.[19]

A second reason is the modest success to date of the far-reaching decentralization that has accompanied democratization. In 1999, under the leadership of President Habibie, laws were passed that decentralized most government functions to the districts and municipalities, bypassing the provinces, where separatist sentiment is most feared.

Between 2005 and 2008, regional executives were directly elected in all thirty-three provinces and more than 450 districts and municipalities. Elections for governors, district heads, and mayors will be repeated from 2010 to 2013. In 2014, provincial and district/municipality legislative elections will be held simultaneously with the national parliamentary election.

Scholars are divided on the implications for democratic consolidation of the 2005–2008 regional executive elections. There is general agreement on two points—one negative, one more positive. First, local-level political and governmental infrastructure in a poor country and after decades of authoritarianism is even weaker than at the national level. Many basic state- and party-building tasks remain before the promise of decentralized democracy can be fully realized.

Second, within that context, the 2005–2008 elections were conducted almost everywhere without excessive violence or (as far as we can tell from the public record) excessive corruption, particularly in the form of vote buying that is ubiquitous in many poor-country democracies. Given the history of violence during the democratic transition and the pervasiveness of corruption in Indonesian government at all levels over the past several decades, this achievement is major. It may also strengthen consolidation by giving local politicians and nongovernmental organization activists a vested interest in democracy as the "only game in town."

The scholarly debate has focused on a different issue: the extent to which the newly elected executives represent and are accountable to the voters. At one end of the spectrum are those who argue that the new executives are mostly members of the Suharto-era oligarchy who have used their political resources (official position, personal wealth, access to state and private business funds for political campaigns) to continue their dominance in the post-Suharto era. The implication is that Indonesia is no more democratic now (in the substantive sense in which these authors define democracy) than it was during the New Order. Nevertheless, within the oligarchic camp a more positive view is that decentralization has allowed for a wider range of competition, but that the elites and their resources are still rooted in the New Order period. Finally, some scholars see a more dynamic election-driven process unfolding in which voters are becoming more and more issue oriented and demanding toward local level officeholders and candidates.[20]

Our view is closer to the last of these three views, emphasizing the effects of local elections, with the caveat that given the recentness of decentralized democracy it is too early to come to firm conclusions. It is also important to be aware that significant structural, policy, and implementation issues concerning decentralization remain to be resolved at the national level. For example, new laws are under consideration for the second Yudhoyono administration (2009–2014) that are likely to strengthen the provinces and perhaps the center at the expense of the districts/municipalities.[21] Decentralization, perhaps more than any other aspect of Indonesian democracy, remains a work in progress.

Democratic Consolidation II: Attitudinal

With respect to attitude, Indonesian democracy appears on balance to be consolidating. There are nonetheless concerns about democracy's meaning and its relative ranking in terms of other values. Indonesians almost universally regard democracy as a good, but they define it diversely. However democracy is defined, public support for it has been strong and growing since 1999. Satisfaction with democratic performance, though lower, has also been growing. Moreover, on key performance indicators, voters are able to distinguish between the nondemocratic Suharto and the democratic Yudhoyono governments. They unfortunately also value economic development more highly than democracy. Though not a current concern, it is possible that a sharp or prolonged economic downturn might significantly reduce public support for democracy.

Data analyzed in this section are responses to nationwide, systematic random-sample surveys of voting-age Indonesian citizens conducted by the Lembaga Survei Indonesia (LSI, Indonesian Survey Institute) and its precursors. LSI was founded in 2003, but the scholars associated with it have been conducting mass political opinion surveys in Indonesia since 1999, when it first became possible to do so after the fall of Suharto.[22]

When asked in 2008 to choose the most important from a range of definitions of democracy, only 22 percent of respondents chose freedom to elect the government, although a further 22 percent chose freedom to criticize the government, for a total of 44 percent who correctly identified basic attributes of democracy. Thirty-one percent chose the availability and affordability of basic commodities, and a further 8 percent chose a small gap between rich and poor, perhaps reflecting Indonesia's history of anticolonialism followed by populist politics and economics.

Asked whether democracy is the best system of government for Indonesia compared to other systems, 68 percent agreed or agreed strongly in 1999. That number remained stable until 2004, when it rose to 75 percent, rising further to 83 percent in 2007 but declining slightly to 79 percent in 2008. Concerning the implementation of democracy or democratic performance, 38 percent expressed strong or moderate satisfaction in 2001. That number grew to 67 percent in 2005, declined to 62 percent in 2006 and 63 percent in 2007 before dropping to 54 percent in 2008. Compared to the Suharto era, most voters by very large margins perceive more freedom of speech and freedom to organize today (81 to 7 percent and 76 to 4 percent, respectively).[23]

On other issues as well, Indonesians prefer the Yudhoyono to the Suharto government—for example, equal treatment by the government of the people, 60 to 8 percent (a 52 percent gap); combating corruption, 65 to 12 percent (a 53 percent gap); providing security and order, 59 to 9 percent (a 50 percent gap); ordinary people's ability to influence the government, 35 to 7 percent (a 28 percent gap); and closing the rich–poor divide, 39 to 18 percent (a 21 percent gap). The smallest gap, though still in Yudhoyono's favor, concerns developing the economy, 42 to 34 percent (an 8 percent gap).

Mass perceptions of governmental economic development success or failure may indeed be the most important variable with ultimate consequences for democratic consolidation. In 2008, we asked: "If you were forced to choose just one of the following two goals, economic development or democracy, which would you choose?" By a huge margin, 76 to 10 percent,

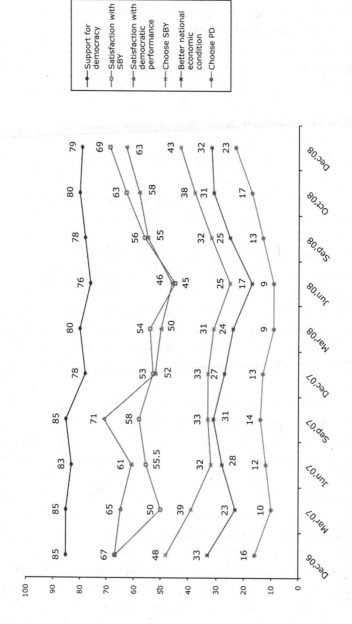

FIGURE 2.1 Parallels Between Political Economy Components: Choice of President, Partai Demokrat (PD), Evaluations of Presidential Performance and National Economic Condition (Responses to Lembaga Survei Indonesia Surveys, in %)

Indonesians chose economic development, a bald statement that they have priorities other than consolidating democracy.

What do our data show about the relationship between satisfaction with the performance of President Yudhoyono and the state of the national economy, on the one hand, and satisfaction with and support for democracy, on the other? For the current presidency, the data seem reassuring, but severe economic crisis or long-term stagnation might have a substantial negative effect on democratic consolidation. (See figure 2.1 and table 2.1.)

Figure 2.1 tracks the parallels in the rise and fall from late 2006 through 2008 in the public's level of support for democracy as a political system, satisfaction with President Yudhoyono's leadership, satisfaction with Indonesia's performance in conducting democratic elections, the decision to reelect Yudhoyono if the election were held on the day of the survey, perception of the condition of the national economy at the time of the survey compared to a year earlier, and the choice of Partai Demokrat, Yudhoyono's party, if the election were held that day.

Not all of these factors are statistically significant. Support for the idea that democracy is the best system of government correlates positively and significantly with satisfaction with democratic performance. Satisfaction with democratic performance in turn correlates significantly and positively with evaluation of the national economic condition but negatively with inflation (as measured by the Badan Pusat Statistik [Central Statistical Bureau]), as one would expect. Evaluation of the economy also correlates positively and significantly with satisfaction with the government of President Yudhoyono and with support for his Partai Demokrat and reelection as president.

The economy is therefore important for democratic consolidation and for strengthening support for the incumbent. But support for democracy and satisfaction with democratic performance are not correlated with support for Yudhoyono and the Partai Demokrat. The latter party won more votes than any other party in the 2009 parliamentary election, and Yudhoyono was reelected by a landslide. Had the outcome been different, with many fewer votes for Partai Demokrat and even a loss for Yudhoyono, support for democracy would not have been affected. Indonesian democracy is not vulnerable to political changes or to changes in national leadership, but it is very vulnerable to mass perceptions of the national economic condition.

TABLE 2.1

Correlation of Political Economy Components and Democracy 2007–2008 ($N = 10$)

	Choose SBY	Choose Partai Demokrat	SBY's Performance	National Economy	Inflation (BPS)	Satisfied with Democratic Performance	Democracy Best System
Choose SBY	1.0	0.95	0.99	0.97	-0.98	NS	NS
Choose Partai Demokrat		1.0	0.93	0.87	-0.91	NS	NS
SBY's Performance			1.0	0.98	-0.99	NS	NS
National Economy				1.0	-0.98	0.95	NS
Inflation (BPS)					1.0	-.76	NS
Satisfied with Democratic Performance						1.0	0.86
Democracy Best System							1.0

NOTE: All correlations significant at P-value 0.01 or better. NS = Statistically not significant. BPS = Badan Pusat Statistik (Central Statistical Bureau).

Democratic Consolidation III: Constitutional

Have governmental and nongovernmental forces alike throughout the country now agreed that conflicts will be resolved within the new democratic constitutional framework? The answer on balance again appears to be yes, although there are a number of methodological and substantive caveats.

The benchmark empirical research on social conflict during the last years of the Suharto era and the first three years of the transition to democracy is Mohammad Zulfan Tadjoeddin's United Nations–supported study based on data from 1990–2001 and published in 2002. His most important finding for our purposes is that there was "a significant upward trend of the number of incidents and the number of fatalities due to social violence during the transition period, reaching their peaks in 1999–2000." In 1997 specifically, there were 131 deaths attributable to social violence. In 1998, the number skyrocketed to 1,343. In 1999, it rose further to 1,813 but then declined in 2000 to 1,617 and in 2001 to 1,065.[24]

Tadjoeddin's sources were reports of conflict in the independent national daily newspaper Kompas and by the state-owned national news agency Antara. Overall in the period studied, he found at least 1,093 incidents of violence in which at least 6,028 people were killed. Communal conflict accounted for 77 percent of the conflicts, and 22 percent were connected to separatist movements in Aceh, Papua, and East Timor. Tadjoeddin's communal category includes ethnic, religious, and migrant–native conflicts because all three of these elements were intertwined in most of the cases reported. Most of the incidents occurred in small towns and rural areas. The major exception is the May 1998 Jakarta riots just prior to Suharto's resignation in which more than 1,000 people died. Much of the violence was concentrated in specific locations in just three provinces—Maluku, Aceh, and Central Kalimantan—out of thirty at the time.

Tadjoeddin argues tentatively that the principal cause of the spike in violence was the national-level transition to democracy. His argument is tentative for two reasons. His data collection ended in 2001, too early to be confident that the two-year decline would continue. Tadjoeddin also recognized that his pre-1998 data were less credible than his post-1998 data because the Suharto government in power until 1998 systematically suppressed reports of violence. Nonetheless, he argues in historical perspective that spikes in violent conflict have long been associated with major political transitions, from the independence revolution in 1945–1949 to the overthrow of Sukarno and the destruction of the Indonesian Communist Party in 1965–1966. In each of these cases, the spike was followed by a long period of a low level of violence.

Tadjoeddin's analysis is supported by political scientist Jacques Bertrand, who argues that Indonesia's founding fathers adopted a "national model" or fundamental conception of Indonesian politics whose components included a single nation, a strong central government, and a commitment to a religious but not Islamic state. During several "critical junctures," the most recent being the 1998–2001 (Bertrand's dates) democratic transition, groups disadvantaged by a particular regime's version of the model mounted violent challenges to that regime. The last critical juncture ended when Megawati Sukarnoputri became president and presided over the passing of constitutional and other reforms. Today's presidential democracy is a renegotiated national model that has led to "a new, relatively stable institutional environment."[25]

Most scholars probably agree with Tadjoeddin and Bertrand that there was a spike in violent social conflicts in the late 1990s and early 2000s, that they have since subsided, that the cause was popular unrest and demands associated with the weakening New Order, and that most conflicts are now being resolved within the framework of the democratic state. New quantitative research is being conducted, however, that may challenge these conclusions and have implications for democratic consolidation as well. The new data include reports from subprovincial as well as provincial and national newspapers and a 2003 Indonesian government survey of all villages in Indonesia.

Based on this ongoing research, Patrick Barron, Kai Kaiser, and Menno Pradhan make three tentative arguments: there may be much more social violence than previously reported; violence may be much more evenly spread across the archipelago; and significant levels of violence may be continuing in the present. Their findings are based so far on data only from East Java and East Nusa Tenggara, but if corroborated they may force other scholars to rethink both their substantive and causal arguments.[26] Relevant to democratic consolidation, it may turn out that a significant number of conflicts are not being resolved within the democratic constitutional framework.

The Five Arenas and Consolidation

In this final section, we identify a number of actual or potential threats to consolidation—that is, problems or weaknesses in Indonesian democratization associated with each of the five interacting arenas in a consolidated democracy specified by Linz and Stepan.

Civil Society

We have already discussed the most specific threat in the civil society arena: the Islamist social movement and its allies in the government and the quasi-governmental MUI. With the passing of an antipornography law and the "freezing," if not outright banning, of Ahmadiyya, Islamists have already succeeded in restricting the rights of Indonesians to speak and worship.

The low level of economic development more generally means that civil society movements are typically resource starved in terms of capable personnel, effective organizations, as well as budgets to fund their programs. They are not effective links between important social groups, political parties, and the governmental process. An example is the labor movement, now totally freed of the heavy Suharto-era repression but still an extremely weak representative of workers' interests. Even organizations that were most developed during the Suharto era, such as legal aid and environmental groups, report the loss of many of their most capable activists to political parties and government.[27]

Political Society

In political society, Indonesians have not achieved consensus on electoral procedures despite three national-level democratic elections. For decades, there has been pressure to make the parties and individual elected officials more accountable through elections, but that pressure has yet to produce an electoral law that can stand the test of time. In 1999, the Suharto-era electoral law, itself derived from the 1955 democratic elections, was continued on an emergency basis. In 2004, electoral districts were shrunk, a genuine achievement in the direction of greater accountability. A half-hearted attempt was also made to open party lists, but without substantial effect on national party leaders' power to determine seat allocations. In 2009, party lists were finally completely open. The cause, however, was a nonpolitical Constitutional Court decision, not the new electoral law passed by Parliament in 2008. Moreover, it remains unclear whether the impact of opening the lists will be to bring Parliament closer to the voters or to further weaken already programmatically weak parties. So the debate will continue at least up to the 2014 election.

Legislators and political party leaders at all levels are more generally not well linked to civil society or to the governmental process.[28] Legislators lack the most basic resources in terms of staff, library, and other investigative or law-making facilities. Legislators also tend to believe that once elected they do not have to be responsive to individual constituents or social groups (and, indeed, constituents make few demands on their elected officials).

Members of Parliament and the regional legislatures are anecdotally said to be chiefly interested in using their position to make money, often corruptly, not to legislate in the public interest. During general elections, vote buying (e.g., the so-called serangan fajar, "dawn attacks," on election day when party workers offer direct cash payments in exchange for a promised vote) appears to be becoming increasingly common. LSI surveys have found that voters have less trust in Parliament than in any other government institution. Indonesian voters also have low levels of political interest and efficacy.[29]

Indonesia's multiparty system interacts uneasily with presidentialism. In the 2004–2009 Yudhoyono administration, the president's Partai Demokrat held only 10 percent of the seats in Parliament, requiring a coalition government with several parties represented in the cabinet. Many of his ministers appear to have given their primary loyalty not to the president, but to their own party. Vice President Jusuf Kalla's Golkar party held an additional 23 percent of seats. This additional support made it possible for Yudhoyono to govern but at the same time set up an additional political tension within the government because of the two leaders' different party affiliations.[30]

Rule of Law

The rule of law has never been strong in Indonesia, and increasing its strength may today constitute the greatest long-term obstacle to democratic consolidation.[31] According to the World Bank's rule-of-law index, Indonesia's standing is among the lowest in the world, although it has been improving slowly since 2003.[32]

The Dutch established the beginnings of a modern legal system before World War II, but it was undermined by the turmoil of the Japanese occupation and lengthy revolution for independence. None of the parliamentary cabinets of the 1950s accorded rule-of-law institutions a high priority. President Sukarno, committed to political upheaval as a governing style, undermined the rule of law further during the Guided Democracy period. Suharto's New Order starved the legal sector of resources, explicitly subordinated the judicial to the executive branch of government, and manipulated legal processes behind the scenes.

After democratization, Presidents B. J. Habibie, Abdurrahman Wahid, and Megawati Sukarnoputri paid little attention to legal reform or rule-of-law issues generally, although the Komisi Pemberantasan Korupsi (Corruption Eradication Commission) was created in 2003 during Megawati's presidency. In his first presidential campaign, Yudhoyono pledged to make rule of law a high priority, and, indeed, both the Attorney General's Office and the commission initiated several prosecutions. Indonesia's improved standing in the World Bank's rule-of-law index may reflect that effort. Yudhoyono also gets very high or high marks from voters for governmental performance regarding criminality, gambling, and combating corruption.[33]

State Apparatus

There is no direct or immediate threat to democratic consolidation from the state apparatus or from a high level of popular demand for better state performance. Nonetheless, it is well to remember that Indonesian democratic governments enjoy only a limited "capacity to command, regulate, and extract."[34] They are constrained by a still small modern economy.

Under Suharto, that economy grew at a substantial rate and steady pace for more than a quarter-century. During those years, the state administrative apparatus, particularly the central government ministries responsible for economic policy formulation and implementation, were also strengthened. Unlike the 1950s, Indonesia now enjoys the basic minimum number of members of an "epistemic community" of trained economists capable of shaping Indonesia's domestic economic future and its international economic policy.[35]

Even after decades of economic growth, however, today's state budget is only about US$70 billion for a population of 230 million, slightly larger than that of the state of Illinois, which is $65 million for a population of 13 million. Corruption from within the Indonesian bureaucracy by all accounts takes a significant portion of that budget.[36] Moreover, government ministers, many of whom represent political parties in coalition cabinets, are unreliable implementers of presidential policy. The armed forces are even more problematic, both because of their history as an independent force and because much of their budget originates outside the state.

Perhaps fortunately for democratic consolidation, few of these weaknesses are reflected in voters' attitudes. Voters tend instead, according to LSI surveys, to give the government good marks across a wide range of substantive concerns. These concerns include demonstrably low-performance areas such as health (where 69 percent strongly agreed or agreed in October 2007 that the government was performing well), education (74 percent), and empowerment of women (67 percent) as well as genuinely higher-performance areas such as law and order and bringing peace in Aceh.[37]

Economic Society

Unlike the eastern European countries that are a principal focus of Linz and Stepan's *Problems of Democratic Transition and Consolidation*, Indonesia has been a mixed economy since independence. Nonetheless, state intervention looms large, with problematic consequences for democratic consolidation. According to the Economic Freedom Network, Indonesia ranked 43rd out of 54 national economies in 1970 and 101st out of 141 in 2006 in terms of level of economic freedom.[38]

The modern private sector has been and is currently dominated by Sino-Indonesian businesspeople. As individuals, they have been particularly vulnerable to extortion by state officials because of their marginal position in Indonesian society. As a group, however, they have substantial economic power and thus the capacity to disrupt the national economy. They can move their financial capital out of the country at the slightest sign of economic crisis (as happened in 1997–1998) or policy change affecting their interests (such as proposed foreign-exchange controls).

In the state sector, there are more than 150 state enterprises, few of them profitable for the state or the national economy, but many providing lucrative sources of income for government officials, political party leaders, and private business associates of those officials and leaders. Pertamina, the state oil company, was a major source of personal and political funds for President Suharto and allegedly remains so for today's democratic politicians.

The possibility of making money from politics is without question a major motive for many members of today's political elite. It also provides a fortunate few with massive resources that can be deployed during election campaigns, as almost certainly occurred in 2009. Relevant to democratic consolidation, some scholars argue that the state–political–business elite constitutes an "oligarchy" that dominates political life today (as it did in the Suharto years) despite formal democratization. In this view, the real issue is not the transition to and consolidation of new democratic institutions, but the concentrated economic power of a few that renders those institutions meaningless.[39]

Between 1998 and 2004, Indonesians managed a successful transition to democracy. A preponderance of evidence suggests that democracy has now consolidated. In terms of behavior, there is no significant group that threatens the democratic regime either by attempting to restore authoritarian rule at the national level or by separating from the Indonesian nation-state.

In terms of attitude, Indonesians strongly support democracy even though many are unsure of its meaning or define it socioeconomically. LSI surveys show that they understand the differences between Suharto's authoritarian rule and today's presidential democracy and much prefer the latter on a wide range of democratic and policy performance criteria. With respect to the Constitution, after a violent transition most Indonesians now appear to want to resolve their differences within the framework of the democratic and importantly decentralized regime.

Despite these successes, there are reasons to conclude on a tentative and watchful note. In terms of behavior, anti- or at least dubiously democratic but politically skillful Islamists have won some battles, both at the local level and the national level, where in the past few years they have restricted both freedom of speech and religion. A few military and civilian secular nationalists oppose democracy and seek opportunities to undermine it. Separatist sentiment remains powerful in Aceh and Papua, in the latter case almost certainly a serious long-term threat. Local-level democracy, still in its earliest stages, is a question mark.

In terms of attitude, support for democracy and satisfaction with democratic performance are hostage to popular evaluations of government policy performance and national economic condition. A major economic crisis, long-term stagnation or decline, might well precipitate a significant rise in antidemocratic sentiment, providing new political resources to antidemocratic actors. With respect to the Constitution, all the data on social violence are not in. Current research may challenge the finding that social peace has been restored after the violent transition to democracy.

In the five interacting arenas, interaction is also less than optimal. Perhaps most troubling is the low gross domestic product and slow rate of economic growth that negatively affect civil and political society, rule of law, state bureaucratic performance, and economic society alike. No democratic government has performed as well economically as did Suharto's New Order. In political society, neither the electoral system nor the relationship between the executive and legislative branches has stabilized. Despite progress under President Yudhoyono, Indonesia has one of the world's worst rule-of-law records. Finally, state enterprises and Sino-Indonesian private businesses that are closely tied to state agencies continue to dominate the economy. The result, although not quite oligarchic control, is certainly too much concentration of economic resources in the hands of a few politicians for the current health and perhaps future stability of Indonesian democracy.

Part II

Attitudes

The Development of a Democratic Consensus by Religious and Political Actors

3

How Pluralist Democracy Became the Consensual Discourse Among Secular and Nonsecular Muslims in Indonesia

Mirjam Künkler

The absence of strong currents of Islamist ideologies and militant movements in much of Indonesia's postindependent history is often portrayed as a consequence of the moderate nature of Southeast Asian Islam. Some even go so far as to attribute it to a certain "syncretism" predominant on the island of Java, which, it is claimed, has produced a religion that integrates Buddhist, Hindu, and local mystical beliefs with an Islamic overcoat. By such accounts, the emergence of liberal theological thought that places a high priority on interreligious tolerance and the equality of Muslims and non-Muslims seems a foregone conclusion. However, to read the failure of the Islamist project in Indonesia as a symptom of a predominantly moderate Islam is problematic in light of the country's postindependent history. Calls for the adoption of Shafii *fiqh*, the predominant Sunni school of law in Southeast Asia, as a source of legislation have periodically surfaced in constitutional and legislative debates. Furthermore, in Indonesia's postindependent history several regions have repeatedly attempted to institute sharia-based by-laws and thereby to circumvent the provisions of the national Constitution of 1945 that insists on the non-Islamic nature of the state. Finally, the survival of the 1945 Constitution must be ascribed primarily to the fact that the Konstituante (Constitutional Assembly of Indonesia) failed to generate a two-thirds majority for either the establishment of an Islamic state *or for the reaffirmation of Pancasila*. Barring any agreement on an alternative constitution, the 1945 Constitution remained in place and with it the Pancasila preamble.

The nature of the state in its relation to religion was openly debated at three junctures in Indonesia's recent history: in the days prior to the 1945 declaration of independence following the capitulation of Japan; in the mid-1950s during the session of the constitution-drafting assembly, the Konstituante; and during the onslaught of constitutional reforms in the aftermath of President Suharto's transfer of power to Vice President B. J. Habibie and the country's transition to democracy in 1998.

The discourse in the 1990s and during the Reformasi (Reformation) years on the nature of the state and a desirable relationship between religion and government closely reflected early postindependence exchanges between intellectuals from the Majelis Syuro Muslimin Indonesia (Masyumi, Council of Indonesian Muslim Associations, an Islamic political party), leaders of the Nahdlatul Ulama (NU, Rise of the Ulama), and secular nationalists.[1] In contrast to accounts that present Indonesia as a society where political Islam took root beginning in the 1980s, a look at the debates of the 1940s and 1950s reveals that a sharia state was always an historical possibility.

In this chapter, I analyze the construction of a pluralist democratic discourse in Indonesia despite this historical possibility. As we will see later, the emergence of a liberal Islamic discourse in Indonesia cannot be understood without tracing why early attempts at establishing group rights and religious law failed.

Islamist Discourse in the Konstituante

Zainal Abidin Ahmad was a leading politician and modernist thinker in Masyumi and a member of the Konstituante.[2] In the 1956 book *Creating an Islamic State*, he outlined the foundational elements of such a state; discussed why countries such as Yemen, Saudi Arabia, and Egypt that called themselves "Islamic" failed in fact to meet this claim; and how Indonesia could establish a genuinely religious state while also remaining true to its cultural identity as a multireligious country with a large part of the population adhering to non-Muslim, mystical, and local variants of faith.

Zainal's envisioned polity presents itself as a curious mix of Muslim supremacy and popular sovereignty. On the one hand, Zainal postulated a political system in which laws of the state must not conflict with Islamic law, the head of state must be Muslim, and demographic factors were to be represented in all legislatures in the form of quotas, so that, in particular, the majority of seats in Parliament would be reserved for Muslims. At the same time, Zainal envisioned that freedom of religion to pay worship to God would be upheld in the widest sense. There would be no coercion, pressure, or persuasion that would remove the sense of freedom and free will.[3]

Zainal also explained that religious or eternal laws "are not numerous, so their character is not to limit or diminish the Supreme Authority of the people's representatives, but to give clear guidance and enduring leadership."[4] Although he thus indicated the possibility of a limited scope of religious law, he failed to delineate clear procedures by which religious law and thereby its scope would be derived. In fact, one may doubt whether his system of government, if ever enacted, would have been able to sustain the people's sovereignty over experts of Islamic law. His further suggestion that "although the right to determine the law and statutes is the right of the people's representatives, the Constitution contains a guarantee that each regulation that is passed is not contrary to Islamic law"[5] would have corroborated that doubt. Notwithstanding Zainal's insistence on religious and other freedoms as well as popular sovereignty, the implementation of his constitutional vision would have resulted in an Islamic state where those endowed with the authority to interpret Islamic law would necessarily have had supreme authority.

Not all Masyumi delegates were as concerned as Zainal with developing an authentically Islamic system of rule for Indonesia. Haji Abdul Malik Karim Amrullah—or "Hamka," as he is usually referred to—was another prominent Masyumi leader and one of the country's most important theologians. Hamka became the first chair of the Majelis Ulama Indonesia (Indonesian Ulama Council), but he focused on normative bases that could unite the Indonesian nation. In a 1957 address to the Konstituante, Hamka tried to remind delegates that it was the spirit of independence and freedom from colonial rule that sparked the regional rebellions against Dutch reoccupation. To portray these separate struggles as a formative and unifying experience for the Indonesian "nation," he referred to them as "the revolution." Even those advocating a Pancasila state would have to concede, cried Hamka, that the source of their revolutionary yearning for freedom and sacrifice was the divine: "If I asked the defenders of Pancasila what they felt in their hearts when their beloved sons died and they took them to be buried—was it Pancasila or Allahu Akbar? Surely they would respond Allahu Akbar."[6]

In contrast to Zainal, Hamka pleaded for the symbolic acknowledgment of Islam as the foundation of the independent state but did not develop an institutional model of Islamic government.

Both Zainal and Hamka were modernist Muslims receptive to a larger transnational discourse about religion, modernity, independence, and government. The NU position was slightly different at the time. Hard-liners within NU also advocated the establishment of an Islamic state, but arguably less so in the context of an engagement with Sayyed Qutb's and Abul Aala Maududi's ideas of Islamic government and more out of a concern for loss of their social and political influence in a postindependent secular state. The pragmatist camp within NU gave greater preference to general jurisprudential maxims than to specific legal provisions. For instance, pragmatists would invoke *amar mahruf nahi munkar* (promoting the good and preventing evil) and *maslahat* (benefit) as general guidelines rather than discuss how codified religious law could be integrated into the emerging constitution.[7] The head of NU's *syuriyah* (advisory) council, the *rais aam*, was Wahab Chasbullah at the time, a pragmatist and political strategist. Most NU politicians and Wahab Chasbullah in particular understood these precepts primarily as justifying political flexibility and expedience. Whereas conservatives placed a high value on Islamic unity, pragmatists were concerned not to alienate non-Muslim Indonesians and were in their policy stances indeed more often aligned with the nationalists than with the Islamic modernists and Masyumi.[8]

Once the Konstituante was dissolved in 1959 and Masyumi was outlawed, President Sukarno proclaimed the return to the 1945 Constitution and reaffirmed Pancasila as the state ideology. Debates about the nature of the Indonesian state then subsided and Islamic organizations invested their efforts primarily in the societal rather than the political sphere. When modernist and traditionalist Muslims aided General Suharto in his quest for power and participated in the killings of thousands of so-called Communists in 1965, many had hoped for accommodation in the emerging Orde Baru (New Order) and a reopening of the debate over an Islamic state. In fact, this expectation may have been the primary motivation for most confessing Muslims to support Suharto's ascendance against Sukarno. When the new president then decided not to relegalize Masyumi, to reaffirm Pancasila as the state's ideational basis in 1966, and, moreover, to force Masyumi's weak successor, the Partai Muslimin Indonesia (Parmusi, Indonesian Muslims Party), and NU into an official opposition party held under strict supervision by the regime, debates over sharia-based legislation became impossible. After 1971, Islamic movements redirected their energies toward *dawa* (propagation of faith) activities in the rural areas and considerably expanded their educational and health programs. The Muhammadiyah (Followers of Muhammad) even proclaimed explicitly in 1971 that it would not join Parmusi and instead devote all its activities to proselytization and education.

An Emergent Liberal Discourse

An important and probably unforeseeable impetus for a major reform in Indonesian Islam came about with the ascendance of one of the most influential Indonesian Islamic scholars of the twentieth century, Harun Nasution (1919–1998), to the rectorship of the Institut Agama Islam Negeri (IAIN, State Institute of Islamic Studies) in Jakarta in 1973 and the curriculum reforms he introduced.

One of Nasution's most profound contributions was his rehabilitation of Mutazilite thought[9] in Southeast Asian Islam. Nasution reexamined the reception of the Mutazila in Indonesia and sought to correct what he felt was a reductionist view of this rationalist strand in Islamic thought prevailing in Southeast Asia. As in other parts of the Muslim world, the discrediting critique of the Mutazila by thirteenth- and fourteenth-century scholar Ibn Taymiyyah had eradicated it from the curricula of Islamic education. The dominance of Ash'arite theology in the *kitab kuning*—the classical books of Islamic instruction in Southeast Asia—discounted the notion of free will in Islamic theology, Nasution argued, and was partially responsible for the discouragement of sciences and technological developments among traditional Indonesian Muslims.

When Nasution became rector of IAIN Jakarta, he seized the chance to integrate his research on the Mutazila and other rationalist approaches to the study of religion into a new vision for Islamic education. He reformed the IAIN curricula by complementing the predominantly Ash'arite Qur'an commentaries with Mutazilite sources and expanding the program of study. Epistemology and hermeneutics were from then on integral parts of the curriculum.

Nasution's vision for a new curriculum was in part also a result of his reexamination of twentieth-century Egyptian reformism in order to determine how its methodologies could be applied to Islamic modernism in the Southeast Asian context. While revisiting the early work of Muhammad Abduh, the Egyptian religious scholar, and exploring its relevance for Indonesian Islam, Nasution excavated the early Sufi influences on Abduh's thought. By making Mutazilite thought accepted again and by reactivating the Sufi and more contextualist elements in Middle Eastern reformism, he laid the groundwork for developing a rational and dynamic interpretation of Islam in the country, facilitated by a new generation familiarized with alternative sources and methodologies to study the religious scriptures.

The new curriculum, called an "Introduction to Islamic Studies," comprised philosophy, mysticism, theology, sociology, and research methods.[10] The reforms not only paved the way to a more critical study of religious sources but also made studies at IAIN more attractive by expanding the non-religious curriculum.[11] Nasution's curriculum development was so successful that the national convention of IAIN rectors in 1973 decided to adopt it in all State Islamic Institutes, and it has been the foundation of all teaching in Islamic studies at IAIN ever since.

Education, in Nasution's view, laid the basis for a more Islamic and ethical society. Instead of being occupied with institutions and symbolism as Zainal and Hamka had been, Nasution was concerned primarily with the role of Islamic education in generating responsible leaders and citizens. To the ulama (religious scholars), Nasution wrote, "Islamic institutions have nothing to do with political parties but are about the spirit or soul of the rule. If the ruler has an Islamic spirit, the Muslim umma will develop; Islam will develop in a country if her leader or power elite is mentally Islamic [and] therefore will be close to the power elite. [It will] [b]ring him or her the spirit of Islam. So men and women who are anti-Islam will regress."[12]

Nasution's project was later complemented by an explicit policy promoted by Minister of Religion Munawir Sjadzali, who instituted a program that would send IAIN students and faculty abroad to receive further education in institutions of Islamic studies in Europe, Canada, and the United States, particularly at the University of Leiden, McGill University, and the University of Chicago. Several of the leading Islamic thinkers of the past twenty to thirty years in Indonesia have pursued Ph.D. degrees at these universities abroad, and several claim that Munawir's program helped relax ideological tensions that were beginning to rise in Indonesia in the 1990s.

Nurcholish Madjid

Among those who pursued their Ph.D.s abroad after having attended IAIN Jakarta was Nurcholish Madjid (1939–2005), who emerged as one of the country's most important Muslim thinkers and public intellectuals. Madjid's religious background was unusual in that he had both strong traditionalist and modernist tendencies in his family: whereas his father remained a Masyumi member when the traditionalist NU split from the political faction in 1952, most of his uncles joined NU. During his education, Madjid was trained in the *pesantren* (religious boarding school) in East Java but also attended Nasution's modernist IAIN in Jakarta and later pursued a Ph.D. with Fazlur Rahman[13]at the University of Chicago. Madjid received his Ph.D. in 1984 with a thesis about the controversial thirteenth/fourteenth-century scholar Ibn Taymiyyah (see the earlier discussion of Nasution), viewed as a Sufi by some and as a literalist by others.[14]

Even though Madjid was elected chair of the Himpunan Mahasiswa Indonesia (HMI, Islamic Students Association) in the year of Suharto's final takeover in 1966 and remained in that position until 1971,[15] he never became a prominent Muhammadiyah or NU member, let alone an activist for either of these two organizations. Rather than working through one of the multimillion-member Islamic organizations and thus risking political appropriation, Madjid remained a distinctly independent voice in society. When Suharto in his final days in 1998 called on nine Muslim leaders to advise on how best to react to the street protests and demonstrations, it was this independence that permitted Madjid—the only one of the nine—to inform Suharto frankly about the state of affairs. The announcement of another reform package would not do, Madjid told Suharto: the people demanded no less than the president's resignation.[16]

Upon returning to Indonesia from graduate studies at Chicago, Madjid published a series of translations into Bahasa Indonesia of writings by al-Kindi, al-Farabi, Mohammad Abduh, and al-Afghani that would build upon Nasution's project of laying the groundwork for dynamic interpretations of Islam in Southeast Asia. Madjid later founded a religious studies institution in Jakarta called Paramadina, which especially catered to the modern middle class and became a popular center for dynamic Islamic thought, including a center for Sufi teachings. As noted later, Paramadina and the discussion circles, networks, and nongovernmental organizations created by its students became major transmitters for Madjid's thoughts.

Renovation of Ideas

Madjid's most influential contributions to Southeast Asian Islam consisted of often unusual and certainly unorthodox reinterpretations of particular

Qur'anic verses. Famously known for his statement "Islam yes, Islamic parties no" and his defense of "secularism" the way he conceptualized it, Madjid often occupied an ambiguous middle seat between faithful Islamic communities and the "secular" New Order, whose project of secular modernization Madjid's thought often seemed to legitimate.[17]

Already in 1970, when Madjid was still national chair of HMI, he gave a visionary speech about the necessity to renew religious thought in Indonesia, which provoked a wave of critical responses. "The paralysis of the *umat* these days is due, among other things," he wrote, "to the fact that it is closing its eyes tight to its bodily defects. This necessitates the existence of a movement aimed at the renovation of its ideas so that the defects may be removed."[18] Only through this renovation of ideas could the Muslim world also start to reacquire an authenticity and autonomy from Western culture that would allow for its political and economic development. Dynamization of Islamic thought was a core concern for Madjid, not only for religious reasons, but also social and political reasons.

In that vein, Madjid proposed to rethink what Islam is and had been over the course of the centuries. Instead of conceiving of Islam as a demarcated religious tradition, he postulated it first and foremost as a way to approach God: Islam as a method, possibly the best available method, of self-surrendering to God. In this vein, he interpreted Sura 3:19, "Inna ad-dina 'inda Allah al-Islam" (often translated as "The Religion before Allah is Islam" or "The only religion at Allah's side is Islam"),[19] as meaning that "the only religion in the sight of God is man's self-surrender to him," conceiving Islam as "self-surrender to the divine" rather than to one singular religion—and, hence, as one of several possible ways to approach God rather than the only way.[20]

He similarly interpreted Sura 3:85, "If anyone desires a religion other than Islam (submission to Allah), never will it be accepted of him; and in the Hereafter He will be in the ranks of those who have lost (All spiritual good),"[21] as implying "All religions are one because there is only one truth. It is the religion that is taught by all prophets"—once again understanding "Islam" here as submission or self-surrender to God. Madjid went so far as to argue that Islam as surrender to God was a generic value common to all religions and that religions were but different vehicles by which to reach spiritual proximity to God.[22]

This supraconfessional or universalist notion of Islam also expressed itself in Madjid's view of the relationship between Islam and Indonesian (multireligious) nationalism, which he viewed as perfectly compatible. Martin Van

Bruinessen comments, "One senses in Nurcholish's understanding of 'Indonesian-ness' the influence of [Islamic scholar and world historian] Marshall Hodgson's concept of 'Islamicate' civilization, with which [Nurcholish] became acquainted during his stay in Chicago. Christians, Hindus, and Buddhists are equal citizens in Nurcholish's view of Indonesian society, but Islam provides the overarching civilizational unity."[23]

Political Islam

As noted earlier, Madjid famously and contrarily to the modernist positions at the time put Islamic parties into question. Reflecting upon the period of parliamentary democracy in Indonesia during the 1950s, he speculated in 1970:

> To what extent were they [Indonesian Muslims] attracted to Islamic parties and organizations? Except for a few, it is clear that they were not attracted to Islamic parties or organizations. Their attitude may be formulated more or less thus: "Islam yes, Islamic party no!" So if Islamic parties constitute a receptacle of ideas that are going to be fought for on the basis of Islam, then it is obvious that those ideas are now unattractive. In other words, those ideas and Islamic thinking are now becoming fossilized and obsolete, devoid of dynamism. Moreover, these Islamic parties have failed to build a positive and sympathetic image; in fact they have an image that is just the opposite.[24]

Although Madjid here appears to diagnose only the relative lack of Indonesian support for Islamic parties (the Islamist parties Masyumi and the Partai Sarekat Islam Indonesia [Indonesian Islamic Union Party] gained only about 22 percent of the vote in 1955), he came to be known as an opponent of Islamic parties because he felt they would reinforce exclusive identities and in the long term divide and polarize the country. The idea of parties catering to an exclusively Muslim community violated his notion of Islam as an overarching civilizational umbrella for the Indonesian nation.

Like many of his Indonesian Christian counterparts and the early Masyumi, Madjid viewed the model of a democratic welfare state as the best institutional arrangement to facilitate a good Islamic religious life in the sense that its socioeconomic ideals of justice and equality enable a believer to live up to his and her religious duties.

Secularism

As van Bruinessen points out, Madjid could also be a shrewd strategist in the dissemination of his ideas. Early on in his career, he alienated many Muslim modernists by suggesting that secularization was necessary in order to desacralize profane things that had been unduly sacralized over the turn of the centuries. The "temporal" character of worldly values had to be recognized, he argued, and the human materialist and social drives differentiated from the spiritual. "The temporal role of man as God's vicegerent on earth [must] be fully consummated. Acting as vicegerent of God provides man with enough space for his freedom to choose and decide for himself, in the context of improving his life on earth."[25] Madjid thus called for the recognition of a demarcation between things in modern life that are fundamentally affected by religion and those that are not. Similar to Abdolkarim Soroush, the Iranian philosopher and religious theorist, he argued here against the totalizing tendencies of some modernist Islamic currents that seek to extrapolate Islamic teachings by the method of precedence and analogy (*qiyas*) to modern phenomena. Secularization, in Madjid's conception, signified the appreciation of the inherently *limited* nature of religion to regulate all realms of modern life.[26] Because this stance could be interpreted as legitimating New Order policies, many modernists remained skeptical of Madjid's supposedly apolitical agenda.

When Madjid started a private exchange with senior Masyumi leader Mohammad Roem[27] during his time in Chicago, he recognized an opportunity to rehabilitate himself by publishing this correspondence, even without Roem's explicit consent. As intended, Madjid emerged from the correspondence and from the discussions sparked by its publication as a "worthy interlocutor" with a senior Masyumi leader, who himself had once been a conciliatory force between nationalists and Muslim modernists during the 1945 negotiations for Indonesian independence.

Madjid significantly pointed out in his exchange with Roem that the revered Ibn Taymiyyah himself had written about the Prophet's ability to err. Madjid used this insight to insist that any law based on prophetic hadith and even the Qur'an could not be beyond human error.

As a consequence, Madjid vigorously opposed any role for the state in promoting religious law: "It is already clear that despite the renovations of the reformists, *fiqh* [jurisprudence] has lost its relevance to the present mode of living. Its complete renovation, however, such that it might become suitable for modern life, would require a comprehensive knowledge of modern life in all its aspects, so that it does not become an interest and [a matter of the] competency of the Muslim umat alone, but of others as well. Its result then, does not have to be in the form of Islamic law per se, but of law that embraces everybody for the regulation of a life shared by all."[28]

How did Madjid's ideas reach the wide audience that they did? How could Madjid, despite the fact that he never became a prominent Muhammadiyah or NU activist, let alone the chairman of either of these organizations, become one of the most—perhaps the most—influential Islamic intellectual of twentieth-century Indonesia?

One major vehicle for the transmission of his thought became the already mentioned Paramadina Foundation, which under Madjid's aegis developed into a major center for nonorthodox Islamic thought and debate and which issued influential publications that further disseminated Madjid's and other reformist thinkers' ideas. Madjid also served as visiting professor in the Lembaga Ilmu Pengetahuan Indonesia (Indonesian Academy of Sciences) and as a senior lecturer at IAIN Jakarta, and he delivered monthly lectures at the Jakarta Klub Kajian Agama (Club of Religious Studies), a network of mainly middle-class Muslims. Several institutions—such as the Lembaga Studi Agama dan Filsafat (Philosophy and Religion Study Circle), the Lembaga Penelitian, Pendidikan dan Penerangan Ekonomi dan Sosial (Institute for Social and Economic Research, Education, and Information), and the Perhimpunan Pengembangan Pesantren dan Masyarakat (Association for the Development of Pesantren and Society)—became recruitment grounds for IAIN graduates and Madjid's students who would transmit his thought into concrete programs for social work, adult education, development, and community building. Dawam Rahardjo, a senior Muhammadiyah member and close associate of Madjid, edited two publications in which he invited authors to discuss social implications of theological approaches (*Prisma* magazine) and to debate theological issues (*Ulumul Qur'an*). As Kamaruzzaman Bustamam-Ahmad has noted, "If Nurcholish Madjid is known as a man of ideas, then Dawam [Rahardjo] may be called a man of practice."[29] Both Madjid and Dawam had been thoroughly trained in the *pesantren* system but later were also educated in modernist institutions such as IAIN. This dual background enabled them to develop sophisticated Islamic thought *and* to connect theology to real-world problems and express ideas in a language accessible to those not trained in Islamic studies.

As was the case for other major Indonesian thinkers, Madjid and Rahardjo's works were published by Mizan, a renowned publishing house that also translated Arabic, Persian, and Urdu works on Islamic thought into Bahasa Indonesia, notably Ayatollah Mottahari's and Ali Shari'ati's works, and therefore provided an important international link.[30] Paramadina also published the *Ensiklopedia Qur'an* in Bahasa Indonesia, which became a new standard in Indonesian modernist Islam and substantially drew on the debates in *Ulumul Qur'an*.[31] Through such discourse-defining publications and a number of regular lectures, newspaper columns, and editorials, Nurcholish Madjid and his colleagues "inundated" Indonesian Islamic thought in the 1980s and 1990s.

NU and the Exit from Regime-Structured Politics

Although the major modernist organizations HMI and Muhammadiyah maintained a distance from the regime and their modernist thought profited from that distance, the same cannot be said for NU. The NU had been a political actor for the greater part of its existence and, in contradistinction to Muhammadiyah, had both formed a political party and run in parliamentary elections since 1955.

The NU was the country's largest Islamic organization, with strong roots in Java's *pesantren* and a membership of 30–35 million in the 1990s. Throughout the Sukarno presidency, an NU member always served as the minister of religion, and the NU probably profited from the ministry's patronage like no other organization or party in the state. After Suharto's takeover, the NU remained a political party, and, as the major faction in one of the two pro forma opposition parties, it often tread a fine line between opposition to and accommodation with the regime. Toward the late 1970s and early 1980s, confrontation between the NU and the regime intensified as Suharto did not deliver on his initial promise to serve only two presidential terms but let himself be reelected in the 1978 session of the Majelis Permusyawaratan Rakyat (MPR, People's Consultative Assembly). Moreover, in that same year (1978), the New Order introduced mandatory Pancasila classes in high schools and two-week-long intensive Pancasila workshops to be held at the start of the semester at all universities. Two years later Suharto elevated the Angkatan Bersenjata Republik Indonesia (Indonesian Army Forces) to the position of "guardian of Pancasila" and the secular order, which triggered wide protest among secular and religious intellectuals and motivated a group of civil society and retired political leaders to publish a slew of petitions and to call for free and direct presidential elections. It is in this climate that NU's 1984 Muktamar (General Meeting) took place, which changed the course of the organization.

It was the NU activist Ahmad Siddiq who must largely be credited with the far-reaching decisions that would be taken at the 1984 Muktamar. Siddiq had served in the country's first elected Parliament from 1955 to 1957 as well as in the first New Order legislature from 1971 to 1979. His career displayed some political ambiguity because in the 1960s he had emerged as a fervent anti-Communist, a position hard to reconcile with his later advocacy of tolerance and balance in theological matters.[32] Despite his anti-Communist zeal, Siddiq became one of the most outspoken advocates of moderation and flexibility in politics in the late 1970s.

When the MPR tabled a bill in 1983 that would force all organizations to accept Pancasila as their sole foundation (*asas tunggal*), it was Ahmad Siddiq who worked out the theological treatise to convince NU members of the reconcilability of Pancasila and Islam. In doing so, he drew heavily on quietist principles in traditional *fiqh*, such as *tawassuf* (moderation, the middle way), *itidal* (equity), and *tawazun* (balance). With reference to these principles, Siddiq argued that confrontation with political rulers—that is, the New Order—should be avoided (except in cases where Islam faces a dire threat, such as communism) and that NU members ought therefore consider withdrawing NU from the political arena.

In this theological treatise, Siddiq drew heavily on his work *Khitthah Nahdliyah* (NU's Line of Action), published in 1980, in which he had reexamined the original motivations for the founding of the organization and the sociopolitical orientations that flowed out of this foundation. During the 1984 Muktamar, he first convinced a group of younger intellectual leaders[33] and then, in a joint effort with Abdurrahman Wahid and others, the majority of NU delegates to return to the 1926 NU *khittah* (constitution). The return to 1926 implied that NU would withdraw from official party politics and direct its efforts again at the societal level to social work, education, and *dawa* (propagation of Islam).

The 1984 decision enabled NU to end a period of increased confrontation with the regime and to evade the possibility of further political cooptation that put NU's legitimacy at risk in the eyes of its members. Signifying the overwhelming support that Ahmad Siddiq and Abdurrahman Wahid were able to secure in their radical effort to change the course of NU's engagement with the state, both were elected to leadership positions at the end of the Muktamar: Ahmad Siddiq was elected president (*rais aam*, head of the organization's *syuriyah* council),[34] and Abdurrahman Wahid the organization's (managerial) chairman.[35] After 1984, NU launched a wide range of community-development and empowerment programs, and a new spirit of intellectual and cultural openness took hold within the organization.

Abdurrahman Wahid

As the grandson of NU founders Hasyim Ashyari and Bisri Syansuri and the son of NU leader Wahid Hasyim (Indonesia's first minister of religious affairs in 1945 and holding that position again in 1949–1952), Abdurrahman Wahid (1940–2009) came from one of the most prominent NU dynasties. When his father suddenly passed away in a car accident that Wahid witnessed at the age of thirteen, Wahid went to stay with preeminent Muhammadiyah leader and modernist Kyai Junaid for three years while attending junior high school. He then studied in a number of leading NU *pesantren* around Jombang in East Java before leaving for Cairo's al-Azhar University in 1964. Perceiving al-Azhar's rigid teachings and methods of memorization as uninspiring, Wahid left it two years later to register at the University of Baghdad, where he studied European philosophy, social theory, and Arab literature before returning to Indonesia in 1971 at the age of thirty-one.

After his exposure to Islamic modernism and foreign educational institutions, Wahid made it a special mission upon his return to advocate the modernization and "dynamization" (*dinamisasi*) of the NU *pesantren* system. Feeling that the pedagogical methods and the limited curriculum centered upon a *kyai*'s (Islamic scholar's) legal opinions were a poor basis to educate and advance the social mobility of the traditionalist youth, Wahid argued for a new model of the *kyai*–student relationship and an expansion of the curriculum.

Wahid would typically make his case with a narrative reference to personal experiences and encounters he had made in his youth and early adult life rather than argue the benefits and drawbacks of a question directly. Instead, he pled by inference, illustration, and analogy. Recalling a dialogue he had entertained with Kyai Ali Ma'shum in Yogyakarta during his studies, Wahid wrote in a 1980 article in *Tempo* magazine: "Along with the classical religious texts, *santri* [students] are encouraged [in Kyai Ali Ma'shum's *pesantren*] to read modern Middle Eastern literature. . . . Together with deepening their knowledge of Islamic law through studies in classical fiqh texts, they are directed to also make a careful comparative study of the legal traditions followed in the West and East. [Someone asked the kyai:] 'Why do you order them to study Abduh's books, aren't you afraid that they might wander away from NU?' Kyai Ali replies, laughing in his inimitable fashion, 'Wide reading will result in a mature NU.'[36]

Although Wahid did not argue a case explicitly by telling this little story, he nevertheless showed his readers why complementing the classical *fiqh* education with other subjects and textual sources from other regions of the world might be important for that education.

The need for reform of the NU *pesantren* system was felt not least due to the growing popularity of both state and Muhammadiyah schools, which offered either a predominantly secular education or an education with mixed curricula, but nearly always one involving training in the natural and social sciences as well as elements of vocational training and the arts. "The most important prerequisite for a wide-ranging and profound process of dynamization is the wholesale reformation of teaching material for religious learning. . . . Mature traditionalism is far better than superficial pseudo-modernism."[37] A major vehicle for Wahid's ideas regarding the reform of the *pesantren* system was the Association for the Development of Pesantren and Society, established in 1983. Its expressed goals included providing intellectual support for ideational renewal in the *pesantren* world. And it published a quarterly journal that examined and disseminated the latest theological and social developments in the country's *pesantren* and offered a forum to examine and discuss further strategies for reform.

Departing from the approach taken by his grandfather Asyari, who had insisted that *taqlid*, or the unquestioning acceptance and adoption of doctrines laid down by the leaders of the *madhab*s (religious school of law or *fiqh*), was necessary, Wahid aimed to show that even in the local Islamic tradition a pure application of *fiqh* principles had never been the case: ulama always used a dose of reason when formulating legal opinions and recommendations, and jurisprudence was not a passive application of law, but, especially before the codification of sharia in the nineteenth century, an act of interpretation.[38] Thus, in an effort to correct an image of the Islamic legal tradition as being rigid and based solely on textual exegesis rather than acknowledging that religious commentary would also always involve the author's individual rationality, Wahid wrote another article published in *Tempo* magazine in 1980 in which he reviewed the position of a senior *kyai* with regard to gender relations. Wahid asked at the outset of the article how one could comprehend the decision by Kyai Sobari of the Javanese NU not to oppose the introduction of coeducational schools when he otherwise rigidly insisted on the modesty of gender relations and entertained a fierce opposition to the government-sponsored family-planning program. Wahid tried to show that the tension between these two seemingly contradictory stances by Kyai Sobari could be understood when acknowledging Sobari's personal investment of rationality in the formation of his legal opinions. "Few places could be safer for the controlled interaction between boys and girls than the classroom," Wahid explained. Coeducation was therefore conceived not as a threat to, but as a vehicle toward establishing modest gender relations. By applying this line of reasoning, Sobari, according to Wahid, exposed his independent use of reason and thereby allowed flexibility in his legal verdicts. "The flexible approach of this unique 'old fashioned' [because of his otherwise conservative views] *kyai* is most interesting," Wahid wrote, "because it has a number of implications. What is clear is that it is not right for us to regard these 'old-fashioned' *kyai* as forming opinions without any rational basis, being only able to pass on the content of classical *fiqh* literature without expanding upon it in any way."[39]

In 1975, Wahid wrote a remarkable article that appeared in *Prisma* magazine (mentioned earlier as an important vehicle of Madjid's thought) in which he argued the necessity of "making Islamic law conducive to development." "In order to become relevant, Islamic law has to develop for itself a dynamic character. In doing this, it needs to formulate itself as supporter of the development of national law in this realm of development.[. . .]This self-development requires a vision that extends well beyond the circle of Islamic legal experts themselves. In other words, it requires taking a multidimensional approach to life, and not simply remaining bound to normative formulations long since settled, that are, in fact, virtually at the point of becoming fossils."[40]

Wahid went on to plead for a greater accommodation of reason in Islamic jurisprudence and an increased sensitivity toward the needs of humanity when applying religious law. "Through this sensitivity, Islamic law will constantly make the adjustments required, without sacrificing its transcendental values as fixed by God who must be praised. Through this sensitivity, Islamic law will continue to contribute to the development of the nation; that is to say, it will create dynamic principles for life based on an awareness of the necessity for men and women to labor within the limits of their ability as mere creatures."[41] The spirit of the law, the *hakikat* (the inner truth), needed to take precedence over the letter of the law. He maintained this position even during the Reformasi era amidst renewed calls for the expansion of sharia in Indonesia's legal system.

In many of Wahid's activities, he increasingly began to focus on the need for democracy for Indonesia. In 1990, he created a broad interfaith group, including Christians, called the Forum Demokrasi (Democratic Forum). The forum's declared goals were "to increase communication between groups of supporters of the democratization process," to loosen existing political arrangements to ensure "that the nation matures politically," and to "build links between a range of efforts in the struggle for democratization."[42]

Pancasila

Wahid's views on Pancasila diverged sharply from those of Nurcholish Madjid. For Wahid, Pancasila provided the quintessential possibility of accommodating religious difference without the need to exclude religion altogether from the public sphere. Pancasila allowed for the religious identification of the state without specifying which religion and thereby provided crucial guarantees to religious minority groups. Madjid, by contrast, although not against Pancasila in substantive terms, did not regard it as a suitable basis of the state because he considered it unnecessary: its teachings were already present in (his interpretation of) Islam and therefore did not need to be stated in a separate doctrine. What Madjid saw as a redundant ideology given (his unusual all-embracing, suprareligious) notion of Islam, Wahid viewed as a politically suitable ideology to guarantee peaceful religious coexistence.

This disagreement is indicative of the two leaders' different approaches to religion. Throughout his career, Abdurrahman Wahid was first and foremost a "manager" of a large Islamic community that he, together with others of his generation, such as Ahmad Siddiq, stirred to accept democratic values for the sake, I would argue, of maintaining interreligious and intercommunal peace as a fundamentally Islamic value.[43] Madjid, by contrast, theologically modernized Indonesian Islam for the sake of the continuing importance of Islamic life and practice—notwithstanding its political ramifications.

Where Madjid embraced democracy primarily on procedural grounds, Wahid did so for both procedural and substantive reasons. Before and during his presidency (1999–2001), Wahid stressed repeatedly that no political system should be based on sectarian politics, an argument aimed mostly at Muslim modernists who for long had publicly favored a religious quota system and power-sharing devices in the spirit of a religious consociational model. Wahid by contrast argued that instead of being concerned with institutional arrangements, Islam ought to be predominantly concerned with culture, including *political* culture.[44] Whereas Muhammadiyah chairman Amien Rais and Nurcholish Madjid embraced democracy as the best method by which to ensure adequate representation of specifically Muslim interests, Wahid saw an intrinsic value in democracy, which he believed coincided with and granted space to the fundamental values of Islam: peace, equality, justice, and dignity. "While religion has an important role as a social and moral force, the political arena should be the realm of political parties. This will allow Islam to function as a force for morality and for the control of authority, and to avoid being entrapped in the ambiguity of power struggles. The relations between the state and religion in the Islamic world will continue to be confronted with many challenges. We should navigate between the two to avoid being entrapped in an absolute secularism or fundamentalism. We should indeed use religious teachings to guide government's actions."[45]

Like Madjid, Wahid profited from the networks sustained by Dawam Rahardjo and other graduates of IAIN, in particular the Institute for Economic and Social Research, Education, and Information, established in 1971 with funding from the German Friedrich Naumann Foundation. As mentioned earlier, the institute published *Prisma*, in which many of Wahid's commentaries as well as articles by Nurcholish Madjid, Fachry Ali, and Dawam Rahardjo appeared. It was one of *Prisma*'s greatest virtues that it featured articles from diverse ideological backgrounds and often included educational essays that would facilitate understanding of complex Islamic discourses even for the layman and a sense of why the theoretical questions under review were of real-world relevance.

It would be futile to attempt a summary of the arguments and debates that Indonesian religious thinkers generated over the course of sixty years to arrive at a new hegemonic discourse that prioritizes religious pluralism, a rationalist hermeneutic in approaching the religious texts, and the defense of democratic norms and processes. Three observations should, however, be highlighted.

First, the extent to which Muslim intellectuals were able to disseminate their message through the careful cultivation of networks of public debate and infrastructures of publication is impressive. Many of these thinkers profited from the already existing infrastructure of the large Islamic organizations, which provided for regular opportunities to engage in debates about the proper place of Islam and Islamic law in a multireligious society such as Indonesia. The regular annual conventions and subnational conferences, the publications that these organizations produced, and their tight network with women's, youth, and student branches all over the country facilitated ample venues and channels for the dissemination of particular ideas. But even thinkers outside of these organizations, such as Nurcholish Madjid, were able to cultivate their own networks of dissemination through regular workshops at the State Islamic Institutes and other intellectual centers in Indonesia's major cities, through independent intellectual magazines, and through a variety of think tanks and nongovernmental organizations that dealt with developmental issues from an Islamic perspective.

Second, the specific nature of the Indonesian Islamic organizations allowed for and, indeed, required intense exchanges between the grass roots and the organizations' *syuriya* councils that would issue fatwas (legal recommendations) and decide on each organization's overall stance regarding key theological questions. This tight connect resulted in a situation where ideas hardly ever remained at the intellectual level but were translated into concrete policies and decisions at the grassroots level. (For example, should NU *pesantren* become coeducational? Should the religious texts be read in the vernacular also? Can Muslims take part in Christian celebrations?) As a consequence, new religious debates often originated in concrete inquiries that had emanated from the organization's local branches and were redefined in a dialogical process between the conceptual and the applied. Thus, religious intellectual developments remained relevant for the average believer and simultaneously informed by and responsive to changing social demands and needs.

Third and finally, it has to be noted that the most influential religious thinkers in Indonesia had both a background in the traditional Islamic instruction in the *pesantren* as well as training in modernist Islamic theology and European philosophy. Although the *pesantren* education would provide these thinkers with elemental training in Arabic language and grammar and introductory level studies of the Qur'an, the hadith, and *fiqh*, a modernist education (often undertaken at the tertiary level) would complement this background with exposure to theories of epistemology and methodology, the place of reason in revelation, and studies in comparative religion, social science, and a history of the Islamicate civilization. It is this dual background in both solid traditional Islamic education and modernist studies of philosophy and theology that enabled Indonesian thinkers both to develop sophisticated Islamic thought that remains in dialogue with the jurisprudential traditions and at the same time to connect theology to quotidian problems and to express ideas in a language accessible to those not trained in Islamic studies.

4

Christian and Muslim Minorities in Indonesia

State Policies and Majority Islamic Organizations

Franz Magnis-Suseno, SJ

In this article, I want to show that the most important factor regarding religious tolerance in Indonesia is state policies. Tolerance, which has deep roots in traditional Indonesian cultures, will prevail as long as the state enforces corresponding legislation and the Constitution.[1]

As a German-born Jesuit Catholic priest who has lived in Indonesia for almost fifty years, has become an Indonesian citizen, and has been an active participant in civil society and interreligious dialogues, I believe it might be useful for me to develop three central points. First, I analyze what I consider to be the basically very good and tolerant relations between Muslims and Christians in Indonesia and discuss factors that have contributed to this tolerance, but I also examine toleration breakdowns. Second, I document and analyze why Muslim-majority intolerance toward Muslim minorities (rather than toward Christians and other minorities) remains, in my judgment, the major religion-related problem in Indonesia's emerging democracy. Third, I explore why I consider *inaction* by the democratic government actually more threatening to the quality of democracy in Indonesia than *actions* by authoritarian and violent religious groups.

Christian–Muslim Relations in Indonesia: The Founding (and Continuing) Pluralist Compromise

On August 18, 1945, one day after Sukarno and Hatta proclaimed Indonesia's independence under the nose of the Japanese occupiers (who had just surrendered to the Allied forces), its Panitia Persiapan Kemerdekaan Indonesia (Preparatory Committee for Indonesian Independence), after sharp debate, adopted the Constitution of 1945, in which Indonesia was declared to be based on five fundamental principles known as "Pancasila." The first principle was "belief in one God" (*ketuhanan yang maha esa*). Paragraph 29 of the Constitution proclaimed liberty of religion and worship.

In Indonesia, nondiscrimination on religious grounds was thus strongly written into the Constitution of 1945 (and all other Indonesian constitutions) and, in a generally satisfying way, into the law. There can be no doubt that there was and still is a strong political consensus in Indonesian society, always kept up by the Indonesian state, that all Indonesians are citizens in the full sense of their rights and duties. Members of minority religions can occupy high positions in politics, the military, and universities. Although the Department of Religion is primarily an answer to the needs of the Muslim community, the other (recognized) religions have their departments within it.

After the fall of Suharto, four amendments to the Constitution of 1945 gave human rights a strong constitutional position. These rights include freedom of religion. In fact, in most parts of Indonesia non-Muslims are free to worship. And unlike in many other Muslim-majority countries, there are no penalties for religious conversion.

How remarkable and extraordinary this philosophical and constitutional base was for tolerance and democracy in Indonesia will be obvious if we look at the religious map of the country. More than 85 percent of all Indonesians are (Sunni) Muslims. Almost 10 percent are Christians, two-thirds of whom belong to Protestant churches and one-third to the Catholic Church; and 1.5 percent are Hindu, most of them being the original inhabitants of Bali. The remaining 3.5 percent belong to indigenous religions, Confucianism, and the Buddhist community. These numbers mean nothing else than that Indonesia was at the time of independence and still is the nation with the biggest number of Muslims on earth. But at the beginning of the existence of the free Republic of Indonesia in 1945, its representatives unanimously decided to build a nation without religious discrimination and without giving Islam, the religion of the vast majority, any special constitutional or legal status. This decision was made with full awareness of its implications because it was preceded by intensive deliberations and bargaining about (as articles by Künkler and others in this volume show), first, whether Indonesia should become an "Islamic state" or not (the decision was *not*) and, second, whether at least the Islamic sharia should be declared binding on Muslims (this stipulation was unanimously *dropped* on August 18, 1945). I am of the opinion that only the willingness of the Islamist representatives not to insist on any special status for Islam made possible the continuance of Indonesia as a single state up to this day.

Since then, religious freedom and nondiscrimination, in spite of many frictions, petty discrimination, and even serious conflicts—which I come back to presently—has been a reality. Even radical Muslim groups have not challenged the principle that in Indonesia non-Muslims have the same legal and civil status as Muslims and are citizens in the full sense of the word. Thus, although there have always been interreligious tensions and petty discriminations, the religious communities of Indonesia have lived and continue to live together peacefully. Catholics, Protestants, Hindus, and Buddhists—all were officially recognized as legal by the state, all have a mandatory and paid holiday in honor of a day especially sacred to their religion, and all have a section in the Ministry of Religion devoted to them from which they receive some subsidies. Confucians were incorporated into this structure in the democratic period under the leadership of President Abdurrahman Wahid. Under the military and Suharto, anything smacking of being "Chinese" was outlawed, and Confucians were forced to register as Buddhists, making Confucian marriages impossible, for example.

Despite this overall legal tolerance of all religions by the state, some intolerant aspects of Indonesian laws must be mentioned. One grave ongoing violation of human rights is that people belonging to tribal religions cannot legally marry due to an extremely one-sided marriage law passed in 1973. Mixed marriages, too, have to be conducted according to the rites of one of the six now officially recognized religions.

Nonetheless, Christianity developed exceptionally well after Indonesian independence. The fact is that religious life in most of the Christian communities on Java, Sumatra, South Sulawesi, and other Muslim regions of Indonesia goes on without any hindrance. There is freedom of worship, freedom of religious instruction, and freedom to baptize and to become a Christian (or a Muslim). Church bells ring out at liturgical hours every day in churches on Java. Although being a Christian has not been an advantage if one wants a career in government or as a state employee, Christians are not systematically discriminated against and can be found in all professions and at all levels of Indonesian society. This is the long history of Christianity in Indonesia. But I would be remiss if I did not discuss a much more troubling short history, roughly between 1990 and around 2005, when the democratic transition was completed.

Worrying Events Starting with Suharto in 1990

In 1990, Suharto took his famous turn to Islam. Many Muslim leaders regarded the change of attitude as long overdue. For them, the twenty-year-long shunning of political Islam by the New Order was an extraordinary discrimination against the majority religion. They also suspected Christian influences behind Suharto's negative attitude toward Islam. Thus, they regarded Suharto's late "conversion" as a question of finally giving justice to the Islamic community.

Christians, however, saw themselves increasingly excluded from public positions; they now felt discriminated against and like a threatened minority. But what really frightened Christians was a growing number of violent attacks on churches. More than six hundred churches were destroyed or violently closed, not counting churches destroyed in connection with the civil wars in the early stages of the democratic transition in eastern Indonesia discussed by Sidney Jones in chapter 6 in this volume. Really traumatic for Indonesian Christians were four completely unprovoked attacks in 1996–1997 in Java, beginning with an attack on ten churches in Surabaya in 1996 (where damage was slight), then in Situbondo, Tasikmalaya, and Rengasdengklok, where *all forty-eight churches* (except one in Tasik) were systematically burned down by mobs. There followed two further mob attacks: one in November 1998 in Jakarta, followed two weeks later by Christian riots in Kupang that led to the expulsion of the Bugis people; and one in January 2000 on the island of Lombok. Especially worrying for Christians is the fact that not a single perpetrator has ever been brought to court for these crimes—at least to my knowledge.[2] During this period, Christians were increasingly asking themselves whether their constitutionally guaranteed right of worship, even their right to openly identify as Christian and remain safe in majority Muslim regions, could be violated with impunity.

Although there have been no more large-scale devastations of churches since 2000, attacks on single and often new small Protestant churches on Java are continuing. Thus, as Christians complain, it is still extremely difficult to build churches in Java and in other Muslim regions even when the Christian community clearly needs a church. Without its own church building, the community is forced to hold its services in a school or a similar building, but doing so is often forbidden because the building has not been zoned as a house of worship. The argument often goes that a church should not be built in the midst of a Muslim community, which, of course, would mean the end of religious tolerance because a minority by definition lives among a majority of another religion. It is, as I have heard, also difficult for Balinese Hindus to get building permits for their *pura* (temples) or for Chinese to build a *klenteng* temple among the Muslims. I have no information on whether similar complaints are voiced by Muslim communities in Christian regions.

Mention has to be made here of an especially terrifying event: the Christmas night in 2000 when fifty bombs were placed in or around Christian churches from North Sumatra to the island of Lombok. Thirty of them exploded, resulting in seventeen deaths and more than one hundred wounded. The police made no serious effort to apprehend the perpetrators. Only after the perpetrators of the Bali bombings in the tourist district of Kuta were caught in 2002 did it transpire that they were also involved in these Christmas bombings two years earlier.

The climax of interreligious conflict were two civil wars that devastated parts of the Maluku Islands and Central Sulawesi for almost four years. These wars raged from 1999 to 2002 and resulted in about eight thousand deaths and hundreds of thousands of refugees, many of whom have not yet been able to return to their homes owing to the uncertain security situation. But it is clear that in both regions the reasons behind the violence were highly complex, including, as Marcus Mietzner and Sidney Jones document in chapters 5 and 6 in this volume, some military involvement as a part of the military's rearguard action against its marginalization by a full democratic transition. But it is also important to stress that some of the conflicts reached back into history or even into local culture (people in the Maluku Islands have traditionally been warriors, and fights between villages were quite common[3]), and others were connected with ethnographic and economic change as well as with both local and national politics, as many Indonesians believe. But to say, as some do, that these conflicts were in fact not religious in character is wishful thinking. The fact is that for more than three years the answer to the question "Are you a Muslim or a Christian?" decided life or death for many people. Although these conflicts were of another nature than the antiminority violence in Java mentioned earlier, being more political, economic, and communal, the disturbing fact is that the conflicts tended to boil down in all these cases to confrontations between Christians and Muslims. Religious hatred can thereby grow and develop its own momentum. The whole atmosphere between the involved communities gets poisoned. Add long-standing suspicions and prejudices, and new outbreaks of conflict can be easily provoked by politically or otherwise interested parties.

Nevertheless, although these conflicts *are* conflicts between communities defined by their respective religions, they have not much to do with the teachings or other specific traits of Islam or Christianity. They should be characterized as communal conflicts, by which I mean that emotions, hatred, and prejudices relate to the collective identity of a group, united by language, local culture, locality, religion, tribalism, and so on. If a member of such a community acts against a member of another one, the victim's community will react collectively against the perpetrator's community.

In fact, the Ambon and Poso conflicts are only a part of a general climate of easy recourse to violence that exists in Indonesian society today. Small frictions, misunderstandings, and confrontations easily evoke violent reactions and physical fighting with weapons. Such fights very often quickly involve whole communities, which then clash with each other. If, for instance, there is a fight between an extortionist and a taxi driver, and the one is a Muslim and the other a Christian (as happened in Ambon), there is always the chance that it may become a war between their respective villages or *kampung*s. Indeed, the conflict may widen, especially if *kampung*s are tribally or religiously homogenous, to become a war between ethnic groups (as happened on Kalimantan) or between religious communities.[4]

These developments have left their scars in religious communities. Many Christians have asked themselves about their future in Indonesia. The existence of hard-line groups that sometimes resort to violence (especially against "sinful places" such as gambling dens and even coffee shops, but in some instances also against Christian institutions that they say are engaging in "Christianization") has added to this atmosphere of apprehension. Hard-line Islamic publications have openly voiced extremely sectarian views, often directly alluding to Christians. There has been, in my view, an unfortunate tendency toward religious segregation. A fatwa promulgated twenty-five years ago by the Majelis Ulama Indonesia (MUI, Indonesian Ulama Council) but only effectively enacted after the fall of Suharto commands that Muslims should refrain from expressing Christmas greetings to Christians. Since then, a whole tradition of grassroots-level interreligious contact has dried up. I have heard Muslim friends express their dismay at the fact that the teacher of religion at their children's schools tell Muslim children not to have contact with non-Muslim and Chinese children. Christians are also worried about the tendency of local authorities to enforce sharia regulations in their regions. Hand in hand with local "shariazation" goes a policy of making religious life for Christian communities more and more difficult in certain districts, often in the name of the newly won "autonomy of the regions."

Positive Muslim–Christian and Democratic Developments

Despite all that I have just acknowledged, the astonishing fact is that relations between Christians and Muslims, although still far from being without problems, are developing well. The democratic period has seen five major developments, undetected by most of the public, that I consider positive for Muslim–Christian relations and, more important, positive for the deepening development of an inclusive, pluralist, democracy in Indonesia.

The first and most fundamental fact I want to stress is that the Pancasila national consensus—that Indonesia belongs to all Indonesians—still stands essentially unchallenged. Political parties that favor making sharia law a state law for Muslims represented only about 17 percent of the 2004 electorate. In that year, the two biggest political parties, Golongan Karya (Golkar, Functional Groups) (22 percent) and the Partai Demokrasi Indonesia Perjuangan (Indonesian Democratic Party of Struggle) (18 percent), but also Abdurrahman Wahid's Partai Kebangkitan Bangsa (National Awakening Party) (14 percent) and Amien Rais's *Partai Amanat Nasional* (National Mandate Party) (6 percent) did not support the introduction of sharia. Even more significant is the fact that the leadership of the two big Muslim organizations, Nahdlatul Ulama (NU, Rise of the Ulama) and Muhammadiyah (Followers of Muhammad), have clearly stated that making sharia into state law does not fit with Indonesia's social-cultural conditions.

A second highly significant and often overlooked fact is that the quasi-war between Christians and Muslims in eastern Indonesia between 1999 and 2002—in which both sides regarded themselves as the victims of violence from the other side—did not spill over to other regions. There were no revenge attacks on Christians by Muslims in the heavily Muslim majority territory of Java and no attacks on Muslims in the Christian majority parts of Indonesia. More amazing still, the much vilified political elite in Jakarta, including the political parties, did not use the terrible conflicts in the Maluku Islands and Poso for political gains during their election campaigns.

Indeed, the third remarkable fact is that during the fiercely contested campaigns during the 2004 and 2009 parliamentary and presidential elections, questions of religion were almost completely absent; even explicitly Islamic parties such as the Partai Keadilan Sejahtera (Prosperous Justice Party) did not campaign in the name of Islam, but against corruption and for social justice. No party campaigned for the introduction of sharia (although some parties have it on their official agenda). All pairs of presidential and vice presidential candidates for the presidential elections were "mixed" between "Islamists"[5] and "nationalists" (all of the "nationalists," of course, were Muslim, too).

A fourth encouraging and notable development during the democratic transition has been a significant warming of relations between Christians and both NU and Muhammadiyah. When speaking about Islamic organizations, we have to distinguish between Muslim organizations in general, no matter how small and possibly noninfluential, and the few extremely large and influential national organizations, especially the "traditionalist" NU and the "modernist" Muhammadiyah. There exists quite a remarkable number of Islamic hard-line organizations of different ideological backgrounds, although many of them might be characterized as somewhat Wahhabist or Salafist. These groups are the hard-liners: promoting intolerance, violently threatening minorities, and very often succeeding in slowly destroying good communicative relations between local majority Muslim communities and non-Muslim religious entities, as discussed by Sidney Jones.

However, NU's and Muhammadiyah's attitudes are of national importance. NU, the big "traditionalist" Islamic organization claiming 40 million members, was for a critical fifteen years of democratic opposition and democratic transition led by Abdurrahman Wahid (often called "Gus Dur"). Gus Dur opened up traditional rural Muslim schools to communications with Christians, Buddhists, and others, a development that can be regarded as one of the greatest social success stories in modern Indonesia. Of course, one should not generalize. There exist within NU, as in other groups, narrow-minded, intolerant people. In general, however, with Gus Dur's leadership, NU takes a tolerant, pluralistic attitude and specifically shows an awareness of its responsibility as a majority group for solving conflicts peacefully. Indeed, Christians are likely to go to NU members if they have difficulties and will very often get at least a sympathetic ear. Without idealizing it, we can say that NU is a very positive element in the social fabric of Indonesia and especially of Indonesian Islam.

But Muhammadiyah, too, the "modernist" organization with about 28 million members, although Wahhabi influenced and—for a long time on principle—adverse toward indigenous Indonesian cultures, has opened up during the past fourteen years or so, beginning with Amien Rais, who at the end of the Suharto government experienced an astonishing transformation from a person occasionally seen as a kind of "Christian and Chinese eater" into a more tolerant, pluralistic personality. His successor as head of Muhammadiyah, Professor Syafii Ma'arif, is one of the most open-minded, inclusive, and on principle, nonviolent people within Indonesian Islam. But even Ma'arif's successor, Professor Din Syamsuddin, whom many regarded as more of a hard-liner and "a typical Muhammadiyah" man, has proved himself to be relatively open-minded, strictly against violence, and open to dialogue with other religious communities. Thus, Muhammadiyah, too, exerts a positive influence on the interreligious climate in Indonesia.

Thus, the influence of the two big popular Muslim organizations, NU and Muhammadiyah, in the democratic transition must be said to be positive and very important. In general, they try to discourage violent intolerant behavior by their followers; they are open to dialogue with minority groups; and they stand ready to enter the public square to counter intolerant Islam with tolerant Islam.

These tendencies got a big boost from the growing terrorist threat hanging over Indonesia. The real watershed was the Bali bombings in Kuta on October 12, 2002. These bombings shocked Indonesians out of their complacent attitude toward the reality of religiously motivated terror.[6] Two closely related changes grew out of the Bali bombings. First, liberal Muslim groups and the popular leaders of NU and Muhammadiyah began to present Islam more forcefully as an inclusive religion that, as the majority religion, felt responsible for the peace and prosperity of the whole of Indonesian society. These Muslim groups publicly condemned terrorism in the name of Islam and initiated prayer meetings among different religions for the victims of the Kuta killings. NU and Muhammadiyah leaders founded the Gerakan Moral Nasional (National Moral Council) consisting of the leaders of all Indonesia religions. Second, extremist groups that had used the new democratic openness after the fall of the Suharto government to come out into the open now retreated into more low-profile positions, and some distanced themselves from terrorist activities.

The fifth encouraging point I would like to insist upon is that during the elections of 1999, 2004, and 2009 there was essentially quiet on the religious front. This phenomenon deserves closer scrutiny. As was the case in the election campaigns of 1999 (in the midst of two civil wars) and of 2004 (peace having been precariously restored), so, too, in 2009 political parties (including parties from an Islamic background) and presidential candidates showed themselves to be inclusive, never alluding to religious or ideological divides. In the same way, all coalition talks between political parties as well as between presidential and vice presidential candidates seemed to avoid anything that looked like the infamous "Islamist versus secularist/nationalist" schism. It was probably that they instinctively believed that taking a "sectarian" attitude would diminish their electoral appeal. But I believe there was more. There was a growing recognition that what I have called the foundational compromise was now the dominant consensus in an increasingly democratic and pluralist Indonesia. There is a deep and growing realization among Indonesians, including the much disparaged political class, that Indonesian unity is such a valued good that it must not to be endangered by cheap religious politicking.

The Problem of Muslim Majorities' Intolerance Toward Muslim Minorities

The question of inner-Islamic tolerance is a completely different story politically, theologically, and psychologically. Islam has always recognized the existence of other religions. In principle, Islam knows there are other religions. These other religions have, in Islamic eyes, their problems with God, but Islam recognizes them. Islam is not "insulted" by their existence and by their unacceptable, for Muslims, teachings and forms of worship. Moreover, Pancasila represents the constitutional recognition and protection of the existence of non-Muslim religions in Indonesia. Even Indonesian Islamic hardliners do not, in principle, deny the right of non-Muslims to full citizenship.

But the situation is completely different regarding sects or movements (*aliran*) within Islam itself in Indonesia. Most of the Muslim community sees such "sects" as direct challenges to their beliefs, as destabilizing their religion from within, and as unfaithfulness directly in the face of God's revealed religion. Sects, of course, have long existed within Indonesian (and other) Muslim communities. But the moment they or different movements get public attention, they can excite intense hatred and easily lead to brutality and violence. This was and is the case regarding Ahmadiyya (Followers of Ahmad), an Islamic sect founded in 1889 by Mirza Ghulam Ahmad, who is revered as a prophet by his followers, in a part of India that now belongs to Pakistan.

On July 28, 2005, the MUI issued a fatwa that condemned the Ahmadiyya sect. The consequence was an upsurge of violence against Ahmadis. Near Bogor, a major city in Java, thousands of men armed with sticks, clubs, and knives—among them many white-clad members of the *Front Pembela Islam* (Islamic Defenders' Front)—encircled the local Ahmadiyya complex, which was then forcefully evacuated by the police. Shortly afterward, an Ahmadiyya kampung near Sukabumi was attacked. In the course of that onslaught, several Ahmadiyya mosques were set on fire, and numerous private residences were looted or destroyed. In February 2006, Ahmadis on Lombok Island were also exposed to violent attacks.

What this example illustrates is that although the Indonesian state (somewhat timidly) tries to uphold the religious rights of non-Muslim religions, it does not offer the same protections to inner Muslim sects. In fact, the government's attitude, up to the highest level, during the brutal anti-Ahmadiyya riots was shameful. When Ahmadiyya facilities close to Bogor were attacked, the president of Indonesia only said that the sect had been banned by the state anyway (which was not even true; MUI had many years earlier banned Ahmadiyya, but the state never had). Not a single word reminding people of their duty to respect the Ahmadis' life and property was ever heard. People certainly would have listened had the president said something along these lines, but it did not happen. The attitude of the great majority of Muslim leaders was more or less the same. They just stood silent while the Ahmadis were driven out of their homes. It seems that the government—and parliamentarians—do not understand that these people have a right to their religious conviction.

The case of Ahmadiyya was eventually resolved by a decree in 2007 that was ambiguously formulated but that, according to Vice President Jusuf Kalla's interpretation (for which he should be given credit), meant that the Ahmadis were free to live and worship according to their understanding of Islam as long as they stayed inside their compounds and did not try to convert others to their beliefs. Significantly for my argument, the number of mob attacks on Ahmadis after this state decree significantly decreased. (Sad to say, they have since 2010 increased significantly and dangerously.)

State "Inactivity" as a Failure of Religious Tolerance

There is a clear difference in the attitude toward non-Muslim religions and the attitude toward so-called heretical groups within Islam. Although non-Muslim minorities face a certain degree of discrimination and experience intolerant attitudes, the principle that all Indonesians regardless of their religion should be recognized as Indonesian citizens in the full sense of the word is not controversial. The state bases its attitudes toward its citizens on this principle, the big Muslim organizations accept it without question, and even more hard-line Muslim groups do not question it openly.

The situation of Islamic "heretical sects" is very different. Only a relatively small number of enlightened Muslims recognize their right to full religious freedom. Most others tend to see these sects as malevolent aberrations from the path of God that should return to the mainstream flock of believers. They are not treated with tolerance and easily can become victims of orthodox violence. The state seems to look at them in the same way and is extremely reluctant to provide protection against attacks.

There is a general problem regarding religiously motivated mob threats or mob violence in Indonesia. The state apparatus, especially the police, is very often slow to protect the property of minorities under attack (usually in connection with worship at "illegal" places or trying to build houses of worship). Here the state clearly fails in its duty to maintain the principle of the rule of law, whose most important element is that no violence in society is tolerated. The state lacks the courage to do its duty and thereby indirectly encourages popular violence and the impunity of intolerant groups and organizations.

There are two worrisome points here. The first is that the state and its organs are generally reluctant to uphold the law, without compromise, in the face of religiously motivated violent mobs. The second is that there is a specific lack of tolerance and understanding of the rights of inner-Islamic "heretical" groups.

But these two unquestionably negative points have to be seen in the context of a sociocultural religious background that has five features I consider positive and that our new democracy might build upon.

First, the fundamental consensus that Indonesia belongs to all Indonesians regardless of their religious beliefs is still intact. Second, Pancasila, the philosophical-ethical basis on which Indonesia is founded, is not questioned. Third, although there are all kinds of petty discriminations against minorities, in general they are not discriminated against, and the existence of non-Islamic religions in Indonesia is firmly accepted by the majority. Fourth, there has been a growing openness and conscious option for moderate positions within the large Islamic organizations NU and Muhammadiyah. This option includes much better communications with representatives of minority religions, specifically Christians. Fifth, on the difficult questions of "errant beliefs" (*ajaran sesat*) there is a growing discourse within Islam urging state enforcement of the law, and the number of Indonesians demanding religious freedom for such beliefs is growing.

Part III

Behaviors

*Challenges to the Democratic Transition and State
and Their Transcendence*

5

Veto Player No More?

The Declining Political Influence of the Military in Postauthoritarian Indonesia

Marcus Mietzner

ew other political actors in Indonesia's democratic transition and consolidation have received as much critical attention—both domestically and internationally—as the armed forces. Such intense scrutiny of the military only seemed natural given its history. As the backbone of Suharto's authoritarian Orde Baru (New Order) government between 1966 and 1998, the military had much to lose if Indonesia's experiment with democratic rule proved successful. Under Suharto's patronage, the military had held key positions in the regime, penetrated all layers of society with its repressive apparatus, accumulated huge economic assets, and monopolized the security sector. These political and socioeconomic privileges were obviously threatened by Indonesia's quest for a more democratic and transparent system of governance. With the generals facing both marginalization from the country's power center and legal investigations into their past human rights violations, many observers believed that the armed forces might seriously undermine Indonesia's process of institutional reform. In fact, despite the existence of various other potential spoilers, in 1998 most Indonesians were convinced that the military would be the biggest obstacle to successful democratization.

Many Indonesian citizens' fear that the armed forces might sabotage the transition to democracy was also echoed by political scientists analyzing democratization processes around the world. In a seminal article on transitions to democracy and democratic consolidation in 1989, Scott Mainwaring maintains that there are usually two decisive actors in transitions that have the power to veto crucial political reforms: the military and the capitalist class. In dealing with the military, newly installed leaders of transitional governments often face a dilemma: they not only have to confront the armed forces but have to cooperate with them at the same time. Despite open interventions by conservative military leaders, political reformers "cannot abolish the militaries or drastically attack the military institution, even if that is what the majority . . . wants."[1] Instead, the strength of the military as a "veto player" often forces civilian leaders to grant concessions to the generals, mostly in the form of residual privileges or pledges to protect them from legal action. In the case of Indonesia, leading theorists warned soon after Suharto's fall that leaving the armed forces with too many privileges could have a disastrous impact on the transition. Richard Gunther, for example, reminded Indonesian policymakers that granting the military continued unelected representation in Parliament could endow "the military with 'reserve powers' that might be invoked to frustrate a democratic mandate."[2]

In the course of Indonesia's transition, comparative analysts continued to express their concern about the military's "veto powers." Most important, Larry Diamond still classified Indonesia as a "hybrid" or "ambiguous" regime several years after Suharto's resignation, pointing to the military's presence in the legislature and its role as a "major veto player."[3] But even after the 2004 elections abolished the armed forces' appointed representation in Parliament, the notion of the military as Indonesia's most formidable veto actor remained popular, both in the country and abroad. In the 2008 Indonesia Country Report for the Bertelsmann Transformation Index, a major quantitative and qualitative tool for political scientists to assess the state of democratic transitions in comparative terms, Indonesia's armed forces were still described as a major threat to democracy. In the report authors' view, "The military remains the main veto actor, and the threat of a coup d'état still exists." Further, the writers claimed that the generals still "reserve the right to interfere with the elected government if they believe the unity and stability of the Indonesian nation to be threatened." Among others, the military was identified as one of the veto actors that obstructed Indonesia's decentralization, leading the authors to doubt "whether the political reformers are able to control the vetoing actors."[4]

Describing the military as Indonesia's most influential veto player has obviously become somewhat of a fixture in the writings of political scientists on the country. But how justified is that assessment? The most prominent theorist of veto players, George Tsebelis, has defined veto players as "individual or collective actors whose agreement is necessary for a change of the status quo."[5] Based on this definition, can the Indonesian military still be categorized as a veto player more than fifteen years after Suharto's fall? Indeed, was the military's classification as a veto player even justified in the early phases of Indonesia's democratic transition or, for that matter, during previous political regimes? This chapter assesses the role of Indonesia's military as a political veto player in several periods. First, it looks at the involvement of the armed forces in Indonesian politics between 1945 at independence and 1998, the year the democratic transition began. Second, it analyzes the extent to which the military influenced the 1998 regime change and the evolution of the post-Suharto polity. Third, the discussion focuses on what I believe were watersheds for Indonesian civil–military relations and the significance of the military as a veto actor: the 2002 constitutional amendments and the Helsinki Peace Agreement for Aceh in 2005. Finally, the chapter evaluates the armed forces' political engagement in the current polity, concluding that although the military remains influential, its importance as a veto player has been widely overstated.

Indonesia's Military Before 1998: Participant-Ruler and Hegemon

Any discussion of the political significance of Indonesia's military must begin with an analysis of its inception during the country's independence war. The main mission of the Tentara Nasional Indonesia (TNI, Indonesian National Military), founded in October 1945, was to fight the Dutch colonial army, which was in the process of reoccupying the territory of the former Netherlands East Indies after three years of Japanese occupation. Sukarno and Hatta had declared Indonesia's independence in August 1945, setting the new Republic on a path of military confrontation with the returning Dutch. In a matter of months, the TNI had to organize a coherent military apparatus out of hundreds of local militias, volunteer groups, auxiliaries trained under the Japanese, and former colonial soldiers.[6] Although this task proved difficult and at times impossible, the formation of the TNI was nevertheless crucially important for the newly emerging nation's self-confidence. The military, like the government led by Sukarno and Hatta, was a symbol of Indonesia's existence, giving it a role that went well beyond being an effective striking force. For millions of Indonesians, the attacks launched by TNI fighters on the superior colonial military emphasized the nation's determination to gain its independence against all odds. Not surprisingly, the military shared and nurtured this belief in its indispensability for the nationalist struggle; indeed, this view is the core of military doctrine and historiography to this day.[7]

It is far from certain, however, whether the army was a "veto player" at that time, despite its importance as a symbol of unity and fighting spirit during the war years. There is no doubt that the military opposed many of the policies defined by the civilian government and that it often acted independently when running its military operations. For example, the armed forces continued their attacks on Dutch forces even after Sukarno had surrendered in December 1948, and the military successfully insisted on electing its own commander despite attempts by the civilian minister of defense to exercise stronger control.[8] But in most key decisions that determined the outcome of the war and the shape of postconflict Indonesia, the military's advice was pointedly ignored. The armed forces were heavily opposed to the negotiations that the government held with the Dutch in Den Haag in 1949, despite the fact that the military situation was unsustainable for the Republic; the generals also rejected many of the agreements reached in Den Haag, ranging from the adoption of a federal system to the exclusion of Papua from the negotiations.[9] The military was likewise not consulted when a parliamentary system was adopted for the new Indonesian state, to which the Dutch transferred sovereignty in December 1949. Overall, it would be difficult to point to a single fundamental policy decision that was the result of military pressure in the nation's early period; there were minor concessions that allowed the military to run its own affairs, but in the greater scheme of things the military was politically marginalized.[10]

The military only gained political strength in the mid-1950s, primarily as a result of the weakening democratic polity. Prior to that—in the early 1950s—the armed forces had still not played a significant role in political affairs: the shift from a federal to a unitary system in August 1950 and the liberal constitution passed in the same year had been negotiated by and among civilian politicians, with little attention paid to the military's interests. In 1952, the frustration in the officer corps over its political irrelevance culminated in a visit of the top brass to President Sukarno, demanding that the Parliament be disbanded.[11] The president, however, found it easy to dismiss both this request and the generals who had voiced it. Had the military been a powerful veto player at the time, its political demands would have certainly carried more weight when forcefully presented to the government, and the shape of early postindependence Indonesia would have been decisively different. Nevertheless, the erosion of parliamentary democracy in 1956 and 1957 offered the armed forces an entry point for its political agenda. The increasing unpopularity of the political parties, rampant corruption, armed rebellions against centralist rule,[12] and Indonesians' unhappiness with the West's refusal to discuss the Papua problem allowed the military to present itself as a viable political alternative.[13] Working closely with Sukarno, who was also displeased with the marginal role he had under the democratic system, the army pushed for the establishment of an autocratic regime in which it expected to possess the very veto powers it had so far lacked.[14]

But many of the institutional privileges granted to the armed forces under Sukarno's Demokrasi Terpimpin (Guided Democracy) between 1959 and 1965 were of a purely nominal nature. In line with TNI's new "Middle Way" doctrine, according to which the generals would receive permanent representation in government in exchange for not seeking to topple it, the armed forces were given seats in the cabinet, special advisory councils, and the appointed legislature. Although these new constitutional rights expanded the military's formal powers, they did not allow TNI to take decisive influence on the political process. In fact, Indonesian politics in the early 1960s drifted into a direction that most military leaders deeply opposed: protected by Sukarno, the Partai Komunis Indonesia (PKI, Indonesian Communist Party) rapidly gained ground and prepared to take over the government after the ailing president's death. Despite TNI's supposed "veto powers," Indonesia's Guided Democracy assumed a revolutionary, left-leaning rhetoric, launched a chaotic military campaign against Malaysia, left the United Nations, and began to rely on the Soviet Union for development aid and defense equipment. None of these key policies had been initiated or endorsed by the military. Thus, although military theorists such as Amos Perlmutter and Eric Nordlinger would have probably termed the army a "participant-ruler" under Sukarno's autocracy, it was not an effective "veto player."[15] With discontent swelling in its ranks, there was a growing consensus in the military that for TNI to have "real" power, much more fundamental change was necessary.

The opportunity to achieve this radical change presented itself on September 30, 1965. Reacting to a clumsy coup attempt by a small pro-Communist faction in the military, the leadership of the armed forces under then Major-General Suharto took control of the situation and entrenched itself in power.[16] Suharto gradually removed Sukarno from power between 1966 and 1968, ultimately installing himself in the presidency. In the early years of Suharto's New Order regime, the military enjoyed all the benefits typically associated with praetorian rule: 80 percent of key local government positions were given to military officers, as was the majority of cabinet seats and senior bureaucratic jobs; generals took over the leadership of state enterprises and substantially expanded their own economic activities; laws and institutions were revised to suit the armed forces' ideological and political interests; and the military became the apex of a repressive system of social control through which all citizens' activities were scrutinized. The military in the early 1970s was evidently much more than a "veto player"; it was a political and security hegemon that could make major policy decisions without taking the interests of other sociopolitical groups into account. It met dissent with intimidation or offers of patronage, effectively removing any opposition to its grip on power.

The biggest structural problem for the military under the New Order, however, was its growing dissociation from Suharto. In the founding years of the New Order, Suharto was concurrently commander of the armed forces and head of government, leading to the impression both in Indonesia and in the rest of the world that the interests of the military and its chief were congruent. Even after Suharto relinquished the commandership, he remained an active general until the late 1970s, keeping in close contact with the officer corps. But the gulf between Suharto and his leading generals began to widen soon afterward.[17] This gulf was not only a generational gap; it also involved divergent personal and institutional interests. Suharto, for his part, was keen to broaden the foundations of his regime by integrating civilian constituencies (such as Islamic leaders and technology experts) into the New Order government. The military, in contrast, rightly viewed this move as a threat to its privileges. In this subtle confrontation between the armed forces and their former patron, Suharto eventually prevailed. By the early 1990s, Suharto had developed the New Order regime into a personal autocracy[18] in which his control was all pervasive and the armed forces were—as in Pinochet's Chile—

"relegated to agent status along with the rest of society."[19] As the number of military officers in key government jobs gradually declined, the armed forces not only lost their institutional status as a political hegemon but arguably were also too weak to play the role of a veto actor.

The previous discussion has demonstrated that the widespread perception of the Indonesian military as the country's most persistent and powerful veto player since 1945 needs to be reassessed. The armed forces did not leave a significant mark on the shape of the various political systems formed in 1945, 1949, and 1950, and despite the military's importance as a symbol of nationalist pride, independence was not won on the battlefield, but at the negotiation table. The only periods in which the armed forces exercised great influence as a political veto player or hegemon were, first, between 1956 and 1959, when the generals successfully negotiated the establishment of a new regime with Sukarno, and, second, between 1965 and about 1978, when the military was effectively running the government. After that, however, there were very few opportunities for the military to act as an independent political player. The one key decision between the 1980s and early 1998 in which the military was able to force Suharto's hand was Try Sutrisno's appointment as vice president in 1993.[20] Other than that, Suharto was firmly in control, and although the military continued to profit from its role as the regime's tool of intimidation and social control, it was no longer in the driving seat.[21] It was only Suharto's political decline in 1997 and 1998 that brought the military back into the spotlight, temporarily providing the generals with the effective veto powers that the longtime autocrat had withheld from them for the previous two decades.

Vetoing Suharto: TNI During the Regime Change and the Transition

As indicated previously, many Indonesian and foreign observers expected in 1998 that the armed forces would emerge as the most influential veto player in the transition, potentially sabotaging democratic reforms. Although the military certainly made use of its revived veto powers (which it owed to both its guns and Suharto's fall), it did so in a much more complex and multi-layered manner. In evaluating the military's political behavior in 1998, some political analysts have overlooked the fact that the regime change could occur only after the armed forces, in line with Tsebeli's definition, lent their necessary consent to the sought change in the status quo—that is, Suharto's removal from power. Without the military's passive but unambiguous approval it is difficult to imagine that the events between March and May 1998 would have transpired in the way they did. If the military used its veto power, then it did so against Suharto—by rejecting the embattled president's suggestions to crack down on the constantly growing student movement.[22] There were significant divisions in the military, but the proponents of a negotiated settlement with the protesters finally prevailed, and Suharto was therefore left with no other choice than to resign.[23] Through its veto against a last-minute crackdown and its tacit support for the regime change, the military thus made a larger contribution to the democratic transition than political scientists tend to admit.

And whereas the military's supportive role in the regime change has often been ignored in the scholarly literature, its obstructive impact on the subsequent democratic transition has been widely exaggerated. To be sure, the military was keen on preserving as many of its institutional privileges as possible, and it used its weight as a political and security force to achieve this preservation.[24] But the results of its efforts were far from satisfactory for the officer corps. To begin with, Suharto handed the presidency to a man who was deeply disliked by many in the army, B. J. Habibie. The tensions between the former minister of technology and the military were legendary, with conflicts over defense procurement being only one of the points of contention.[25] Habibie's ascension, therefore, was not the result of intensive military lobbying but followed a consensus among the civilian elite that the constitutional succession of the vice president was preferable to a transitional government led by nonregime figures. The armed forces simply supported this scenario as the most obvious default position, but they were not the initiator of Habibie's rise to power. Hence, it is difficult to ascertain whether the regime change could have assumed a more grassroots-driven, democratic format had the armed forces played a less significant role in May 1998. Habibie's interim presidency would most likely still have emerged as the only viable solution, especially because he was prepared to accommodate key civilian groups by offering fresh elections and extensive political liberalization.[26] Overall, the character of the 1998 regime change was shaped more by broader sociopolitical dynamics than by military interventionism.

After Habibie launched his program of wide-ranging democratic reforms in June 1998, TNI tried unsuccessfully to veto several of its most important elements. For example, then chief of staff of sociopolitical affairs Susilo

Bambang Yudhoyono declared publicly that the military wanted only a limited number of parties to compete in the upcoming elections.[27] By contrast, Habibie insisted that no significant restrictions be imposed on the formation of new parties (with the exception of pro-Communist ones). The president won this dispute: more than two hundred parties were founded, forty-eight of which participated in the 1999 elections. In the same vein, senior generals warned against lifting all limitations on press freedom, releasing political prisoners, and liberalizing the labor union laws. On all three accounts, the military was unable to convince the government to go along with its position. In essence, the polity that had emerged by late 1998 could not have been less attractive to the armed forces: parties were formed on an almost daily basis; politicians competed for support by the previously depoliticized masses; different ideologies and religious identities began to express themselves; one of the freest press markets in Asia developed; and regions talked with great self-confidence about their dissatisfaction with Indonesia's unitary constitution.[28] In the formation of the post-Suharto polity, TNI's veto powers were much less effective than its leaders had hoped and its critics had feared.

This does not mean, however, that TNI's attempts to defend its interests were completely unsuccessful. Most important, military leaders were able to protect themselves from public demands for their prosecution, and they managed to stay in control of TNI's internal organization. Fending off attempts by civilian politicians to revamp the military's institutional structures and subordinate it firmly to the government, TNI convinced Habibie that reforming the armed forces was a job that only the generals were qualified to do. As a consequence, the military leadership was allowed to define its own reform agenda, with officers prioritizing less crucial areas and excluding those that were of vital importance to TNI.[29] Among the latter was the territorial command structure, which had anchored the military in local politics since the 1950s and had served as a major tool for off-budget fund-raising. Maintaining this system was essential if the army wanted to insulate itself from the reforms occurring around it, and it achieved that goal during much of the early post-Suharto period.[30] It is important to emphasize, however, that the military, despite the successes in defending its internal autonomy, hardly ever could influence policy decisions that affected the direction and format of the postauthoritarian state as a whole.

Even when the armed forces as an institution or rogue elements within them tried to sabotage government policies through covert operations, they often suffered setbacks that further undermined their position. The East Timor debacle is the most prominent example. When President Habibie in early 1999 announced his decision to let the East Timorese decide in a United Nations–supervised referendum whether they wanted to remain in or leave the Indonesian Republic, the military felt too weak to oppose this move publicly.[31] Instead, senior generals developed plans to engineer an Indonesian victory in the former Portuguese colony through intimidation and intelligence operations. In case East Timor still opted for independence, these plans envisaged that TNI-supported militias would declare open war on the pro-independence movement, leading to complete chaos and a potential breakup of the territory.[32] Needless to say, this strategy ran counter to Habibie's declared aim of settling the East Timor problem peacefully and—possibly—getting nominated for the Nobel Peace Prize in the process. But TNI's approach damaged its own interests as well. The mayhem after Indonesia's defeat in the popular ballot attracted an international intervention force, which not only restored stability but also identified TNI as the main culprit in causing the chaos. The United States and other Western countries imposed sanctions on TNI as a result, embarrassing the military internationally and weakening it domestically.[33]

By and large, there was a significant gap between the military's ability to veto interventions into its internal affairs and its impact on the political architecture of the early democratic state. Although mostly successful in maintaining its autonomy as an institution, TNI was much less able to influence major decisions on what Indonesia's new polity should look like. There were only small victories for TNI in the latter field: it initiated the removal of an attorney-general who was determined to bring Suharto to court; it pushed through limitations on the freedom of assembly; and it negotiated continued military representation in the 1999 parliament, despite heavy resistance by civilian politicians.[34] But in almost all groundbreaking decisions that created post-1998 Indonesia as a competitive, open, and pluralist democracy, TNI's input was ignored. Beside the already mentioned political liberalization program, Habibie also launched an extensive decentralization project, effectively turning Indonesia from one of the most centralist into one of the most decentralized countries in the world.[35] The military, deeply engrained in paradigms of centralist hierarchy and thus opposed to decentralization, found no way of opposing it. By 2002, four years into the post-Suharto transition, the armed forces could not point to a single key element of the new polity that had been adopted because of their insistence. Struggling with its reputation as Suharto's repressive palace guard, unable to stop the strong ambition of civilian forces to rule, and weakened by factional divisions dating back to the late New Order years, TNI had to get used to the idea that it was now only one among many actors in Indonesia's new democracy.

TNI Vetoes Overruled: The 2002 Constitutional Amendments and the Aceh Peace Process

The year 2002 marked a watershed in Indonesian civil–military relations in several ways. To begin with, it was a year of significant political stabilization after a severe constitutional crisis in 2001, when President Abdurrahman Wahid was controversially impeached by the country's legislature and replaced by his vice president, Megawati Sukarnoputri. During the political upheaval that led to Wahid's removal, the armed forces had been able to consolidate their position temporarily, and many generals believed that TNI would emerge from the crisis reenergized and with new political might.[36] Although it may have appeared that way at the time, in hindsight it is evident that Wahid's impeachment initiated a political process that would result not in an increase but in a further decline in TNI's veto powers. Shocked that the absence of clear constitutional arrangements for political competition had brought the country to the brink of collapse, the civilian elite decided that a new set of regulatory rules was needed to stabilize the polity. The way to achieve these new rules was through a fourth round of constitutional amendments; the three previous rounds in 1999, 2000, and 2001 had empowered the legislature and strengthened civil rights but had not led to a coherent and effective political system. All political parties accordingly agreed that the 2002 amendments had to finalize and complete the political transition, ending the experimental phase of Indonesian democracy and entrenching a new, workable regime.[37]

Whereas the political elite viewed the constitutional amendments as an opportunity to expand and consolidate the democratic state, the armed forces sensed a chance to roll back reforms that they had never endorsed in the first place. The military's excessive self-confidence was apparently based on a misreading of its powers in the post-Wahid period: the generals believed that because they had assisted Parliament in Wahid's removal, the elite would have to grant TNI wide-ranging concessions. Indeed, Megawati fully surrendered the management of internal military affairs to the armed forces leadership upon taking power and allowed TNI to play a greater role in battling domestic insurgencies and communal violence in Aceh, Papua, Maluku, and Central Sulawesi. In addition, TNI's unitarian rhetoric about the sanctity of Indonesia's territorial integrity now gained wide acceptance in the elite and society.[38] But these concessions—although substantial in terms of strengthening TNI's autonomy—once again had little impact on the military's ability to influence the design of Indonesia's overall political framework. Falsely believing that it could dictate the terms of the fourth round of the constitutional amendments and revive some of the nondemocratic elements of the pre-1998 polities, TNI was about to suffer one of its greatest defeats in the post-Suharto era.

During the debates on the constitutional amendments in August 2002, TNI intended to exploit disagreements among civilian groups in order to achieve the annulment of all previous revisions and reinstate the original 1945 Constitution. The 1945 Constitution was popular within the officer corps because of its brevity and manipulability: it had enabled both Sukarno and Suharto to establish their autocratic regimes despite some vague references to democracy and elections. The reenactment of the 1945 Constitution thus would have allowed the military to cancel many of the reforms implemented since 1998 without exposing the antidemocratic agenda behind this proposal. But key civilian elites were determined to defend and consolidate the post-1998 reforms. In a rare show of unity, all major parties finally agreed on a package of amendments that would lead to direct presidential elections, much more complex impeachment procedures, and the establishment of a constitutional court as a referee between conflicting state institutions. The military resisted this consensus to the last minute, until its chief negotiator conveyed to the TNI commander that "if we don't agree to this, they [the civilian elite] will just walk over us."[39] Faced with the prospect of public humiliation, TNI dropped its opposition and ultimately endorsed the amendments. And if the crushing defeat of TNI's proposal to restore the 1945 document was not sufficient evidence for the ineffectiveness of its veto powers, the civilian elite drove home that point by deciding to terminate the military's representation in the Majelis Permusyawaratan Rakyat (People's Consultative Assembly) in 2004, five years earlier than initially planned.[40]

The second watershed in the relationship between the Indonesian state and its armed forces came in August 2005, when the government signed a comprehensive peace agreement with the separatist rebel movement Gerakan Aceh Merdeka (GAM, Free Aceh Movement). The military had been fiercely opposed to negotiations with insurgents, believing that any settlement would only allow the separatists to regroup.[41] In 2002 and 2003, the armed forces had therefore torpedoed a half-hearted "cessation of hostilities agreement" negotiated between the Megawati government and GAM, the failure of which triggered an all-out war in the troubled province. Although in 2003 TNI still could undermine the cease-fire easily (the civilian government and GAM were not serious about it either), in 2005 the situation was dramatically different. This time around, the government under Susilo Bambang Yudhoyono was firmly committed to ending the conflict peacefully, and GAM was prepared to drop its demand for Acehnese independence in exchange for full political rights and other concessions.[42] In order to pave the way for the agreement, Yudhoyono removed a number of conservative generals who had sabotaged earlier negotiations with GAM. In their stead, Yudhoyono appointed loyalists who ensured that the internal opposition within TNI to the peace deal was no longer voiced publicly.[43] Most important, they also prevented possible covert operations (such as the ones in East Timor) that could have endangered the peace process.

The significance of the Aceh Peace Accord for Indonesian civil–military relations cannot be overstated. For the first time in Indonesian history, the government had been able to make considerable concessions to a separatist rebel movement without the military sabotaging the effort. In East Timor in 1999, Papua in 2000, and Aceh in 2003, the military had actively undermined attempts by Jakarta to seek settlements with insurgents, and although it had hurt its own interests and international reputation in the process, the various peace initiatives had suffered irreparable damage as well. In all these cases, TNI had crudely tried to use its veto powers as a security force when its vetoes as a political actor had been ignored. In 2005, however, TNI did not even have the chance to embark on such a course. Yudhoyono had established tight executive oversight over the military, preempting any move by discontented generals to veto the Aceh Peace Accord politically or physically by force.[44] The irritation within TNI over this powerlessness was immense, with many commanders urging their superiors to take action.[45] But Yudhoyono's supporters in the armed forces stood firm, arguing that the military had no right to overturn policies determined by the democratically elected government. Two years after the military had lost its quest for a major dedemocratization of Indonesia's political system, it now had to accept that its ability to influence government policies on separatist conflicts was declining rapidly as well.

In combination, the collective agreement on constitutional reforms and the successful implementation of the Aceh Peace Accord highlighted the fact that whenever civilian elites were united on a particular policy, the armed forces found it impossible to veto it.[46] The unsteadiness of earlier phases of the democratic transition had offered the military some limited opportunities to veto planned reforms of TNI's internal management, but the stabilization of the political system from 2002 onward made such interventions increasingly difficult. The last important policy decision that the TNI had been able to undermine was arguably the "cessation of hostilities agreement" with GAM in 2002–2003, and even this influence was possible only because Jakarta's civilian elite was happy to see the initiative fail. But the collapse of the 2002 agreement boomeranged on TNI: it was followed by a much more substantial peace treaty in 2005, which included concessions that had not even been remotely considered in 2002. By 2005, Indonesia had already entered the stage of democratic consolidation, with the constitutional amendments adopted in 2002 becoming fully operational in 2004. These changes strengthened civilian state institutions and further reduced the political weight of the military, which lost its representation in Parliament and was no longer needed as a mediator in intracivilian conflicts. The portrayal of the military as Indonesia's "main veto actor," which even in the pre-2004 phase of democratic transition was more of a conventional wisdom than a political reality, became increasingly questionable.

TNI in Indonesia's Consolidating Democracy: How Strong Is Civilian Control?

In 2008, Indonesia both witnessed the death of former president Suharto and commemorated the tenth anniversary of his fall. Although Suharto's slow and public demise led to some nostalgic reevaluations of his regime, there was no doubt that Indonesia had seen a decade of tremendous political change. Suharto's monotonous autocracy had been replaced by a competitive electoral democracy, and the armed forces had been reduced from a political hegemon in the 1970s and a participant-ruler in the 1980s to a much less influential player in postauthoritarian politics. The shape of Indonesia's political system was no longer determined by the military's interests in the way it had been in the late 1950s and late 1960s, and TNI was struggling to prevent civilian state authorities from intervening into its affairs. Most important,

Indonesia's new democracy appeared surprisingly stable. At ten years of age, it had already outlived the country's first attempt at a democratic polity between 1950 and 1957, and there were no signs of a credible political campaign that aimed at the replacement of the current system.[47] To be sure, there was widespread discontent with political parties, corruption, and government inefficiencies, but such complaints were not dissimilar to those widely held in other functioning democracies.[48] The military, for its part, did not seem to have the strength to challenge the democratic system, instead withdrawing into its professional niche of national defense and the very few fields of domestic security that it was still allowed to engage in. Overall, Indonesia's democracy ten years after the end of the New Order was consolidating at a slow but steady pace, and that remains true today.

But the assessment of TNI's decline as a decisive veto player in Indonesian politics has to be qualified in several ways. First of all, the erosion of TNI's powers as an institution did not automatically translate into the complete marginalization of active and retired military officers from the political landscape. In fact, former generals have become major actors in electoral politics, particularly after the constitutional deadlock of 2001. Many former commanders have used their nationwide name recognition to run for political office in the center as well as in the regions. For instance, three retired officers ran in the 2004 and 2009 presidential elections, with ex-general Yudhoyono emerging as the winner in both cases. The scholarly literature on former generals in democratic politics has repeatedly wrestled with the problem of how to classify this phenomenon analytically,[49] with most observers arguing that retired officers holding key positions cannot be equated with military interference. Although former Indonesian generals espouse very diverse viewpoints and interests,[50] there is no doubt that they share a common code of military values and doctrinal convictions. For that reason, the involvement of retired officers in post-Suharto politics is not an entirely "civilian" affair, as the generals themselves argue. Instead, it relates to the issue of how the military and its top brass have adapted to the new democratic polity; the successful political careers of some of Suharto's leading generals suggest that at least some senior generals have adjusted reasonably well.

Despite some former officers' success in elections at the national and local level, this trend seems to be less pronounced than it was at the time of Yudhoyono's first inauguration. Since then, retired TNI leaders have lost some of the country's key governorships. For example, during the direct local elections conducted between 2005 and 2011, the formerly military-held governorships of Jakarta, East Java, North Sumatra, South Sulawesi, Central Sulawesi, and East Kalimantan went to civilians, in some cases for the first time since the 1960s.[51] As of 2012, only three of Indonesia's thirty-three governors—those of Maluku, Central Java, and West Papua—are retired military generals. Thus, the percentage of former military officers serving as governors, which had already dropped from around 50 percent in 1998 to 27 percent in 2005, has now declined further to 9 percent. The explanation for this development lies largely in the shrinking stock of former New Order military leaders who can use their celebrity status to compete in elections. Most candidates for senior positions owe their prominence to their elevated status under Suharto's regime—Yudhoyono, Wiranto, and Prabowo Subianto being only some examples. Under the post–New Order governments, by contrast, much fewer active military leaders have acquired the high levels of name recognition necessary to win regional elections after their retirement. In contemporary Indonesia, many citizens do not even know the name of the incumbent TNI chief; this decline in sociopolitical significance is set to negatively affect military retirees' electoral chances in the long term.

The second area in which TNI's influence remains significant is that of internal military organization. Although the armed forces have been unable to design the post-Suharto polity according to their politico-ideological priorities, they have managed to maintain a certain degree of institutional autonomy. For instance, senior generals still enjoy legal impunity, with not a single key TNI leader sent to prison under democratic rule for human rights violations committed during the New Order or the transition. The reform of the military justice system—designed to make officers more accountable—was aborted in 2009 after the armed forces and the Department of Defense managed to drag out the deliberations of the bill until the legislature's term had expired.[52] Similarly, the military continues to raise a significant percentage of its operational income from off-budget funds. This percentage has dropped from around 70 percent at the beginning of the transition to around 25 to 30 percent today, perhaps even lower if TNI's official numbers are to be believed. Regardless of the concrete figures, however, the practice of self-funding needs to be terminated completely if Indonesia intends to establish strong democratic control over its armed forces.[53] Finally, the preservation of the territorial command structure has allowed the military to keep a foothold in the country's regions. TNI units remain operational in almost all of Indonesia's villages, subdistricts, districts, cities, and provinces, providing it with the logistic infrastructure to intervene in government administration should circumstances ever allow it to do so again. At the moment, the political context is unsupportive of such a scenario, but there is no guarantee that this situation will not change in the future.

Third, there are a few provinces and districts in which the military remains disproportionately powerful. In these territories, the armed forces continue to exercise political and economic control. In general terms, the higher the level of sociopolitical, ethnic, religious, or separatist tensions in a locality, the deeper the military engagement in that locality's politicoeconomic affairs. The number of such areas has dropped sharply since the end of most of the large-scale communal conflicts in 2003 and the successfully implemented Aceh Peace Accord of 2005. In Papua, however, TNI maintains a much higher profile than in any other territory in Indonesia. This is due to widespread concerns among Jakarta's political elite, both civilian and military, that Papua might secede from Indonesia in the same way that East Timor did in 1999. As a consequence, the central government and legislature are often prepared to turn a blind eye to some of TNI's continuing transgressions in the province, believing that they are necessary to contain the separatist movement there.[54] The military arguably remains an effective veto player in some parts of Papua, marking a sharp contrast to its status in the rest of the Indonesian archipelago.

TNI's ability to hold on to some privileges and territories is evidence of the structural deficiencies in Indonesia's control over its security forces. The Department of Defense, for example, has not yet developed the capacity to fully control the armed forces, and the members of Indonesia's legislature still struggle to acquire the necessary expertise to effectively supervise security operations and the agencies involved. Indeed, it is remarkable that TNI has been unable to take more advantage of such institutional shortcomings in security-sector governance. The fact that the armed forces have been politically marginalized despite problems in the bodies charged with their control highlights the continued relevance of Samuel Finer's focus on stable political cultures as the most effective barriers to military intervention in politics.[55] In post-Suharto Indonesia, it was the stabilization of the polity, the decline of communal conflicts, the empowerment of democratic institutions, and the relative solidity of the economy that allowed civilian actors to sideline the armed forces without controlling all aspects of their affairs. In the absence of any initiatives to replace the current political system, Indonesia's civilian politicians could afford to leave the armed forces with the power largely to regulate themselves. Although this approach might have been risky in a climate of political instability and economic crisis, it has proved workable within the framework of continued democratic consolidation.

Of course, some comparative scholars might argue that a democracy in which the military is not fully subordinated to objective civilian control can hardly be described as "consolidating."[56] However, Indonesia appears to be a compelling example of a gradually stabilizing democracy that has succeeded in entrenching its democratic institutions without aggressively pursuing Western ideas of complete civilian authority over the military. In Indonesia, the erosion of the military's powers occurred almost as a side effect of a comprehensive political reform program, which focused on the institutionalization of competitive elections, the strengthening of civilian actors, the development of effective legislative and executive bodies, as well as extensive decentralization. This process has not produced a flawless democracy; serious defects remain in the areas of rule of law, social equality, good governance, and the security sector. But there is no doubt that Indonesia's democracy has fared much better than many observers would have predicted in 1998 and has consolidated much faster than it has in its Southeast Asian counterparts Thailand and the Philippines. In the 2009 Freedom House report on political rights and civil liberties around the globe, for example, Indonesia was the only country in the Association of Southeast Asian Nations classified as "free" and an "electoral democracy"—a predicate it was first awarded in 2006 and continues to hold in 2012.[57] Such assessments indicate that Indonesia has made significant progress in its democratization process, even without having addressed all remaining problems related to the institutional control of its military.

TNI—Veto Player No More?

In this chapter, I have critically reassessed widespread claims by scholars and policymakers that TNI was and continues to be Indonesia's most formidable veto player. Analyzing the role of the armed forces in several key periods of Indonesian history, I have shown that the importance of the military in shaping the political system tends to be overstated. In the independence war, which many analysts have identified as the source of the military's political power, the army was unable to influence the decisions civilian politicians made about the future format of the Indonesian state. Appreciated more as a symbol of national unity than feared as a powerful "veto player," the armed forces spent the first half of the 1950s at the political margins. It was only in the turmoil of the mid- and late 1950s that the military could, for the very first time, shape key political developments in a way that served its interests. Sukarno's Guided Democracy offered the military institutionalized political participation, acknowledging TNI's increased importance after its successful suppression of regional insurgencies in Sumatra, Sulawesi, and Java. But TNI's new powers were short-lived: under Sukarno's autocratic rule, Indonesia's domestic and foreign policies increasingly drifted to the left, leaving the army with little room to maneuver. Frustrated over its lack of influence, the military elite used the opportunity of a failed pro-Communist coup attempt to take power in October 1965. In the formative years of the New Order regime, the military was not only an effective veto player, but a hegemon that single-handedly determined the shape of the political system.

The military's overwhelming political dominance in the late 1960s and early 1970s is the foundation for the frequent description of TNI as the country's most powerful veto player. This depiction has become so deeply engrained in both foreign and domestic observers' analyses that even significant changes during and after the New Order regime could not alter this fixture of political science writings on Indonesia. In the 1980s and 1990s, Suharto transformed the initially military-dominated regime into a personal autocracy in which he presided over a network of patronage relationships. In this authoritarian system, the military still played a significant role as Suharto's primary instrument of repression, but it was no longer an independent political actor whose interests dictated government policies. Since 1998, many analysts have pointed to the armed forces as Indonesia's "main veto player," implying that it used—and still uses—its powers to obstruct Indonesia's democratization. This assessment misses two important aspects of the military's political behavior: first, the armed forces consented to the regime change in May 1998, clearing the way for the democratic transition. Second, their veto powers in the new polity were subsequently very limited; TNI's proposals regarding the design of the post-Suharto state were mostly ignored, and one of the most democratic regimes in Asia emerged as a result. Although the military made many attempts to influence policies and roll back democratic reforms, only very few of these initiatives succeeded.

But it would be misleading to interpret the decline of TNI's veto powers as evidence of the successful establishment of full democratic civilian control over the Indonesian armed forces. The institutional mechanisms of security sector governance remain deficient, allowing the military to continue its long-

standing tradition of managerial self-regulation. Principles of legal accountability have still not been enforced for military officers; the problem of off-
budget funding has yet to be resolved (despite a recent government initiative
to take over TNI-owned businesses); and there are no signs that the territorial
command structure will be reformed anytime soon. In addition, TNI is still
very influential in the province of Papua, where it effectively runs a parallel
government to the civilian administration. However, the surprising aspect of
these residual TNI privileges is not that they still exist, but how little impact
they have had on Indonesia's overall process of democratic transition and consolidation. By all accounts, Indonesia has made significant progress in reforming its polity, turning it from one of the world's most persistent autocracies
into a competitive electoral democracy. No serious political scientist would
describe Indonesia in 2012 as a "hybrid regime" or "semidemocracy," thus
marking a notable break with the pre-2004 period, when such terms were still
widely used. Contemporary Indonesia is, in Larry Diamond and Leonardo
Morlino's scheme, a low-quality democracy facing myriad challenges,[58] but
TNI's potential veto powers seem—at least for the time being—no longer the
most pressing of these issues.

6

Indonesian Government Approaches to
Radical Islam Since 1998

Sidney Jones

To the extent that extremist Islamic movements reject democracy or actively try to destabilize the state, they can become "veto actors" in young democracies. How governments respond to them can strengthen or undermine the transition process. In post-Suharto Indonesia, the only time these movements had the potential to unravel the democratic experiment was in the first two years of the transition, and, even then, it was only because some within the security apparatus tried to exploit them for short-term domestic political gain.

In general, the transnational links of some of these movements had little if any bearing on the severity of the threat they posed. At no time, for example, did Jemaah Islamiyah (JI, Islamic Group) or later splinter groups that at certain points looked to al-Qaeda for ideological inspiration and funding constitute a serious destabilizing force in the sense that their bombing campaigns weakened the government. If anything, their attacks strengthened it by leading to a greater professionalization of law enforcement agencies. Nor were those attacks ever directed primarily at weakening the state, undermining the economy, or punishing apostate rulers. The broader objective of JI as a movement was indeed to establish an Islamic state, but the attacks per se were aimed at avenging the deaths of Muslims at the hands of either the United States and its allies or local Christians.

JI, with its ties to al-Qaeda, its branches around Southeast Asia and Australia, and its international media coverage, was thus never as dangerous to the state as the alliance between local radical groups and individual army officers or politicians jockeying for power during the Habibie and Wahid administrations. (Contrary to the thesis that jihadi mobilization occurred as a result of frustration over lack of inclusion in or influence over post-Suharto governments, JI leaders were never interested in joining the political process in the first place.) In fact, as democracy consolidated, the role of these domestic radicals evolved, in some cases coming to be seen by their government partners as defenders of the Indonesian state, including against global jihad.

Successive post-Suharto governments reacted to radical Islam only when it crossed the line into crime. B. J. Habibie and his allies saw militant Islam as an asset, not a threat, a conservative counterweight to the radical student movement. Abdurrahman Wahid saw all radical violence as evidence that his enemies were out to unseat him. Megawati Sukarnoputri was president when the terrorist attacks in the United States happened on September 11, 2001, and the extent of Indonesia's own terrorist problem became clear; the combined result was a strengthening of the security apparatus, but civilian, not military. Susilo Bambang Yudhoyono (SBY) had the benefit of a stronger democratic base and had to wrestle more than his predecessors with the dilemma of how to cope with radical Islam as an authentic civil society voice. Through all these administrations, however, the governments never spoke with one voice, and there were always multiple actors with different and often contradictory agendas: fighting terrorism, fighting separatism, gaining votes, seeking political power, upholding the Constitution, protecting the country against foreigners, and protecting the country's image.

Democratic consolidation has meant in general that the fight against the criminal side of extremist Islam has worked. The much more difficult problem is how to address nonviolent radicalism, where Suharto-era tactics such as book banning, are unacceptable, but where innovative ideas are in short supply.

Habibie: May 1998–October 1999

The short-lived Habibie government was in office at the time of several key developments in the radical movement. One set of developments was linked:

the emergence of militant Muslim groups as major actors instead of bit players in Jakarta politics; the outbreak of communal violence, some perhaps provoked, from Jakarta to Maluku between November 1998 and January 1999;
and the involvement of security forces in the radical response to deaths of
Muslims in Ambon.[1] Most of these developments played out very publicly.

The Indonesian government was completely oblivious to another set of
developments that took place over the same period: the consolidation of the
JI network inside and outside Indonesia; the graduation in Mindanao of the
first class of JI's military academy there; the adoption by some senior JI leaders of the al-Qaeda interpretation of jihad; JI's establishment of a special forces unit; the dispatch of the first JI fighters to Maluku; the establishment of
a JI jihadi offshoot, Mujahidin KOMPAK; and the return from Malaysia of
many senior JI leaders.[2] Some JI members believed that Suharto's fall meant
the opportunity for an Islamic revolution was at hand or that at least there
was a window of opportunity to build an Islamic state. The outbreak of the
Ambon conflict for them was an unexpected bonus in this regard because it
allowed JI to put its teachings on jihad into practice in a way that could serve
these larger goals by attracting new recruits and giving them combat experience.[3] However, JI, which claimed two thousand members across Indonesia
at this time and some five thousand additional sympathizers, had no interest
in joining forces with other radical organizations in Indonesia.[4] Its members
were not interested in promoting or seeking backing from political players;
they were simply interested in how the political changes might facilitate an
Islamic state. The type of government, the state of the economy, and maneu-
verings of the political elite—all were largely irrelevant.

It was very different for hard-line Islamic groups in Jakarta that depended
on political patronage. The main political battle in the immediate post-Suharto
era was over the legitimacy of Habibie as successor to Suharto. It took place in
an atmosphere where tensions within the security forces were high and where,
in the aftermath of the May 1998 riots, serious concerns over the ability to control Jakarta's streets remained. Top political actors, such as Minister of Defense
and Armed Forces Commander Wiranto, wanted street support; the groups
that could provide it wanted political influence or funding or both.[5]

As a result, Wiranto and one of his allies, Jakarta garrison commander
Djaja Suparman, together with the then national police chief Noegroho Dja-
joesman, became major backers of groups that had support among Jakarta
thugs (preman). These groups included the Front Pembela Islam (FPI, Islamic Defenders Front). Formed on August 17, 1998 (Indonesia's National

Day), the FPI became one of twenty Muslim organizations that the military mobilized as "civilian volunteers" (pam swakarsa) to provide security for a special session of Indonesia's highest parliamentary body, the Majelis Permusyawaratan Rakyat (MPR, People's Consultative Assembly), in mid-November 1998.[6] Salafi groups, normally apolitical, were also brought in for the first time.[7] Trained by the army and equipped with bamboo spears, these Muslim militias, some thirty thousand strong, clashed with anti-Habibie protestors and caused far more mayhem than they curbed.

A decade later the idea of key state actors' recruiting and training thirty thousand militia members in Jakarta would be unthinkable. But Habibie's supporters needed a show of force against the students and middle class who had brought down Suharto, and the Muslim street could provide it. Many of the groups mobilized were conservative in the sense of being committed (at least publicly) to the implementation of Islamic law in some form; some were ultranationalists who later, after Ambon erupted, could be rallied to defend the homeland against "Christian separatists."

The Habibie government had no policies against the more extreme edge of the spectrum, notably JI, because it had no idea of their existence. (With developments in East Timor, there were also other priorities.) The extremists in turn had no interest in Habibie or political patronage. They had been hoping for major conflict in Indonesia that they could turn into a jihad for an Islamic state, and when that did not materialize, the eruption of conflict in Ambon seemed like a godsend.[8] The first JI contingent arrived there in June 1999; the need to get people into the field more quickly than allowed by the normal JI indoctrination period led to the creation of another group, Mujahidin KOMPAK.[9] For both KOMPAK and JI (and some Darul Islam factions as well), defense of fellow Muslims was important, but even more so was the need to gather the combat skills and experience that could be put to use for a larger struggle.

Abdurrahman Wahid, October 1999–July 2001

It was during the presidency of Abdurrahman Wahid (Gus Dur) that Indonesian democracy was in the most peril because of the president's disastrous ineptness, his tensions with the military, and his opponents' deliberate efforts to destabilize the country. It was during his tenure that the conflicts in Maluku and Poso escalated out of control and that JI reached its peak strength, with Maluku and Poso providing undreamed of recruiting opportunities and the justification for a bombing campaign because Muslims were dying at Christian hands on Indonesian soil.[10] The bomb attacks included the attempted murder of the Philippines ambassador to Jakarta and the bombings of churches across eleven cities on Christmas Eve 2000. Gus Dur's response to Islamic radicalism was to assume that any major incidents were the work of his political enemies, real or imagined, while his enemies in the military continued to make political use of mass-based hard-line Muslim organizations. There was still no knowledge of JI's existence, and although Laskar Jihad (Jihad Militia) sent thousands of fighters to Maluku, there was little appreciation in the palace that they were anything more than army stooges.

Gus Dur came to power at the end of 1999 as the result of a parliamentary alliance that included the main Muslim organizations joining forces to prevent Megawati Sukarnoputri from coming to power. His incompetence convinced many in the military and some outside it that Indonesia was not ready for civilian government and would be better off with the military in power. Every step he took as president seemed to alienate the military more. The military was already deeply unhappy over the loss of East Timor and became more so in January 2000, when Gus Dur invited a Geneva-based nongovernmental organization to help solve the Aceh conflict. The invitation came as Gerakan Aceh Merdeka (GAM, Free Aceh Movement) guerrillas, returning from Malaysia, had embarked on a serious recruitment and mobilization program in Aceh.

January 2000 had seen a huge rally in Jakarta to mobilize Muslims in defense of their fellow faithful in Ambon, financed in part by a well-established member of the political elite. That same month Muslims rioted in Lombok in a project that seemed to be orchestrated by a Wiranto ally. In February, Gus Dur sacked Wiranto, allegedly because of the latter's responsibility for human rights violations in East Timor, and tensions escalated further.

In March 2000, as the situation in Maluku and North Maluku continued to deteriorate, the deputy Speaker of Parliament and the head of Gus Dur's party, Matori Abdul Jalil, was attacked by a man with a machete. Police arrested the man and some of his accomplices but made no effort to understand the organization behind them, called AMIN (Angkatan Islam Mujahidin Nusantara, or Islamic Mujahidin Forces of the Indonesian Archipelago). If they had, they might have begun to understand the impact that Ambon was having on radical Islam: it was fueling or in some cases reviving a commitment to jihad. In this case, the attackers were members of a radical Darul

Islam faction, who told police that Matori and by implication Gus Dur had not done enough to defend Muslims in Ambon and that Ambon was in danger of being taken over by Communists. There is some evidence that the group was approached by military intelligence officers and offered funding, which they said they rejected.[11]

Then in April 2000 Gus Dur very publicly failed in his effort to stop thousands of Laskar Jihad volunteers from going to Maluku to fight. This Salafi militia, led by the Yogyakarta-based Ja'far Umar Thalib, was backed by the army, received training from it, and, in the militia's view, made common cause in defending a Muslim government from assault by Christian separatists.[12] Laskar Jihad fighters arrived to find a much smaller but better-trained contingent of fighters already present. This contingent included JI, Darul Islam, and Mujahidin KOMPAK and was collectively known as "Laskar Mujahidin" (Mujahideen Militia). Very few in Indonesia or, indeed, the outside world paid any attention to the smaller group, but unlike Laskar Jihad, its members were not interested in collaboration with the government; they wanted to topple it.

When a major massacre of Muslims took place in Poso, Central Sulawesi, in May 2000, many in Laskar Mujahidin shifted there to recruit and train local recruits. The point was not just to fight Christians; it was to use the jihad to establish the conditions for turning Poso into a base for the gradual expansion of an Islamic community. Again, the government, consumed by problems in Jakarta, made no effort to understand what was happening.

The first attacks by JI to cause fatalities outside Ambon and Poso took place in August 2000, when the Philippines ambassador in Jakarta was nearly killed after a remotely detonated bomb went off by his car as he was returning to his residence for lunch; two others died in the blast. Gus Dur suggested that one motive of the attackers was to show that he could not control security in the city; in fact, it was a revenge attack for the Philippine army's "all-out war" on the Moro Islamic Liberation Front camp where JI had trained. No arrests took place, however, and the police investigation went nowhere.[13]

When a coordinated series of bombs went off on Christmas Eve, Gus Dur blamed a former top army officer and another official close to the Suharto family, saying the motive of the bombing was to destabilize his government.[14] This motive was as plausible as any other, although it is clear that at least the Badan Intelijen Negara (BIN, National Intelligence Agency) knew who some of the real perpetrators were—a JI group led by a man known as "Hambali," now imprisoned at Guántanamo. Very few saw extremist Muslims as responsible; most saw the army or the Suharto family as the culprits.[15] The problem was that in a period of high political tension, there were just too many possible suspects and motives, and there was no reason to believe a serious terrorist group was involved.

If there was a danger to the state from radical Islam during this period, it was not from those who subscribed to the global jihad. Their numbers were too small, and they had no interest in playing politics in the sense of getting immersed in the day-to-day power struggles going on in Jakarta. The dangers were from elements of the security forces—Gus Dur was probably right on the main point if not on the details—joining forces with local players for their own political interests. The intensity of the communal conflagration that resulted proved far easier to start than stop and did serious damage to Indonesia's efforts to present itself as a pluralist democracy.

Megawati Sukarnoputri, July 2001–October 2004

It was during the early part of the Megawati administration that the attack on the World Trade Center in New York City took place and that Indonesia woke up to the terrorist threat at home from JI and its splinter groups. Three of the major suicide bombings in Indonesia were undertaken during her administration: the Bali bombing in October 2002, the Marriott Hotel bombing in August 2003, and the Australian embassy bombing in September 2004. The bombings had no impact on national stability, except, if anything, to reinforce it. What they did was to expose the police force's limitations and the urgency of turning it into a more professional agency. With virtually unlimited amounts of counterterrorism funding from abroad, first the police, then other parts of the legal system, and finally even the deservedly maligned Attorney General's Office became the focus of grants and training. The military received relatively little, which helped promote the police as the main internal security agency, as it was in law but not initially in practice. Thus, the silver lining to the bombings was the strengthening of key government institutions.

Until Bali, the government was inattentive to a possible threat from radical Islam. A JI bombing at the Atrium shopping mall in Jakarta in August 2001, where church services attended by Ambonese Christians were held, netted a Malaysian bomber (who blew his foot off) and one other, and a few members of the police criminal investigation squad began to connect the dots with the Christmas Eve bombings. They found more Malaysians who had taken part in a training course in West Java prior to embarking for Ambon. Other churches were bombed in Jakarta during the year, but no one paid much attention. Then the world changed with the World Trade Center attacks in New York, and the dangers of radical Islam suddenly seemed to enter a new dimension. Megawati was President George W. Bush's first state visitor after the attacks and pledged to work with the United States in fighting terror. Neither she nor anyone in her cabinet, however, really believed that Indonesia itself had a problem.

In December 2001, then coordinating minister for people's welfare Jusuf Kalla successfully brokered an end to the communal fighting in Poso, effectively buying off the main players. The agreement, known as the Malino Accord, was successful in that it ended Christian–Muslim fighting. When one-sided attacks continued, however, government officials refused to recognize them for what they were, assaults on Christians—and much more rarely transmigrant Balinese Hindus—by radical JI members trained in Afghanistan and Mindanao. Instead, they were dismissed as "pure criminality"; no one, least of all Kalla, wanted to suggest that the Malino Accord was less than a triumph. But for the first time, government officials had shown a serious interest in trying to resolve conflict rather than foment it, and Kalla's success led him to try the same in Maluku in early 2002 and Aceh in 2003 in an initiative that eventually led to the 2005 Helsinki Agreement, ending a three-decade insurgency.

The arrests of JI members in Singapore and Malaysia in late 2001 and revelations that they had been trained in Afghanistan, had links to al-Qaeda, and looked to Abu Bakar Ba'asyir for leadership were greeted with disbelief in Indonesia. Vice President Hamzah Haz made a point of showing solidarity with Ba'asyir, as did other Muslim leaders.

The Bali bombings that killed more than two hundred people put things in a different perspective. Given the number of foreigners killed, Indonesia had no choice but to accept outside help, and some of the best local police investigators, who had begun to put some of the pieces of the puzzle together after the Christmas Eve and Atrium bombings, were brought into a new counterterrorism unit, Detachment 88. On-the-job training and access to state-of-the-art equipment was provided by Australia with additional assistance from the United States and others. It may not have been the donors' primary aim, but by making the police rather than the army the main recipient of counterterrorism assistance, the role of civilians over the military in internal security was strengthened (and also probably worsened relations between them).

The Megawati government quickly enacted an antiterrorism decree that the Parliament adopted as law in 2003. It was far less draconian than the Internal Security Act of neighboring Singapore and Malaysia but provided the legal basis by which those accused of the Bali bombings could be tried. The debate over the law produced an interesting alliance of human rights defenders and hard-line Muslim groups, both arguing against a harsher law: the former concerned about a return to Suharto-era repression, the latter fearing that it would lead to stigmatization of Islam and a mass round-up of Muslim activists.

There was huge public curiosity about the bombers once they were arrested. They were tried relatively quickly in 2003 on the basis of solid forensic evidence in open trials that bore none of the preprogrammed characteristics of the political trials the previous year of Indonesians accused of human rights violations in East Timor.[16] The courts used were part of the deeply flawed Indonesian legal system, but the evidence was so overwhelming and the defendants so defiant that it was hard to question the guilty verdicts at the end.

From the beginning, the bombers justified their attack as a revenge for Muslim deaths at the hands of America and its "lackeys." They wanted to make clear they were playing on an international stage, not an Indonesian one. Efforts to undermine the Indonesian government never entered the equation. In his interrogation deposition, Imam Samudra, field commander for the bombings, said the main reason for choosing Bali was that it was "the gathering place of international terrorists—that is, Israelis/Jews, America, Australia, and other countries involved in the destruction of Afghanistan during Ramadhan 2001."[17] He said he had taken part in earlier church bombings because Christians had blown up mosques in Ambon.

Another bomber wrote: "We want to retaliate for the brutality of the leaders and armies of these states that have killed, annihilated our women and our children, but at the moment, we don't yet have the capacity to attack and kill them. So we attack their people, whose religion is the same as theirs— that is, they are all kafir [unbelievers]—as a way of retaliating for their attacks against us."[18]

In a way, the international attention to al-Qaeda and the sheer enormity of the Bali carnage kept the domestic focus on the crime rather than on the ideology behind it. There was a sense that if this group could be rounded up, the problem would be over. Bali thus generated little introspection about radical thought in Indonesia or about where JI, still a poorly understood group, had come from.

The mass-based organizations that relied on thugs bashing up karaoke bars and nightclubs to promote the application of Islamic law continued to have their government backers: in the trial of a senior JI figure in 2003, one prosecutor was so afraid that the man's supporters would disrupt the proceedings that, with police help, he hired FPI to stack the courtroom with men in white robes and turbans who had been paid not to cause trouble.[19] The FPI continued to enjoy near total immunity for its vigilante violence, as did Laskar Jihad. Even when the latter's leader, Ja'far Umar Thalib, was arrested in 2001 for imposing a death sentence by stoning on a follower accused of adultery, pressure from other conservative organizations eventually led to his release.[20]

The Marriott bombing in August 2003, which seemed to cause more domestic outrage than the Bali bombing because it was in the heart of Jakarta and all but one of the victims were Indonesians, was quickly solved. Evidence pointed back to some Sumatran-based members of JI, many of whom had links to Ba'asyir's school in Ngruki, Solo, as well as to two Malaysians, Noordin Mohammad Top and Dr. Azhari Husin. Good police work continued, but the involvement of Malaysians in both this attack and the Australian embassy bombing the following year—which was an entirely Noordin-led, not JI, operation—led many in the Parliament to conclude that the root of the problem lay with Malaysia, not at home.[21]

There was ludicrous speculation in the Australian press that the embassy attack had been aimed at trying to influence the Australian elections or the Indonesian elections scheduled for September 25. But, again, the bombers had no interest in Indonesian politics. Their main aim, in the words of one of the bombers, was to "make Western nations tremble."[22]

The government continued to be oblivious to the connection between JI and the ongoing violence in Poso, nor was there much interest in the international community for any act of terrorism where only Indonesians, but not foreigners, were killed.

Susilo Bambang Yudhoyono, October 2004

SBY's administration took the first steps toward looking at radical Islam in terms of the message more than just the crimes, but it also succumbed to pressure from hard-line civil society groups that over a decade of democratic reform had become adept at using political space to advocate a more intolerant agenda. Failure to stand up for minorities emerged as a major shortcoming of a government that was otherwise doing most things right. Police reform continued, still fueled by counterterrorism funding, and increasing concern about radical recruitment in prison directed some of that funding to prison reform—so, again, state institutions were strengthened.

The line between the mass-based, nonviolent radicals and the Salafi jihadists represented by JI also began to blur as members of JI increasingly moved into above-ground activities. Although parts of the government had begun to look at radical Islam writ large as a generally antidemocratic force—and the erstwhile terrorists focused more of their attention on nonviolent criticism of democracy—there was some evidence that members of the security and intelligence agencies still looked to mass-based above-ground radical organizations as partners in countering terrorism and curbing separatism.

The new government had its first brush with terrorism when the second Bali bombing occurred on October 1, 2005. The chief perpetrator was Noordin Top again. His partner, Azhari, was tracked down and killed by police a month after the bombing. But police found a document on Azhari's computer that explained the rationale for the bombing:

> It can no longer be denied that Islam's main enemy is America and its allies. They are waging war on Islam around the world, in every corner of the earth—in Afghanistan, Iraq, Chechnya, Kashmir, and Philippines. They are giving financial and technical support to apostate rulers to arrest mujahidin in Saudi Arabia, Egypt, Pakistan and Indonesia. That's why, around the world, [mujahidin] are making war on them—just recently in July 2005, they were attacked in London. Now they will be attacked in Bali, too.
>
> Why Bali? Because an attack in Bali is an attack with global impact. Bali is known around the world, better known than Indonesia itself. An attack in Bali will be covered by the international media. In this way, the world will get the message that an attack has been directed at America and its allies.[23]

A few weeks after the bombing, three teenage Christian schoolgirls were attacked with machetes and beheaded in Poso. The government had largely ignored all the bombings and murders in and around Poso that had taken place since the 2001 Malino Accords; most were unsolved, and all were dismissed as "ordinary" crimes. The attack on the schoolgirls was so brutal and so risked reigniting communal conflict, however, that the government took action.[24] The national police commander sent a crack team of investigators from Detachment 88, who reasonably quickly solved not only this crime, but most of the others. The perpetrators were JI members, and their stated motivation was revenge for attacks by Christians at the height of the conflict. Most were based at an Islamic school in Tanah Runtuh, Poso, run by a JI sympathizer named Adnan Arsal; some had been trained in Mindanao.

Led by Vice President Kalla, the government finally began to look beyond arrests to counter the radical message, trying to provide educational alternatives to radical schools and to co-opt local JI leaders through trips to Mecca and other perks. Some of these measures were constructive, such as the establishment of a state-of-the-art branch of an Islamic pesantren (boarding school) known for its progressive teaching methods, although it attracted fewer students than the government hoped. The school was built on a site just down the road from Adnan Arsal's pesantren in Tanah Runtuh.[25]

Other steps created an uproar, as when Kalla seemed to suggest that all students at pesantrens should be fingerprinted.[26] He claimed that he had only intended that there should be a better national identification system that would include everyone, including students, but the outcry probably set back any thoughts of such a system for years.

Poso brought out all the complications of the government's stance toward radical Islam. In their anxiety to stop the Poso violence, police went back to their old friend, FPI head Habieb Rizieq, and sponsored a speaking tour for him across Central Sulawesi. (In a speech in Luwuk on November 29, Rizieq paid tribute to his sponsors, saying that in their commitment to law and order the FPI and the police were "like husband and wife.")[27]

The police were operating on the assumption that if young men could be turned into moralist thugs, this was at least better than turning terrorist. "The problem is to find out who the radicals will listen to. They'll listen to Arsal, but he's not always giving the right message. We brought Habieb Rizieq up here to talk to them because he may be hard-line, but it's a different kind of approach: we thought it would be useful."[28]

The government tried a similar tactic in early January 2007, when officials sought support of Muslim leaders after police operations against JI-linked fugitives ended up killing fourteen militants. One of those summoned out of obscurity was Ja'far Umar Thalib, the former leader of Laskar Jihad, who had taken a low profile ever since Laskar Jihad disbanded in early October 2002.[29] Ja'far obligingly criticized Abu Bakar Ba'asyir and JI as heretics who had gone astray, but there was a distinct sense that officials had a sense of "bad radicals" and "our radicals"; Ja'far Umar Thalib and Habieb Rizieq were still on the good side.

It took events of July 2008 and the sight of FPI thugs thrashing peaceful demonstrators at a rally in central Jakarta in support of religious freedom to convince the government that FPI's actions were harming Indonesia's image. (The rally had been sparked by government moves against the Ahmadiyya sect in response to hard-line pressure.) Public pressure to ban FPI intensified, and Habieb Rizieq was arrested, tried, and sentenced to a brief term in prison. The spectacle of FPI thugs beating up witnesses inside the courtroom, with seemingly no effort made to keep them out, outraged even members of the public who supported a ban on Ahmadiyya.

But if FPI's image was tarnished, elements of the security apparatus still saw the group as an ally when there was a perceived political need to play the Islamic card. In Aceh, the sudden prominence of FPI members in the lead-up to elections at a time when the government was trying to portray Partai Aceh, the party of the former rebels, as anti-Islamic, suggested that the partnership was still useful in certain contexts.[30]

By the end of the SBY administration's first term, the threat of terrorism seemed to have declined substantially, due in part to the stepped-up law enforcement efforts that began in response to the first Bali bombing. Within the JI leadership, there was also a general consensus that the bombings had been counterproductive.[31] No major bombings had taken place since the second Bali bombings; Poso and Ambon were quiet; and a police-led "deradicalization program" had attracted worldwide praise, although it was more an exercise in economic co-optation than in ideological counseling.[32] In the aftermath of the November 2008 execution of the Bali bombers and the appearance of a rash of books glorifying their "martyrdom," the government had even begun to look gingerly at the problem of countering jihadist content in radical publications.

Just as complacency was setting in, however, the calm was shattered. Noordin, in what would prove to be his last operation, emerged from hiding to direct the July 2009 bombings of two Jakarta luxury hotels, the Marriott for the second time and the Ritz-Carlton. Now calling his group "al-Qaeda for Indonesia," he worked with a disparate collection of operatives, including a Yemen-trained cleric and several JI members. Police tracked down most of those involved and killed Noordin near Solo in September 2009.

Even as the hotel attack was under way, a different alliance of jihadis was setting up a training camp in Aceh, defining themselves strategically and tactically in opposition to both Noordin Top and JI. Noordin, they claimed,

aimed only at weakening the enemy through bombings but had no long-term vision; his operations also caused unnecessary Muslim casualties. They argued it was better to have a secure base that could both serve as the nucleus of an Islamic state—the long-term goal—and be a place to retreat to after operations. They saw JI as having abandoned jihad and castigated some of its leaders by name in a video produced to raise funds for the camp.[33]

By 2010, police and other security officials had a very good idea of the jihadi network and how it had operated in the past. It understood the thug organizations because it had worked with them, but it had very little understanding of radical nonviolent mass organizations such as Hizbut Tahrir Indonesia (HTI, Indonesia Party of Liberation), whose stock in trade is not rent-a-mob violence, but intellectual input into Islamic advocacy organizations and the government bureaucracy. Dealing with purveyors of intolerance that use classic civil society techniques may be more of a challenge for the Indonesian government than fighting terrorism.

The Anti-democrats

Although there are major ideological differences between the Salafis represented by Ja'far Umar Thalib, the Salafi jihadists represented by Abu Bakar Ba'asyir, and the utopian radicals represented by HTI, they have in common a deep antipathy to democracy. Their major argument is that democracy relies on man-made rather than God-given law.

All rely on different texts and interpretations. HTI, which advocates the restoration of a worldwide caliphate, points to how capitalism has failed and marshals economic arguments to show that the poor will be better protected and social justice better served under Islamic law.[34] JI and some of the Salafi jihadists now use the writings of the Jordanian radical Abu Muhammad al Maqdisi as their major reference, but they also cite others in the radical pantheon, such as Sayyid Qutub and Abul 'Ala Maududi.

On January 26, 2009, the quasi-governmental Majelis Ulama Indonesia (MUI, Indonesian Ulama Council) issued a fatwa that choosing a devout, honest leader who could meet the aspirations of the umma (Muslim community) was obligatory and that to choose someone who did not have those qualities or not to vote at all was forbidden (haram) under Islamic law.[35] The radical community immediately responded. FPI, mindful of its backers, welcomed the fatwa as being appropriate as long as it was interpreted to mean that "it is obligatory to vote if a leader is available who meets the conditions of leadership according to Islamic law."[36] HTI argued that without Islamic law, even the most well-intentioned leader cannot succeed. If MUI in an earlier fatwa (2005) said that secularism was haram, it followed that any secular system or any not based on Islamic law was also haram. In any case, the obligation to choose leaders did not rest with individuals, but with the community.[37]

Ba'asyir's new organization, Jamaah Ansharut Tauhid (JAT, Group for the Oneness of God Partisans), and others on the Salafi jihadi side stepped up public book discussions at mosques around Java related to the un-Islamic nature of democracy. These events were advertised in Friday mosque bulletins, short text messages, and JI magazines. A handout distributed at one such discussion outside Jakarta in mid-February said:

This is what democracy users say:

- We don't have to reject everything that comes from kafir [unbelievers]; we can take democracy as an opening for our struggle.
- Democracy is policy formulation [ijtihadiah siyasah—by implication, with an Islamic precedent], so it's okay.
- Democracy allows for dakwah [propagating Islam], including in Parliament.
- To vote is obligatory, to abstain is haram, according to the MUI fatwa.
- And many other reasons. . . .

But know you have been trapped; in fact, you've voluntarily trapped yourself by the poison of democracy. . . .

- Democracy is a kafir system that leads to NONBELIEF and APOSTASY.
- Going along with democracy may bring partial benefits, but it sacrifices the fundamental principle of being free from rule by anti-Islamic forces.
- Islam should be fought for through DAKWAH and JIHAD, not by punching ballots![38]

The problem was that democratic participation was too popular. Even Abu Bakar Ba'asyir, who himself abstained from voting, intimated to his followers that he would not forbid them to vote in the 2009 elections as long as they voted for parties or individuals committed to Islamic law. JAT, founded in September 2008, initially attracted many JI members who saw little point in being a clandestine organization when there was no jihad to fight at home and when it was possible to campaign openly for Islamic law.[39]

Antidemocrats such as Ba'asyir constitute no threat to Indonesia's democracy. HTI is more insidious because it has mastered the art of political lobbying, starting from issues that resonate with the public, such as the Ahmadiyya ban, and finding friends in government to press for policy change. The government's reaction to HTI is one of guarded tolerance. It allowed an international conference in Jakarta in July 2007 that drew some seventy thousand people; its only intervention ironically was to put pressure on the organizers to disinvite Abu Bakar Ba'asyir. The police have little knowledge of HTI because its members do not commit crimes; it is known to the intelligence agencies not because of its message or style of working, but simply because it is an international organization, and in the xenophobic world of Indonesian security any local organization with international links is suspect.[40]

In Indonesia today, HTI appears to be growing rapidly, particularly on university campuses and in places such as Aceh where it never had a presence before the 2004 tsunami. It managed to bring under its thumb the health minister in SBY's first term, who called for an end to immunization against certain childhood diseases on the grounds that she did not want Indonesian children becoming guinea pigs for testing by Western pharmaceutical firms. HTI is one of the hard-line civil society organizations that post-Suharto democracy has brought to prominence, but it is not a threat to the state. It is rather an effective advocacy group that has shown an ability to affect public policy.

The concern about radical organizations is not that they preach against a popular political system that they have no hope of changing, but that they foster hostility toward non-Muslim minorities, in particular Christians and Jews, and toward any group considered "deviant," such as the Ahmadiyya movement. The government's response to this hostility should be active promotion of minority rights and inculcation of pluralist views from elementary school on up. It is the one area, however, where all post-Suharto governments have failed.

Indonesians should be grateful that they got past the worst of their post-Suharto uncertainty and turmoil by the time the first Bali bombings hit in 2002. The phase of mobilizing thugs on the streets was over. The tension between army and civilians had been resolved in favor of civilians. If an attack of that magnitude had come while Abdurrahman Wahid was in office, the military might have demanded a greater role.

No post-Suharto government has spoken with one voice on radical Islam. After a spate of FPI attacks on churches and on meetings of gay activists, the national police commander could still suggest in late 2010 that the organization would be a welcome partner with the government in providing security, but this statement generated public outrage. As for terrorism, its overall impact on Indonesian democracy has been to strengthen state security institutions—but civilian, not military ones. The police may still be the most hated institution in Indonesia, as most surveys show, but it is becoming more professional. The need for prosecutors in terrorism cases to be able to use more forms of evidence than allowed by the existing criminal procedure code led to a redrafting of the code itself in ways that are likely to facilitate broader criminal justice reform. Some of these changes would have happened anyway, but the need to respond to terrorist attacks and the money that came with it from abroad expedited the process.

The biggest issue for Indonesian democracy, however, is not terrorism, but intolerance, which is moving from the radical fringe into the mainstream, as surveys from 2001 to the present by the State Islamic University and a major polling organization, Lembaga Survei Indonesia (Indonesian Survey Institute), have charted. The number of attacks on churches has risen in recent years, and government attitudes toward the Ahmadiyah sect have hardened. Any Indonesian government that wants to curb radical thought will have to move beyond putting pressure on publishers not to print jihadi texts and start thinking of how to inculcate religious tolerance in young citizens.

7

How Indonesia Survived

Comparative Perspectives on State Disintegration and Democratic Integration

Edward Aspinall

In the mid-1990s, following the end of the Cold War, the long and near-sacrosanct international consensus against secession and the dismemberment of states seemed to be in tatters. Experiences in the former Soviet Union and Yugoslavia showed how rapidly multiethnic states could disintegrate and how readily secessionist regions could gain recognition as full members of the community of nation-states. To some observers in 1998–2000, the sequence of events in Indonesia looked similar, superficially at least, to what had happened in Yugoslavia and the Soviet Union, and there was much fearful speculation about whether Indonesia might also break up.[1]

In the Soviet Union and Yugoslavia, long-standing nondemocratic regimes had suppressed oppositional political mobilization by ethnically or regionally defined groups. When those regimes began to unravel, slowly at first, after the death of Josip Tito in 1980 and Mikhail Gorbachev's reforms from 1985, fissiparous pressures mounted and, startling participants and observers alike with their speed, led to state collapse and the emergence of new successor states. In Indonesia, it was the Asian economic crisis of 1997 and then the collapse of Suharto's thirty-two-year old Orde Baru (New Order) regime that opened Pandora's box. The disintegration of the regime opened the way for rapid spread of political mobilization and violence, some of which took separatist form. The population of East Timor, a former Portuguese colony incorporated into Indonesia by military occupation in 1975, voted in August 1999 in favor of independence in a United Nations–supervised ballot. Separatist mobilization dramatically escalated in two other provinces, Aceh and Papua, both sites of long-running separatist insurgencies. Early signs of agitation in favor of independence appeared in several other provinces where such a goal was historically novel. Remembering how pro-independence sentiment and deadly conflict had spread to regions in Yugoslavia and the Soviet Union that had previously lacked nationalist aspirations, such early signs of separatist contagion in Indonesia seemed to herald a disintegrative mobilizational spiral. To add to the atmosphere of crisis, between 1997 and about 2001 numerous nonseparatist ethnic and religious conflicts erupted in different parts of the archipelago. Nobody knows the precise figure, but at least 19,000 people lost their lives, with another 1.3 million people displaced.[2]

Yet in terms of state disintegration, Indonesia was the dog that did not bark. Today the country's crisis has passed. East Timor has made the transition to independence, albeit not very successfully, and no longer causes much concern to Indonesia's policymakers or its public. In Aceh, a peace deal brokered in mid-2005 has brought the thirty-year-old insurgency to an end, at least for a time. Separatist sentiment has certainly not disappeared in Papua, but it has receded to manageable levels for now. All the other nascent separatist movements of 1998–2000 died in the bud. Most communal violence burned itself out or was ended by negotiations and improved security measures, and most had in any case not fundamentally challenged Indonesia as a nation-state.

There has been less interest in explaining Indonesia's survival than there was a decade ago in speculating about its possible collapse. The international affairs commentators who prognosticated most luridly on Indonesia's fate have since moved on to focus on other countries in crisis. Most Indonesia experts, in contrast, dismiss the very notion that Indonesia was ever seriously threatened. Yet we should be careful about adopting such a teleological approach. Mark Beissinger reminds us that although the "prevailing view of Soviet disintegration today is that the breakup was inevitable," in fact this outcome was not considered even possible at the time. However, "within a compressed period of history the seemingly impossible came to be widely viewed as the seemingly inevitable, turning a world once unthinkingly accepted as immutable upside down."[3] With such a major historical example before us, it seems valid to ask why an outcome so many people feared did not come to pass in Indonesia.

How did Indonesia survive? This essay points to three key factors. The first is the suite of concessions offered by Indonesian national leaders to the regions, and the second concerns the policies of force they applied there. The combination of these approaches resulted more from internal divisions and ad hoc decision making among the political elite than from careful design, but it was the combination that mattered. By ceding greater control over their own affairs to local elites and potential local dissidents, while harshly suppressing those who sought to break away from the state, Indonesia's national leaders reduced the incentives for secession and increased the costs, thus preventing a separatist spiral.

The third factor is the legacy of the institutional form taken by the subnational units in Indonesia's state structure prior to democratization. During the Suharto years, observers often saw the fact that Indonesia was divided into provinces in a unitary state rather than into states in a federation as a source of future fragility. Many rightly pointed out that the unitary state heightened grievances in the periphery by suppressing regional sentiment and fostering inequitable division of resource wealth.[4] However, it turned out that the unitary state form also removed from Indonesia's crisis some of the most explosive ingredients that helped to produce state disintegration in Yugoslavia and the Soviet Union: the institutional and identity resources that federal statehood provided to regional dissidents. In those two countries, once central controls began to weaken the symbolically powerful federal republics were readily turned by local elites into weapons to be used against the central government, speeding the process of state collapse. In Indonesia, the provinces were relatively marginal politically, and their populations did not view them as ethnic homelands, so they played relatively little role in Indonesia's political crisis. In short and not without some irony, Indonesia's prior history of centralized government was as important as its policies of decentralization in inoculating the country against state disintegration when democratization began.

Reform

One reason why Indonesia weathered its storm is that its government after 1998 recognized the depth of its crisis and opted to manage it by implementing a far-reaching policy of regional autonomy. Autonomy is the main piece of equipment in the international peacemaking tool box, at least in instances of territorially based ethnic conflict. In 2000, for instance, Ted Gurr argued that states' growing willingness to offer autonomy arrangements was one of the primary causes of a downward trend in armed conflicts driven by ethnopolitical grievances then becoming apparent.[5] Over the past decade or so, decentralization of governmental authority has also been promoted as a salve for all manner of governance ills, with the rationale being that bringing decision making closer to the people will make the provision of services more responsive and efficient.[6]

With both goals in mind, soon after the Suharto regime collapsed, Indonesia's government implemented what has frequently been described as a "big bang" decentralization. In two pieces of legislation passed by the final Suharto-era legislature in 1999 with minimal debate or amendment, the government transferred wide-ranging authority to the country's several hundred districts (the second level of its regional government, below the provinces). President B. J. Habibie, Suharto's successor, had spent many years in Germany and was impressed by that country's federal system. Some of his ideas, such as making the police force responsible to provincial governors, were not accepted, but in the end the law on regional government that was passed reserved only limited government functions (notably, foreign policy, defense and security, monetary policy, the legal system, and religious affairs) exclusively to the central government. A second law on "fiscal balance" dramatically reallocated government funds from the center to the districts, with the result that within a year of implementation, according to a group of World Bank experts, "regional spending rose from an estimated 17 percent of all government spending in 2000 to over 30 percent in 2001; two thirds of central civil servants were re-assigned; over 16,000 public service facilities were handed over to the regions. . . . Over time, the regional share in spending is likely to rise to 45–50 percent, making Indonesia one of the most decentralized countries in the world."[7]

Habibie and other government leaders justified decentralization in part as a means to bring decisions about public expenditure closer to the people they were supposed to benefit, an approach that international development agencies enthusiastically backed. But the dominant public justification was that decentralization would respond to swelling discontent in the regions and so bolster national unity. Numerous politicians, intellectuals, and other commentators argued explicitly that Indonesia needed to decentralize if it wanted to avoid the fate of the Soviet Union and Yugoslavia.

Indeed, at the time these policies were formulated, Indonesia was arguably in the early stages of a cycle of mobilization of the sort that had brought down the Soviet Union. Beissinger has written about a "tide of nationalism" that arose out of this earlier cycle: "The *glasnost* tide of nationalism was . . . a period of 'thickened history'—one in which the pace of events accelerated, in which action came to play an increasingly significant role in its own causal structure, and in which the seemingly impossible, under the daily onslaught of challenge and change, became the seemingly inevitable."[8]

The years 1998–2000 were a similar phase of "thickened history" in Indonesia. First, in the brief period between late February and May 1998 a wave of antigovernment student protests and violent unrest by the urban poor splintered the New Order regime and forced Suharto to resign.[9] After the resignation, mobilization focused on national issues continued. The most dramatic confrontations in the second half of 1998 were between protestors, most of them students, and security forces in Jakarta and other big cities, in which the protestors sought to force Habibie to step down, the army to withdraw from politics, and the authorities to put Suharto on trial. By the time the legislature began to draft decentralization laws in mid-1999, however, this wave of national-level mobilization had already peaked because Habibie's offer of democratic elections—eventually held in June 1999—offered a constitutional way to resolve the political crisis.

A second form of unrest, which began to gather pace only once Suharto resigned, was less dramatic but more widely dispersed and focused on local goals. Many protestors in Indonesia's regions sought to force the resignation of corrupt and unpopular government leaders, from provincial governors down to village chiefs. In many regions, such protests were accompanied by complaints about how the central government had badly treated or exploited the region. Many local officials and politicians tried to keep pace with the new mood, themselves criticizing Jakarta, giving voice to local grievances, and calling for greater autonomy. Some new political parties followed suit, notably the Partai Amanat Nasional (National Mandate Party), led by the modernist Islamic leader Amien Rais, who publically promoted the idea of transforming Indonesia into a federation.

In the three provinces where there had been histories of secessionist movements and brutal counterinsurgency campaigns—East Timor, Papua, and Aceh—protests about human rights abuses, economic inequity, and other grievances crystallized in renewed demands for independence. In February 1999, President Habibie flabbergasted his own cabinet and the rest of the Indonesian political elite by offering East Timor a referendum on independent statehood. This move greatly encouraged independence campaigners in Papua and Aceh, leading to a surge of mobilization in both places.

What is now largely forgotten is that the specter of separatism also began to stalk, albeit unsteadily, through other regions where it previously had been absent. In Riau, an oil-rich province in central Sumatra across the Straits of Malacca from Singapore, an academic called Tabrani Rab established the Riau Merdeka (Free Riau) movement. His main grievance was that Riau received only a tiny fraction of the vast revenues it provided to the central government from its oil industry (he said that on one occasion Riau provided 62 trillion rupiah [US$7 billion] in revenues, but only 0.07 percent of the sum was returned to the province in the state budget).[10] Tabrani attracted some support from local student activists and others, and there were even ominous warnings that the movement would take up arms.[11] And some of the Christian fighters and activists involved in Christian–Muslim violence in Maluku began to revive the dream of South Maluku independence that had briefly flourished among pro-Dutch Moluccans immediately after Indonesia's independence struggle in the late 1940s. Some formed the Forum Kedaulatan Maluku (Maluku Sovereignty Forum) and raised nationalist flags every year on the anniversary of the 1950 declaration of the Republic of South Maluku. In another category of cases, protestors in some regions almost playfully introduced the threat of secession to dramatize their demands or highlight their anger about how they felt their region had been treated. A tiny Bali Merdeka (Free Bali) movement among a few intellectuals was largely motivated by anger about alleged mistreatment of Megawati Sukarnoputri, a decidedly nationalist politician who had part-Balinese descent, by her political rivals.[12] A similar example occurred when the favorite son of South Sulawesi, B. J. Habibie, failed to be reelected as president in October 1999, and student activists in that province threatened to secede.[13] Local politicians in Christian parts of eastern Indonesia several times made similar threats when Islamic interests were, in their view, being accorded too much weight in national policymaking.[14] In these and similar cases, there is no indication those concerned seriously planned to secede, but the threats showed how long-standing taboos about the sacrosanct nature of national unity had been broken.

Few observers believed that separatist sentiment beyond the three main centers of unrest in East Timor, Aceh, and Papua was serious. Most Indonesia specialists who have considered these other movements are dismissive of their attempts to develop serious justifications for independence on historical, cultural, or legal grounds.[15] In none of them did separatism become mass based or seriously challenge the central government. In most cases, especially obviously in oil-rich Riau and East Kalimantan, separatist statements were instead a bargaining ploy used by local political elites to wrest greater concessions out of Jakarta in the decentralization process they knew was already under way. In fact, political elites in these provinces made more calls for "expanded autonomy," "special autonomy," or federal status than for outright secession.

However, the wisdom conferred by hindsight can be a powerful suppressant of curiosity. With a little effort, it is possible to imagine a different scenario in which these early discontents might have become the beginning of a cycle of separatist mobilization that spread rapidly across the archipelago. As already noted, there are precedents for such mobilizational spirals escalating quickly: in the Soviet Union and Yugoslavia, nationalist sentiment eventually took hold in regions where it was initially weak or virtually nonexistent (such as Bosnia or Belarus) and which at first had seemed unlikely candidates for national independence. It is possible that a similar process of learning and emulation might have happened in Indonesia had the early mobilizations met greater success (East Timor's success certainly had such a stimulatory effect on Papua and Aceh).

Swift design and execution of decentralization policies played a major role in heading off severe state crisis in Indonesia. Whether this policy has provided better governance, as its supporters promised, or has not is a controversial point that cannot detain us here. But decentralization did have important and immediate taming effects on local political elites, the very groups who in the Soviet Union and Yugoslavia were primarily responsible for mobilizing state-destroying political movements. By passing political responsibility and economic resources to these groups, decentralization in Indonesia shifted the focus of political contention dramatically toward the base of the political system. Regional political elites no longer saw a remote and exploitative government in Jakarta as their main political adversary or patron but instead concentrated on local political competition and alliance building. Indeed, this shift arguably contributed to the communal or "horizontal" nature of much of the worst post-Suharto violence in Indonesia, whereby ethnic or religious groups fought each other, rather than encouraging a "vertical" type of violence in which local communities were pitted against the state. An accelerant of such violence in conflict areas such as Maluku, West and Central

Kalimantan, and Central Sulawesi was competition between local elites who were vying for control of local government as well as for the enhanced resources and authority that control brought.[16]

More broadly, many local elites who might otherwise have challenged Jakarta were placated by the new fiscal and political arrangements. Tabrani Rab, the head of the Riau Merdeka movement, was appointed as a member and later as chairperson of a national consultative body on regional autonomy directly responsible to the president. An even more dramatic example occurred in the oil-rich district of Kutai Kartanegara in East Kalimantan, a province where there was initially considerable agitation in favor of greater provincial and district rights. In this district, the flamboyant district head, Syaukani, used the greatly expanded funds provided to his district under decentralization to become a major dispenser of government patronage, winning considerable popularity: "Syaukani has used the money to build a tourist resort in the jungle, complete with a 1,300 meter cable car and a planetarium. He has also made interest-free loans of up to [5 million rupiah] available to each household to help them start small businesses, granted each village [1 billion rupiah] to improve infrastructure, and ensured access to free education."[17]

Syaukani also used government funds to enrich himself and his allies, as did so many other local political leaders, becoming one of the many regional government heads to be tried, convicted, and jailed for corruption, a fate that befell him in 2008.

In considering the effects that democratization and decentralization may have in forestalling state disintegration, scholars have pointed out that the sequencing and design of reforms can be crucial. Alfred Stepan and Juan Linz, for example, argue that one reason why Spain withstood disintegrative pressures during the democratic reforms that followed Franco's death was the sequencing of its elections, with national elections preceding regional ones and impelling parties to emphasize broad cross-regional coalitions rather than local interests.[18] In this regard, two points about the design of Indonesia's reforms were significant.

First, although the political system was deregulated, one important limitation was introduced: political parties had to show that they had a broad national presence, with branches in a large proportion of the country's provinces and districts, in order to register to run in elections.[19] Local political parties were thereby excluded from Indonesia's new democratic system. Would-be aspirants for local political power were required to affiliate to national parties, dramatically reducing their ability to depict themselves as solely representative of local or ethnic interests. The absence of local parties in turn prevented the party system from encouraging localization of political identity, becoming a vehicle for ethnic outbidding or prompting polarization of relations between center and regions. This measure, although arguably representing a serious limitation on democratic freedoms, significantly checked the potential for decentralization to accelerate disintegrative pressures; indeed, "scholars who argue that decentralization increases ethnic conflict and secessionism are, by and large, observing the effect of regional parties on ethnic conflict and secessionism."[20] This factor made the Indonesian party system also very different from those in Yugoslavia and the Soviet Union, where, even before political deregulation, there were separate and at least notionally autonomous Communist parties for each federal state, parties that quickly learned to flex their muscles and demand greater autonomy as democratization began and that eventually led struggles for independence.

A second feature of Indonesia's decentralization was that authority was deliberately devolved to the district levels, the second level of Indonesia's government, rather than to the larger provinces. As with the restriction on local parties, this choice was also deliberate. As M. Ryaas Rasyid, the chief architect of Habibie's decentralization policies explains, "Any attempt to shift power to the provinces would have been read by the conservative Unitarians as promoting federalism, by extension placing at risk national coherence and integrity."[21] Secessionist sentiment had previously always been expressed at the provincial level. Devolving power to the several hundred districts rather than to the few dozen provinces strengthened only those regional governments that lacked the population, history, and economic or political bargaining power to mount serious secessionist challenges. Unlike many provinces, no district represented a potentially viable independent state.

By introducing these elements to Indonesia's democratic and decentralizing reforms, the country's national leaders managed to produce the beneficial effects of decentralization for state survival without bringing about any of the negative effects. Grants of political and financial authority bought off local political elites and largely neutralized regional discontent. But by granting the new powers to the districts rather than to the provinces and by excluding local political parties, the national government did not cede crucial institutional resources that could help to crystallize and politicize regional identity against the center or otherwise strengthen the regions as bastions of secessionist activism.

Force

So far the story is a familiar and perhaps even comforting one: a democratizing regime tries to survive the wave of popular mobilization that accompanies its birth by granting concessions to popular and regional opinion that would have been inconceivable under its authoritarian predecessor. However, reforms were not the only factor resolving Indonesia's crisis. Sidney Tarrow reminds us that Alexis de Tocqueville's dictum, "The most perilous moment for a bad government is one when it seeks to mend its ways," applied in the case of the former Soviet Union.[22] In the Soviet Union, the government gave plenty of concessions, but these concessions tended to fuel the cycle of mobilization rather than to dampen it. Concessions encouraged previously passive groups to escalate their demands.

Why did such an outcome not occur in Indonesia? After all, in Indonesia, too, autonomy also failed to satisfy the regions that were on the leading edge of the cycle of separatist mobilization. East Timor was a special case: it was offered an independence referendum as an alternative to autonomy before the regional autonomy laws were even drafted; its political evolution followed a distinctive path. But the 1999 regional autonomy laws had no appreciable impact on reducing separatist sentiments in Papua and Aceh. Indeed, separatist mobilizations reached an all-time high shortly after these laws were passed. In November 1999, there was a massive demonstration (some estimated it involved half a million or more people) on the streets of Banda Aceh calling for an independence referendum, and before long the Gerakan Aceh Merdeka (GAM, Free Aceh Movement) insurgency controlled most of rural Aceh. In Papua in May–June 2000, the Papuan People's Congress brought together delegates from many organizations and regions and passed a resolution that declared, "The people of Papua have been sovereign as a nation and a state since December 1, 1961."[23] The central government was so concerned about the strength of separatist sentiment in both places that in 2001 it granted both provinces special autonomy laws that went much further than the general autonomy laws. But these new laws also had little effect on separatist mobilization, with separatist leaders in both provinces angrily rejecting them and continuing to demand independence. Had their movements continued to grow and been successful, it is surely conceivable that the mobilization cycle would have restarted in the territories that had only toyed with independence in 1998–1999 and then been satisfied with decentralization.

The second lesson of Indonesia's survival is therefore not so comforting for those who see the gradual emergence, in the words of a recent United Nations sponsored report, of a "war-averse world."[24] Indonesia's leaders combined their policy of decentralization with ruthless military force and repression against those who threatened to secede. One compelling explanation for the collapse of the Soviet Union is that it experienced a dramatic loss of confidence at the center and that its leaders were, in the main, strikingly unwilling to use coercion against regional dissenters. According to one assessment, the "central element in Gorbachev's *modus operandi* [was] an almost physical aversion to violence, political repression, and coercion."[25] With a few relatively minor exceptions, Gorbachev did not authorize the use of force against regional dissidents and pro-independence movements.[26] After the failed coup of August 1991, the political initiative passed from Gorbachev to Boris Yeltsin, who had previously been elected president of the Russian Republic and who, far from trying to prevent the destruction of the Soviet Union, became a chief architect of its demise. Overall, there was relatively little loss of life in the Soviet Union in the period leading to its disintegration. The breakup of the Soviet Union was certainly a much less bloody affair than was Indonesia's survival.[27]

Indonesia's new democratic leaders did not share Gorbachev's scruples. Far from wanting to be Indonesia's Gorbachev, President Megawati Sukarnoputri compared herself to another world leader when she addressed an audience in Washington, D.C., on September 19, 2001: "I would like to make it clear once again that the integrity of our country is of the highest importance, and we will defend it at all cost. Abraham Lincoln, one of your greatest heroes, carried out a similar policy about one and half centuries ago. America became great because, among others, the principle of national integrity was upheld by Lincoln and other heroes of that era. As I said, we will certainly pursue a peaceful political approach. But as did Lincoln in the United States, we will defend the integrity of Indonesia no matter how long it will take." [28]

From about 2000–2001, the explosion of separatist sentiment that in 1998–1999 had followed Suharto's fall was in turn followed by a hardening of mood against separatism among politicians in Jakarta as it became evident that autonomy policies were not stemming demands for independence in Aceh and Papua. Conciliatory policies, in particular special autonomy in Papua and Aceh, were not abandoned, but civilian politicians increasingly justified military action against those threatening the integrity of the state and condemned negotiations with separatists or the granting of further concessions to them. Numerous national leaders warned that allowing Aceh and Papua to secede would set off a domino effect as in Yugoslavia and the Soviet Union and lead to the disintegration of the country. Even otherwise liberal intellectuals who had been supporters or even designers of the decentralization policies stated that secession was not a legitimate matter of public debate.[29]

In this context, the security forces took increasingly harsh measures to suppress both violent and nonviolent separatists. We do not know how many people were killed in the attempt to hold the country together. Most of the fatalities were in Aceh, where armed separatism was strongest. There, several thousand people died at the hands of the military, which revived many of the techniques of state terror it had used in the province during the Suharto years, including massacres of civilian protestors, routine torture and killing of prisoners, targeted assassinations, revenge attacks on villages accused of supporting the rebels, and forced relocation of civilian populations away from rebel zones.[30] In Papua, armed separatist groups, notably the Organisasi Papua Merdeka (Free Papua Organization or Movement), mounted a much less serious threat, but there was nevertheless also concerted suppression of pro-independence sentiment, bringing to an end the short-lived Papuan Spring of 1999–2000. Theys Eluay, the leader of the main civilian separatist group, the Presidium Dewan Papua (Papua Presidium Council), was strangled to death by soldiers from the army's elite Special Troops, men who were (notoriously) praised by the then chief of staff for the army as "national heroes" for taking this action. In subsequent years, people were arrested and imprisoned for raising the Papuan nationalist Morning Star flag and interrogated for even doing such seemingly innocuous things as possessing bags with the symbol of the flag displayed on them.[31] In other provinces, too—in an important exception to the generally much improved state of political freedoms since the end of the Suharto period—the authorities have taken swift and harsh action against individuals who have espoused separatist goals, often arresting and trying them for *makar*, sedition. Such individuals include members of rather unlikely groups that lack popular support in their places of origin, such as members of a so-called Gerakan Negara Sunda (Sunda State Movement) in West Java, as well as members of groups that are somewhat more grounded, such as the Maluku Sovereignty Forum in Ambon.[32] Continuing and legally sanctioned suppression of expression of peaceful secessionist political views arguably remains the greatest ongoing restriction on civil liberties in postauthoritarian Indonesia.

But repression achieved results. Just as the East Timor referendum in 1999 boosted the optimism of secessionists in Aceh and Papua, the subsequent coercion in both places killed off that optimism and prevented it from spreading elsewhere. In particular, in Aceh a series of military offensives from 2001, especially severe after 2003 when a state of military emergency was declared, succeeded in greatly weakening the GAM insurgency. The iron hand of repression, combined with offers of concessions, convinced GAM's leaders in 2005 to abandon their armed struggle and their goal of independence and instead agree to the Helsinki Memorandum of Understanding.[33] At the core of this compromise settlement were opportunities for expanded autonomy and political participation for the Acehnese (including in the form of local parties, with Aceh now being the only place in Indonesia where such parties may contest elections), but on condition that GAM give up secessionism. The violence meted out to achieve this outcome in Aceh had not only an important impact on the rebels there, but also salutary effects on other would-be secessionists. There was considerable alarm in Papua around 2003 that it would be next in line for martial law. We can only speculate about the effects that repression in Papua and Aceh had on people in other provinces who might otherwise have been tempted to toy with secessionist ideas. In the Soviet Union and Yugoslavia, successes by early secessionist regions encouraged others to follow suit. In the Indonesian case, repression played a part in preventing the cycle from getting far, as unpalatable as this conclusion may be.

Institutions

In an unfortunately timed remark in 1986, the influential scholar of nationalism Anthony Smith suggested that Yugoslavia might be a model for countries such as Indonesia that wanted to strike a balance between central authority and regional diversity and thus avoid disintegration. He argued that "the Yugoslav model of recognizing ethnie [ethnic communities] as nations in a federal constitutional context offers real hope for the consolidation of the state and the authority of its institutions . . . and might well provide a model for the more intractable 'state-nation' conflicts in Africa and Asia, even if the minimal unity of Yugoslavia is lacking in the new states."[34] As we now know, it was the Indonesian model of the unitary state that proved more able to survive the shock of rapid transition from authoritarian rule rather than the Yugoslav or Soviet federal or multinational model. Indeed, as Valerie Bunce has put it, "national federalism was central to the story of state dismemberment in the socialist world."[35] As well as the reforms and repressive actions taken by post-Suharto national government leaders, the institutional legacies they inherited from the Suharto era also counted in preserving Indonesia intact.

It was certainly not ethnic diversity alone or even arguably ethnic conflict that led to state breakup in the Soviet Union and Yugoslavia. Instead, the prior institutional arrangements existing in those states played the key role in determining how and why they fractured. Both the Soviet Union and Yugoslavia were organized as federations of republics. In both cases, it was not ethnic homelands that became independent, but the constituent federal states. Both federations disintegrated along the preexisting borders between the federal units. Most attempts to redraw boundaries along ethnic lines as part of the process of state breakup (for example, by partitioning Bosnia or carving off the Republic of Serb Krajina from Croatia) were unsuccessful. Ethnicity was important for mobilizing populations, but it did not determine how these states fractured. Thus, in the former Soviet Union, republics in which populations felt great ethnic affinity with Russia (Belarus, for example) became independent, along with republics marked by a strong sense of ethnic difference. The international community failed to recognize as independent certain regions with very strong independence movements that happened to be located inside the Russian Federation or other federal states (e.g., Chechnya, Abkhazia, South Ossetia, Transinistria) even when they achieved de facto self-rule. The pattern was broadly similar in the former Yugoslavia.

The importance of the federal structure for the Soviet and Yugoslav breakups was in part a matter of legal niceties. In both cases, the federal states were formally sovereign. In the Soviet Union, according to Article 72 of the 1977 Constitution, each of the fifteen union republics had "the right freely to secede from the USSR." In Yugoslavia, chapter I of the Basic Principles in the Constitution referred to "the right of each nation to self-determination, including the right to secession" and called Yugoslavia "a state community of freely united peoples and their socialist Republics." Of course, these rights were merely formalities that had no possibility of being exercised while state socialism remained intact. But they became more consequential once it weakened, in part because they counted—or could be made to count—when it came to international law and recognition. The international community is reluctant to recognize secession where the state from which secession is sought opposes it. In the case of the independence of Slovenia, Croatia, and Macedonia (and later other Yugoslav republics), this obstacle was overcome when the Badinter Commission advised the European Economic Community that they were not instances of secession, but rather of dissolution of the Yugoslav Federation, in effect holding that states that constitute a federation have the right to assert their sovereignty and dissolve their unions if they choose. By the same token, the commission ruled that Serb minorities in the constituent federal republics could *not* exercise a right to self-determination but were owed only minority rights and that the boundaries between the federal republics would become borders protected by international law.[36] International recognition was less crucial in the case of the Soviet breakup, but here, too, the process of state breakup arguably took the form of the dissolution of an existing federal structure rather than a series of unilateral secessions.

The federal form of the Soviet Union and Yugoslavia was also important for how it shaped the self-perception and identification of the populations that lived in the constituent republics and for the political and mobilizational resources it provided their leaders. Ethnic identity, of course, did matter in the Soviet and Yugoslav breakups but principally insofar that it was linked to, was shaped by, and gave legitimacy to substate administrative and territorial units. The Soviet Union and Yugoslavia were not merely federal states, but *ethno*federalist states in which "at least some of the subunits exist[ed] for the purpose of representing and empowering specific cultural communities." As Bunce points out, "Ethnofederation, therefore, guarantees that some cultural communities sharing the same state will have at their disposal both geographical and institutional platforms for the expression of their interests and the exercise of political power."[37]

Each federal state was seen as representing not merely distinct cultural groups, but nations whose special status in these federal states was reinforced by language policy, education systems, and other aspects of cultural policy. As Rogers Brubaker puts it, "The Soviet state not only passively tolerated but actively institutionalized the existence of multiple nations and nationalities as fundamental constituents of the state and its citizenry."[38] Ronald Grigor Suny makes a similar point: "There was shockingly little effort to create a 'Soviet nation.' While everyone in the USSR carried a passport inscribed with a nationality, no one was permitted to declare him- or herself a Soviet by nationality. The Soviet idea of nationality was based on birth and heredity, the nationality of one's parents, but with its almost racial finality nationality was rooted in the substate units."[39]

Little wonder that when the Communist Party regimes in these countries entered into crisis, it was substate nationalism that became the main organizing foundation of political movements aiming either to dismantle the Communist order or to take over from it. Local national identities had long been inculcated in the populations of the federal units, and as the old regime began to falter, leaders at the substate level inherited an institutional framework that could readily be turned against that regime. As a result, "nationalist mobilization was far more common when nations had republics—than, for example, when they had lower-level administrative units or when they were deprived of any administrative identity."[40] The Communist parties, legislative bodies, presidencies, and other political organs of the federal states turned against the old order, either mobilizing nationalist movements and issuing independence declarations or else being challenged by alternate leaderships who tried to outbid them. The political authority and sovereignty enjoyed by the federal units only on paper in the old order suddenly became real, and state dissolution was the result.

The institutional and identity framework inherited in Indonesia could hardly have been more different. The Indonesian state for most of the independence period was single-mindedly focused on constructing a single Indonesian nation and, with few exceptions, expended more effort in suppressing political manifestations of regional and ethnic identities than in institutionalizing them. The imperative to forge a strong overarching national identity and to downplay regional identities had been a central and defining urge of Indonesian nationalism ever since its birth in the early decades of the twentieth century, both because of the nationalist leaders' consciousness of the diversity of the population of the Netherlands East Indies and because the colonial Dutch rulers they opposed "systematically preserved difference within their political order."[41] This urge reached an early high point during and immediately after the Indonesian national revolution (1945–1949), when the Dutch tried to counter the nationalists by organizing a federal state in which the outlying regions that were effectively under Dutch control would be able to hedge in the more militantly republican areas in Sumatra and Java, thus allowing the Dutch to continue to dominate an independent Indonesia. The republic was forced to adopt the federal model in negotiations leading to independence but repudiated it within months of the transfer of sovereignty in 1949, with the result being that the very concept of federalism has since been close to anathema in Indonesian political discourse. Instead, Indonesia adopted a unitary state form in which there was no place for the divided sovereignty of federalism or the inculcation of strong substate political identities associated with ethnofederalism.

In Indonesia, the provinces had very limited political authority, especially in the highly centralized Suharto period (1966–1998). There was certainly no sense in which they were even notionally viewed as having sovereign powers independent of the central government, nor was there even much sense of subnational units being especially meaningful politically. Indeed, the heads of provincial and district administrations in formal terms "simultaneously . . . served as regional political leaders and central administrative representatives in the regions."[42] In practical terms, they were always appointees of the central government. This situation began to change with the post-Suharto democratization, but, as noted earlier, when decentralization policies were introduced, meaningful political and budgetary authority devolved directly to the much smaller districts, bypassing the provinces and robbing them of the potential to become more important sites of political contestation and organization. As a result, the provinces remained relatively marginal to political life, as they had always been.

Moreover, the Indonesian provinces, unlike the federal republics in the Soviet Union and Yugoslavia, were not seen as representing distinct ethnic communities. For one thing, ethnic and provincial boundaries mostly did not coincide. As Robert Cribb observed when Indonesia entered its crisis, "Few of the borders or island coastlines of the 27 provinces make sense as nations-of-intent." Only a few provinces (Cribb names Bali, South Kalimantan, West Sumatra, and East Timor, and we might add Aceh) are "both ethnically relatively coherent and more or less coterminous with the local dominant ethnic group."[43] Indeed, in the 2000 census, only in twelve of the then thirty-one provinces did a single ethnic group constitute more than 50 percent of the province's population.

More important (because state institutions can construct regional or ethnic identities in even initially heterogeneous populations over time), the provinces also did little to institutionalize distinctive identities in their populations, as happened in the Soviet Union and Yugoslavia. To be sure, there was some celebration of local cultures as the wellsprings of tradition from which Indonesian national identity originated. But, for instance, local languages were not afforded even semiofficial status and were used as a medium of instruction at only the very lowest levels of the education system. Instead, propagation of the Indonesian language was (and continues to be) viewed as a central unifying task of Indonesian nationalism. Likewise, ethnic identity played little formal role in official politics. Although every citizen was compelled to carry an identity card (like the passports of the Soviet Union), these cards did not record ethnicity. So strong was the impetus to national unity that even the census did not ask questions about ethnicity (at least between the Dutch colonial census of 1930 and the first post-Suharto one of 2000), in sharp contrast to the Soviet Union and Yugoslavia, where bureaucrats were obsessed with measuring and quantifying the various national groups.

This background of only weak intermeshing of ethnic identity and regional political institutions meant that when the crisis of authoritarianism came, the cards were stacked against separatist nationalism emerging as a model of political organization and mobilization that could easily be transported across the country. The previous state form had not served to institutionalize substate nationalism as an alternate framework for political identity and mobilization.

The main separatist provinces—East Timor, Papua, and Aceh—were in some respects the exceptions that proved the rule. In each case, local histories that were strikingly distinct from the Indonesian norm provided local nationalists with a plausible claim for sovereignty. Two of these territories, Papua and East Timor, had come late into the Indonesian nation-state (Papua in the 1960s, East Timor in the 1970s) by processes that were highly coercive and generated deep grievances. Military occupation gave rise to strong beliefs in the Papuan and East Timorese populations that sovereignty had been stolen from them and that they had a right to reclaim membership in the international community of nation-states. Aceh was a different case, but here, too, separatist nationalism was marked by a strong outward gaze and a belief that the Acehnese sovereignty had been violated by the Indonesian state. This separatist nationalism was also importantly founded on several decades of official recognition, institutionalization, and even celebration of Aceh as a "special territory" that deserved unique rights, a status conferred as a result of negotiations that had ended an earlier conflict in the 1950s.[44]

In contrast to the separatist provinces, one particularly important legacy of the Indonesian unitary state model and the preceding history of anticolonial nationalism was the absence of a strongly institutionalized and politically salient alternate sense of nationhood in Indonesia's heartland. As Cribb has pointed out, a key factor leading to state disintegration is the emergence of alternate nationalisms not at the periphery, but at the center. Hence, the rise of Serbian and Russian national awareness was central to the disintegration of Yugoslavia and the Soviet Union. In Indonesia, there was no equivalent sense of Javanese self-assertion, although Java is the heartland of the Indonesian nation-state, with about 57 percent of the country's population living on the island and about 42 percent of the population being ethnically Javanese. Despite occasional accusations of Javanese domination made by regional politicians, in fact the hand of Java has rested lightly on Indonesian national identity.[45]

Between the extremes of the separatist provinces on the periphery and the heartland of Java, in most provinces democratization and decentralization did not produce political movements that sought to pit the province against the center. Instead, a host of cross-cutting communal and political identities became salient.[46] Provincial institutions and, even more so, district institutions became sites of contestation between local actors rather than weapons they turned against the center. This pattern did not immunize Indonesia against communal violence in its democratic transition, but it did ensure that most such violence did not take separatist form.

During its democratic transition, Indonesia faced the prospect of a "stateness" crisis. As Linz and Stepan explain, stateness problems occur in democratic transitions when "the crisis of the nondemocratic regime is also intermixed with profound differences about what should actually constitute the polity (or political community) and which demos or demoi (population or populations) should be members of that political community." Such challenges often seriously impede democratic transition and consolidation. They do not mean, in Linz and Stepan's view, that "democracy cannot be consolidated in multinational or multicultural states, [but] . . . that considerable political crafting of democratic norms, practices, and institutions must take place."[47]

In this essay, we have seen that one method that Indonesia's leaders used to overcome the country's stateness problems did indeed seriously strain Indonesia's democratic transition and consolidation, even as it proved to be effective. National leaders applied coercion against independence movements in East Timor, Papua, and Aceh, reducing the attractiveness of the secessionist model in other provinces and helping to prevent it from spreading. Although this repression contributed to Indonesia's survival and therefore can arguably be seen as indirectly contributing to the country's successful democratic transition, it also seriously compromised the quality of Indonesia's democracy. In East Timor, major crimes against humanity were committed amidst the security forces' attempts to preempt and then respond to the United Nations–supervised vote in favor of independence; similar state crimes also occurred in Aceh and (to a lesser extent) in Papua, along with a host of other abuses against civilians. The proscription of even peaceful advocacy of independence remains a significant curtailment of civil liberties, and political prisoners remain in Indonesian jails as a result.

At the same time, transitional governments also engaged in particularly effective political crafting of the sort needed to resolve stateness problems while keeping democracy intact. Most obvious, the Habibie government took the steam out of centrifugal pressures by quickly devolving political authority and fiscal resources to the regions, reorienting political contention away from a region-versus-center axis toward multiple struggles for position and resources in the regions themselves. Decentralization thus did not avert violent political mobilization at the local level—in some places it encouraged it—but it did ensure that most such violence was about local issues instead of being directed against the national state. In those places where anticenter ethnonationalist grievance and mobilization were most severe, notably East Timor, Papua, and Aceh, successive national governments went even further, offering (in the case of East Timor) or implementing (in Aceh and Papua) special autonomy provisions that involved the devolution of much greater powers than to other parts of the country. Yet, equally important, national leaders built safeguards into the decentralization process, devolving power in ways that did not strengthen would-be separatists' institutional or identity resources. By ceding power to the second-level districts, national leaders further marginalized the provinces. By excluding local political parties, they helped to prevent the crystallization of intermeshed regional-ethnic identities as alternative sources of political authority.

Finally, Indonesia was also assisted in surviving its stateness crisis because it had inherited a relatively favorable institutional legacy, at least when compared to countries that did experience state disintegration, such as the Soviet Union and Yugoslavia. Indonesia's unitary state form and its rather politically inconsequential provinces meant that the provinces, or most of them, did not provide a congenial framework for the spread of ethnonationalist mobilization. In the Soviet Union and Yugoslavia, the federal states had been central to political organization and citizenship for decades and therefore rapidly became vehicles and legitimating bases for independence movements once the center began to loosen its hold. In Indonesia, ethnic identities were only weakly articulated with provincial administrative boundaries, and local political actors in most regions did not view their provinces as putative national homelands or alternate sources of sovereignty.

The Indonesian case helps to reconcile two starkly contending views in the literature on the relationship between democratization and the accommodation of ethnic and regional difference. On the one hand, observers have noted that in multiethnic or multinational societies, democracies that survive

tend to be those that make concessions to ethnic and regional minorities. Alfred Stepan, Juan Linz, and Yogendra Yadav, for example, argue that "virtually every long-standing and relatively peaceful contemporary democracy in the
world whose polity has more than one territorially concentrated, politically-
mobilized, linguistic-cultural group that is a majority in some significant part
of the territory, is not only federal, but 'asymmetrically federal' (Belgium,
Canada, India and Spain)."[48] On the other hand, as we have seen, leading
analyses of the disintegration of Yugoslavia and the Soviet Union suggest
equally forcefully that ethnofederal states are most vulnerable to disintegration during democratic transitions. The Indonesian experience helps to demonstrate that state structures that accommodate ethnic and regional diversity
may be a source of state fragility *during* democratization, but a source of
democratic robustness *after* it. As we have seen, Indonesia's democratic transition enjoyed the best of both worlds, as it were, with an institutional legacy
inherited from authoritarian rule that privileged national political structures
and identities over regional ones and with a series of transitional governments that were willing to make dramatic concessions to regional sentiment
in the process of democratic transformation. Both democratic progress *and*
state survival were the result.

Part IV

Constitutionalism

The Role of Law and Legal Pluralism

8

Contours of Sharia in Indonesia

John R. Bowen

L et me begin with a paradox. In more than one-third of Indonesia's provinces, at least one region or city has enacted regulations intended to introduce sharia (or the spirit of sharia) into local public life. These measures range from requiring couples to recite from the Qur'an before they can marry to requiring certain forms of dress in public (head coverings for women, Islamic dress for male and female civil servants) and to instituting Islamic criminal penalties for adultery. The fact that some politicians saw such regulations as enjoying some public support and were able to enact the regulations suggests that at least in those places considerable numbers of people support raising the profile of sharia in public life.[1]

But election results seem to show the opposite. The parties receiving the highest vote totals in the 2009 parliamentary elections did not call for more Islamic law, with the exception of the Partai Keadilan Sejahtera (PKS, Prosperous Justice Party), which received almost 8 percent of the vote but ran a campaign that played down sharia and even praised former president Suharto (the "Father of Development") in its television campaigns. In Aceh, the only province to which the national government has devolved the right to pass laws explicitly based on sharia, the governors elected in 2006 and in 2012 as well as the party winning the 2009 parliamentary elections did not support expanding Islamic legal regulations. These politicians sensed that voters did *not* want more sharia in public life.

So in the democratic climate of post-Reformasi (Reformation) Indonesia, sharia appears either to have great political appeal or very little appeal at all. The paradox may be due to a difference in scale—here and there some portion of an electorate supports politicians who urge more sharia, but most people nationally feel otherwise—although the Aceh case should give us pause.

I make a different argument here: that trying to gauge "support for sharia" is taking the wrong analytical tack and that we ought to ask instead how political actors invoke sharia in particular settings. They do so, I argue, in order to mobilize concerns for authenticity, autonomy, or the right to say what counts as Islamic. To understand the genesis of the debates and thus the force of the arguments, we must look at how political actors have evoked the category of sharia in colonial and postcolonial political debates nationally and locally. After an analysis of the changes wrought by judicial centralization during the Suharto period, I turn to two examples of local usages of sharia in the era of reform and decentralization: in South Sulawesi and in Aceh. My argument is in a very broad sense a methodological one in that it calls for us to look to local and national processes of differentiation as a way to understand ways in which people attach meanings and value to calls for sharia.

Adat, Islam, and Judicial Centralization

Debates about governance of the Indies/Indonesia have often turned on the role, if any, to be played by Islamic law. Islamic law is always thought of in opposition to two other sources of law: local ways of resolving disputes (*adat*) and statutes and regulations (positive law). If in the early twentieth century colonial rulers marginalized the role of Islamic law, by the end of that century a series of legal reforms had created a centralized Islamic judiciary with jurisdiction over matters of marriage and divorce (and, optionally, inheritance) among Muslims.

In the mid–nineteenth century, colonial administrators assumed that Muslim natives were already governed by Islamic law, an idea reinforced by certain local rulers, who played up the glorious sultanates of the past. Working from this assumption, the Dutch created Islamic tribunals on Java and Madura in 1882, each with a panel of judges empowered to hear disputes over matters of marriage, divorce, and inheritance.[2] By the 1920s, however, scholars led by Leiden's C. Snouck Hurgronje had convinced the government that Dutch interests lay in supporting a pietistic version of Islam over and against a legalistic one and that in any case native people had their own rules for governing themselves—rules that were based on long-standing local practices and sensibilities and that, unlike sharia, were organically part of the societies. The field of *"adat* law" (*adatrecht*) studies grew up around this political and sociological precept. Snouck Hurgronje argued that an Islamic rule could be applied only if it had been "received" into local practice—if it had in effect *become adat*. And by and large, continued Snouck, such was not the case because Indonesians shared certain postulates that were anathema to Islam: that adopted children should inherit from their adoptive parents, for example. This "reception doctrine" shaped late colonial policy, including the decision in the 1930s to withdraw jurisdiction over inheritance disputes from the Islamic courts and give it to the civil courts.

The "reception doctrine" also empowered those local rulers who claimed authority on the basis of *adat* vis-à-vis those local leaders who claimed authority on the basis of Islam. During the political uncertainty that followed the declaration of Indonesian independence in 1945, local struggles in some regions pitted these two power bases against one another: leaders claiming a vision of the future based on Islam and others defending long-standing institutions associated with *adat* bases for rule.[3]

In independent Indonesia, *adat* lived on in several guises. As a set of rules and procedures limited to a particular district, the older Dutch notion of *adatrecht* continued to be invoked and often applied in civil courts. As a looser notion of customs and ceremonies, *adat* provided a way to assert local authenticity and identity under the radar of centralizing political projects. More precisely, as customs and ceremonies but *not* locally embedded systems of rule, a defanged notion of *adat* (sans the *recht*) underpinned the Orde Baru (New Order) state. The Indonesian Mahkamah Agung (Supreme Court) advocated a reconstruction of *adat*, as a broad sense of "Indonesian ways of life" or "the living law of society," along lines of gender equality. Finally and especially after Suharto's fall in 1998 and the measures taken to decentralize political and financial power, *adat* came to stand for "not the state": regional or local norms and practices that could provide an alternative to state control of everyday life. *Adat* communities and *adat* assemblies called for taking over control of local natural resources and reviving means of resolving disputes (especially during the violent conflicts in Kalimantan and Ambon).[4]

Such has been the trajectory of *adat* as a conception of normativity and rule in Indies/Indonesia. As for sharia, it had a brief fling with constitutional destiny, one that continues to haunt certain Muslim currents with dreams of what might have been. In 1945, drafters of the Constitution considered a clause that would have included "the obligation for Muslims to carry out the sharia." They did not, in the end, include these "seven words" (as they are in Indonesian) for two reasons that remain relevant to current debates. First, the success of the national project was by no means assured, and Christian regions in the East might have seceded from an Islamic state even if the clause would not have directly affected them. Second, many Muslims were not at all happy with the idea that the state would enforce Islam. In the end, the state remained constitutionally monotheistic, but not Islamic. Was the omission of this clause, often referred to as the "Piagam Jakarta" (Jakarta Charter), the victory of national unity over efforts to divide society along religious lines? Or was it a stab in the back of the overwhelmingly Muslim majority in its efforts to become truly self-governing and finally free of colonial oppression?

Strong reactions against the elimination of the "seven words" probably gave greater impetus to the creation of a Ministry of Religion and to the eventual creation of a Directorate of Religious Justice within the Ministry of Religion, which, in the absence of a national religious court system, assumed de facto the role of performing judicial review and circulating decisions to lower courts. In the early decades of independence, those religious courts that already existed in various parts of the country continued to operate on the basis of two decrees: the 1882 Dutch decree that had initially established Islamic courts on Java and Madura and a 1957 government regulation that authorized creating new courts everywhere else. But this dual legal legitimacy created a jurisdictional disparity because the courts authorized in 1882 had seen their jurisdiction over inheritance matters withdrawn in 1937, whereas courts authorized by the 1957 regulation enjoyed jurisdiction over inheritance as well as marriage and divorce, reminding some Muslims on Java of the continuing weight of the colonial period.

Three particularly important legal steps give us the rest of the historical framework needed to understand the current climate. In 1974, a marriage law gave the Islamic courts sole authority to recognize marriages and divorces—including the husband's unilateral repudiation of his wife, the *talaq*, which in previous years he could effectively perform on his own. But the early draft of the bill would have produced the opposite result, giving *civil* courts, not Islamic ones, jurisdiction over marriage and divorce, and the ensuing, often vociferous arguments raised fears that a parliamentary majority was trying to snuff out hope for any role for Islamic law. A 1989 law created a uniform set of jurisdictional rules for courts throughout Indonesia and in particular extended the jurisdiction of Islamic courts on Java and Madura to include inheritance matters, finally bringing them into line with Islamic courts elsewhere in the country. But it, too, raised disputes, this time over perceived dangers to the nation that a full-blown Islamic legal structure would pose. Sharia could be taken to stand for either the final emancipation of Muslims from colonial sidelining or the dangerous division of the nation along religious lines. It continued to evoke hopes and fears far beyond the concrete effects of specific laws.

The third measure created a legal substance for the new courts and had less political visibility. In 1991, President Suharto ordered that a new Compilation of Islamic Law in Indonesia be followed by all civil servants, including judges. The Compilation consists of a set of lawlike rules concerning Islamic family law—in effect, rendering as positive law one set of possible interpretations of sharia.[5] But it, together with the 1974 marriage law, did transform the way the state recognized marriage and divorce by transferring the moment of legal performativity from Muslims acting on their own to state-appointed judges.

Consider a divorce initiated by the husband, a *talaq*, as defined by the 1974 Marriage Law and as confirmed in the Compilation of Islamic Law. According to generally accepted understandings and practices of Islamic law predating these two laws, when a husband pronounced the *talaq*, it was immediately effective. The couple was divorced in the eyes of God *and* in the eyes of a judge, whatever the civil requirements might be to register the divorce. But the 1974 law and the 1991 Compilation require that the husband show grounds for divorce in court and stipulate that the divorce occurs if and only if the judge permits the husband to pronounce the *talaq*. A legal ambiguity remains in the eyes of many Indonesians and not a few judges: if a man divorces his wife out of court by pronouncing the *talaq* at home, for example, is he divorced (albeit in violation of the requirement to go before a judge), or is he still married? Although one can find Supreme Court decisions on both sides of the question, Mark Cammack, Helen Donovan, and Tim Heaton have argued persuasively that the overall effect of Court rulings is to maintain that marriages and divorces occur only if the persons involved follow the requirements of the law—in the case proposed here, the husband and wife are still married. In other words, the Court has effectively curtailed

Muslims' power to marry or divorce on their own and given that power to state-appointed judges.[6]

By the end of the twentieth century, then, as the era of reform and decentralization began, all provinces and districts in Indonesia had Islamic courts, with the same jurisdictions and the Supreme Court exercising the powers of cassation. Furthermore, the Court had made clear that general lines of civil law thinking applied to Islamic law as well: that the executive and legislative branches made the law and that the courts enforced those laws. Islamic law was to be treated in the same way as other laws, and Islamic judges were to be thought of first and foremost as judges occupying their place in a national, uniform legal system. Whatever one might say about sharia in one's private life, it had become positive law in public life.

Morals and Sharia Under Decentralization

But this perfected centralizing of judicial power came just as local governments were given the power to define more of their own political and cultural priorities. Soon after Suharto's resignation in May 1998, Parliament passed laws transferring some powers from the central government to provinces, cities, and regions (*kabupaten*). The Regional Autonomy Laws of 1999 (later revised in 2004) gave regions responsibility in the domains of finance, public works, health, and other matters, but not in the domains of public order and religion. Moreover, regions and cities could not simply promulgate whatever measures they wished; they had to draft regulations that did not violate national laws or the Constitution. Since that time, a number of provinces, regions, and cities have issued regulations regarding a wide range of matters. According to the respected legal-monitoring site *Hukumonline*, 5,054 such regulations were passed from 1999 until March 2006. The Indonesian Home Office considered 930 of them to be problematic; 506 were overturned. But almost all of them had to do with financial matters, not our concern here.[7]

Some of the new regulations concerned morality and conduct, and it is these regulations that have received the most attention within Indonesia and abroad. Although many commentators have written as if all the morals-related local regulations have been efforts to enforce aspects of Islam, many of them target specific issues of morality without mentioning Islam. The West Java region of Indramayu was one of the first to issue such regulations in 1999, banning prostitution on grounds that it violated "[r]eligions and [m]orals." In 2004, the mayor of Palembang, the largest city in South Sumatra, issued an order that also banned prostitution, as did the mayor of Tangerang, a satellite city of Jakarta in West Java, in 2005. In 2004, the governor of North Sulawesi issued a regulation against human trafficking, targeting women and children illegally brought in to work as prostitutes, beggars, or household servants.[8]

Now, had these regulations been carried out in a fair and thoroughgoing way, they might have been applauded nationally and internationally as instruments to crack down on the exploitation of women and children. But all too often they were interpreted and enforced in ways that clearly targeted poor women. Most notorious were incidents when women traveling home from late-night factory work were picked up as suspected prostitutes, such as in the 2006 case of Lilies Lindawati, arrested in Tangerang along with other women waiting for public transportation or eating at a café, a case that made international headlines. These regulations did not on the face of them derive from Islam; they were intended to enforce morality or build "good character."[9] Their problematic outcomes had to do with the patriarchal nature of their content and the ways in which they were enforced, not with a reliance on Islam. They were sold as responses to popular demands for law enforcement.

Other regulations clearly *did* set out to enforce certain behaviors on Islamic grounds. In 2001, the region of Cianjur (in West Java) issued a circular (*surat edaran*) that took as its purpose "urging all Muslims in the region to practice Syaria'at Islam"—specifically that they pray at the required times, pay the *zakat*, and recite the Qur'an on a regular basis and that women wear the *jilbab* (head covering).[10] In nearby Tasikmalaya, officials (men and women) were ordered to wear Islamic dress on Fridays, and schools were told to ensure that all pupils could recite the Qur'an. The region's 2003 strategic plan makes it clear that local politicians saw these and other measures as ways to build character and thereby to produce better workers for the region's agribusiness.[11] Tasikmalaya also urged that steps be taken against prostitution and alcohol; on these and other matters, the government solicited fatwas from the regional Majelis Ulama Indonesia (Indonesian Ulama Council). In 2009, the Tasikmalaya city government passed a regulation aimed at developing "values for living together based on the teachings of Islam and the society's norms" and that included a wide range of measures. The law specifies that all Muslims must fight against corruption, fornication, prostitution, gambling, alcohol and narcotics, abortion, pornography, interest (usury), traditional healing if it leads people to polytheism (*syirik*), the exploitation of women and children, banditry (*premanism*), and the spread of heterodox sects. Everyone is urged to ensure that everyone else respects these norms, "following the principle of amar ma'ruf nahyil mun'ar [*sic*]," or the obligation to do good and avoid wrongdoing. But the same regulation also urges everyone to respect the rights of others to carry out their own religious practices.[12] Most of these measures are not particularly Islamic in character, despite the general reference to Islamic teachings.

We then have two types of regional morally relevant regulations that have accompanied decentralization. "Morals rules" seek to ban drinking, gambling, and prostitution. Patriarchal assumptions about behavior and morality as well as textual vagueness and irregularities of enforcement have led to infringements of the rights of individuals, usually poorer women. Indeed, the Komisi Nasional Anti Kekerasan Terhadap Perempuan (National Committee on Violence Against Women) emphasized that it was mainly poor legal drafting rather than a religious antipathy to gender equality that led to the discriminatory outcomes of some of these rules.[13] Such rules are most often the objects of criticism from within Indonesia and from international sources, but when they have been tested in court, they have been upheld as legal because improving morality is clearly within the jurisdiction of regional or municipal government.[14]

"Islamic rules," on the other hand, compel people to follow certain precepts said to be basic to an Islamic religious life, including paying the *zakat*, learning to recite portions of the Qur'an, and wearing Islamic dress. The latter clause usually requires women to wear head scarves (and it is sometimes limited to civil servants, perhaps only regarding dress on Fridays), but in other instances it compels civil servants (men and women) to wear recognizably Islamic clothing or prohibits men from wearing shorts. The enforcement of head scarf rules aside, these rules have come in less often for criticism than have morals rules, but in the long run they are much more likely to be overturned by the national government or courts as violating the laws on decentralization in that they arrogate to the regions matters of religion, which remains under the purview of the central government. Indeed, in 2008 the president of the Mahkamah Konstitusi (Constitutional Court) declared that he thought that these regulations should be overturned.[15] However, as of mid-2010 none had been overturned.

It is understandable that many commentators have made blanket statements supporting or deriding all such "regional regulations" without distinguishing between morals rules and Islamic rules. Their detractors can highlight the more internationally condemned morals cases as blackening the whole lot. Their proponents can point to the Islamic character of some of them and the moral value of others to extol their virtues. Those groups who long have wished to revive the Jakarta Charter as a basis for *national* law now come to the defense of these *regional* regulations, arguing in key pro-sharia publications—such as *Sabili*, *Media Dakwah*, and *Gontor*—that enforcing Islamic law for Muslims would not threaten national unity but would restore to Muslims "their" law. At the peak of the debates over the regulations in August 2006, the covers of all three magazines spoke to this issue. *Gontor* depicted a map of Indonesia surrounded by prayer beads and proclaimed that "the ulama [religious scholars] care for the unitary state of the Indonesian Republic." *Media Dakwah* reviewed the history of postindependence Islamization in Indonesia and proclaimed that the Jakarta Charter was "the solution, not the problem." *Sabili* argued that those who opposed the local regulations were "attacking sharia" and emphasized that the implementation of the Jakarta Charter posed no danger to non-Muslims.

Playing down the regional character of the Islamic rules and morals rules, these national pro-sharia movements argue explicitly that Islamization does not undermine national unity because the state ideology, the Pancasila, has monotheism as its first principle and that this concept is moral in nature. One writer for *Media Dakwah* said that each community has its own sharia and quoted Vice President Jusuf Kalla, who called for opposition to sharia to cease because "in truth we have always each carried out our own sharias, with everyone long respecting those of other groups."[16] Finally, these pro-sharia authors point out that the state has already implemented aspects of sharia with the creation of Islamic courts, the promulgation of the Compilation of Islamic Law, and the laws giving Aceh special rights in this regard.

The rhetoric of these groups makes it seem that local regulations are part of a nationwide drive for sharia and the natural realization of the Muslim community's desires. This way of framing the debate suits their interests in pressing for an implementation of the Jakarta Charter. But their claims should not be mistaken for a sufficient analysis of local dynamics, to which we now turn.

Qur'anic Sensibilities in South Sulawesi

Since the passage of laws authorizing decentralization, it has become more politically acceptable for local actors to do exactly the opposite of what is advocated in the national pro-sharia publications: to frame demands for special legislation in terms of regional identity rather than in terms of Islamic self-rule. South Sulawesi is a case in point: it was one of the first provinces to capture international attention for local efforts to promote sharia-based law. The Komite Persiapan dan Penegakan Syariat Islam (KPPSI, Committee for the Preparation and Creation of Islamic Sharia) grew out of the economic and political turbulence of the years just before and after Suharto's fall from power, 1997–2000. One recent study of the region argues that in various parts of the province mass movements grew up to combat what they saw as rising problems of theft and a collapse in moral restraints.[17] They cited "sharia" as the umbrella concept for their efforts to do what the police and army had failed to do: keep public order. When President Habibie left office thereafter, and Jusuf Kalla was dismissed from his position in Megawati Sukarnoputri's cabinet, some saw the departure of these two favorite sons of South Sulawesi to be offenses against provincial honor, and they reacted with a new attempt to regain that honor. In 2000, a group of activists began to promote Islam as the ideology that would recall the past greatness of Sulawesi Islamic kingdoms and provide an effective basis for opposing decisions taken by Jakarta's leaders. They extolled the province's identity as the "Veranda of Medina," echoing Aceh's nickname, "Serambi Mecca" (Veranda of Mecca). Among them was Abdul Aziz Kahar Muzakkar, a son of the famous Kahar Muzakkar, who had led the region's Islam-based rebellion in the 1950s. His participation added to the credibility of the movement's claim to be reviving a Sulawesi political identity.

By framing its movement as based primarily on a provincial identity, KPPSI was able to argue for autonomy within the discursive space provided by decentralization. In December 2001, KPPSI held the first of what were to be several congresses, attracting many of the political and academic elite of South Sulawesi, and produced a draft autonomy law based on the laws granting autonomy to Aceh.[18] Shortly thereafter the movement threatened to take political or, if necessary, military action if the province were not granted special autonomy akin to Aceh's. Their arguments were based on the Islamic identity of the province's major kingdoms—Gowa, Tallo, and Bone. The leading historians and anthropologists at the province's main university underscored this Islamic political identity. The congresses made it possible for provincial leaders to ask Jakarta for the creation of a sharia-based legal and political system as part of the decentralization process. This framing process converted what could have been branded as a dangerous move against the unitary state into a formally acceptable search for provincial identity. It also allowed local representatives of Muhammadiyah and NU, organizations that on a national level oppose the creation of an Islamic state, to support the Sulawesi sharia initiative. Sulawesi's measures were presented as about creating the cultural basis for decentralization, not about challenging Pancasila or resuscitating the Jakarta Charter.

But Jakarta made no move to accept the demands for a Sulawesi sharia code, and KPPSI refocused its attention on the efforts of one region, Bulukumba, to develop public sharia. Bulukumba leaders had seized on Islam as the basis for its regional identity, drawing on religious references already existing in the region, in particular the grave of Datu di Tiro, said to be the *alim* who brought Sufism to South Sulawesi. Emphasizing the Islamic character of Bulukumba also served to distinguish it from the provincial capital, Makassar. Whereas Bulukumba added Arabic script to its public signs to emphasize its Islamic character, Makassar added indigenous script, the *aksara lontara*, or palm-leaf alphabet, in order to emphasize its cultural and historical distinctiveness.

The implementation of sharia in Bulukumba was the work of the regional head, Patabai Pabokori, who engineered the enactment of four regulations between 2001 and 2003. In 2003, he ordered that every man and woman who wanted to marry as well as all students and civil servants demonstrate their ability to recite from the Qur'an. When a Bulukumba couple sought a marriage license, the religious officer was directed to certify that both of them could recite al-Fatiha, the first, very short chapter of the Qur'an and the one that most Muslims would be likely to have mastered because they recite it as part of every prayer. If either the bride or the groom could not recite the verse, the religious officer was supposed to ensure that the village imam delay the wedding until such time as they could demonstrate their capacity to do so. Almost certainly, there were quite a few cases of couples unable to recite from the Qur'an, but their weddings were never delayed because it would have violated strong notions of dignity and honor to do so. Other regulations required female students and civil servants (men and women) to wear Islamic dress, prohibited alcohol, and created a body to collect and distribute the *zakat*. Patabai apparently was persuaded that creating a local *zakat* board would bring in relatively large sums of money—much needed because Bulukumba became more financially dependent on Jakarta after decentralization.[19] Patabai argued repeatedly that the regulations were matters of education and social life and indeed were handed over to the local Department of Welfare and Social Affairs, not Religious Affairs.

Patabai made these regulations into the public signs of Bulukumba identity. As a visitor approaches Bulukumba from Makassar, he or she passes by a large monument marking the regional boundary. The building resembles a mosque and lists the government's eight "crash programs" in religion and its four regulations on large signs. The regional head also plastered Qur'anic verses and hadith on traffic signs, on walls, and on government cars. Official signs had Indonesian directions duplicated in Arabic script. Indeed, Arabic script and Qur'anic literacy became the hallmarks of Bulukumba reforms.[20] This emphasis picked up on the long-standing centrality of the Qur'an in Bulukumba lives, where children grow up learning to recite. Since the 1980s, a celebration of having completed a reading of the Qur'an has been part of wedding celebrations. (The imam recites; the groom points to the place in the open book where the recitation is written.) During this period of Islamization through Qur'an, Patabai gave out copies of the Qur'an at every competition sponsored by the region, including swimming contests. The state asserted its presence by drawing on locally acceptable signs of religious potency.

The particular thrust of the Bulukumba initiative depended on the specific way in which Patabai combined local sensibilities with the idea of a sharia-based identity. When in 2005 Patabai was replaced by a new regional head, one less enamored of the sharia initiative, signs of sharia diminished in intensity and performance. At the same time, other groups developed alternative ways of framing the importance of local identity and attachments to Islam. The stance taken by KPPSI was opposed by the Makassar-based organization Lembaga Advokasi dan Pendidikan Anak Rakyat (Institute for Legal Advocacy and for Popular Education) in which younger scholars trained at *pesantren* (religious schools) took the lead. They cite the idea of *maqasid ash-shari'a* (sharia's objectives) over and against KPPSI's draft. They argued that promoting health and education were more important than the regulations passed in Bulukumba. Other Islamic leaders argued that other practical matters took priority among the *maqasid*. Taking a different tack, the chair of the Bulukumba Indonesian Ulama Council branch argued that the major emphasis of Islamization should be on practical knowledge, such as learning how to properly bathe deceased Muslims.[21]

The Bulukumba measures are thus best understood as efforts by a political entrepreneur to base his career on local practices and sensibilities. His project marked Bulukumba as "Islamic" vis-à-vis the neighboring city of Makassar, drew on ingrained cultural practices concerning Qur'anic knowledge and literacy, and offered a positive outcome to what otherwise was the failed effort to win Jakarta's acceptance of Sulawesi sharia-based autonomy. Far from being either a groundswell call for shariazation or a plot by a nationwide Islamist conspiracy to restore the Jakarta Charter, the enactment of these regional regulations came about because of a very specific, locally contextualized political gambit. When the leadership changed, so did the local tenor of sharia.

Sharia and Autonomy in Aceh

Aceh long has constructed its special identity around its Islamic history and culture, and it now, alone among Indonesian provinces, has the legal right to reconstruct its legal system on the basis of sharia. But Aceh also long has been sharply divided along political and religious lines, and today these divisions are worked out over divergent and discordant ideas about what "sharia" ought to mean. The postindependence rebellion against Jakarta, Darul Islam (House of Islam), was intended to gain greater autonomy for Aceh and to create an Islamic basis for the Indonesian nation. In its early years, the Gerakan Aceh Merdeka (GAM, Free Aceh Movement) retained this Islamic tenor but increasingly focused its military activity on liberating Aceh from Jakarta control, which it identified as resting in the hands of the ethnic Javanese. Although bathed in popular Islam, GAM was mainly about resisting Jakarta colonialism, not about installing an Islamic system, and as its leaders sought international recognition, they played down Islam as a part of their platform.

But the GAM position on sharia also was a reaction to Jakarta's efforts to do an end-run around the group on the Islam question. When in 1999 and 2001 the national Parliament granted Aceh the right to create a sharia-based legal system, GAM responded negatively. It also opposed student Islamic groups in Aceh that called for recognizing Islam in the Indonesian Constitution and for worldwide Islamic solidarity with the Palestinians and against the American invasion of Afghanistan. Jakarta's measures were intended to win over these and other Islamic elements in the national Parliament and in Aceh as well as to isolate GAM. For GAM, sharia now stood for Jakarta trickery. Some GAM leaders sought to counterpoise the natural Islamic identity of Aceh to Jakarta's ideas of enforcing Islamic law.[22]

These laws, followed by the Helsinki Agreement of 2005 and the 2006 Law for the Government of Aceh, have transferred substantial powers to the Acehnese government, including the right to pass laws based on Islam. But the national government retained jurisdiction over matters of justice (giving the Supreme Court the power to quash any decisions taken by courts in Aceh) and the right to annul Acehnese statutes should they conflict with public order or with national laws.

The Acehnese Parliament passes laws, now called *qanun*, often at the behest of a new body, the Majelis Permusyawaratan Ulama (MPU, Ulama Deliberative Council), which is composed of local Islamic scholars (ulama) and representatives of local government. Although Aceh long has had an Ulama Council, the MPU has a new formal role in proposing laws and issuing fatwas on the religious acceptability of new laws or regulations. The Dinas Syariat Islam (Office of Islam Sharia), located in the governor's office, oversees proper Islamic conduct in public and private life—including dressing appropriately, attending Friday prayers, not drinking or selling alcohol, and not insulting religion—and makes legislative recommendations to Parliament. The office has its own enforcement arm, the Wilayatul Hisbah, or Sharia Police, which in 2008 was merged with the civil police.[23] Members of the WH, as this arm is known locally, are supposed to "socialize" Islamic law, meaning educate the people about what they ought to do. It is up to local prosecutors to decide whether they should carry out enforcement of the new rules, such as caning for gambling or drinking. They are not required to do so de jure.

But the Aceh sharia situation is rife by tensions that are at once theological, legal, and political—tensions largely ignored in the international press in favor of the sensationalism surrounding coverage of canings and (very legitimate) concerns about former GAM members' willingness to return to civilian life.[24] First, long-running divisions between reformist and traditionalist Islamic scholars have taken on new institutional form through the creation of multiple Islamic councils and disputes over civil law and ritual practice. The MPU includes both university-trained scholars from the Institut Agama Islam Negeri (State Institute of Islamic Studies) and conservative ulama based in Aceh's rural Islamic *dayah*, boarding schools, who in the 1950s and 1960s had lost power to reformist scholars.[25] But the *teungku dayah* have created a new body intended to reflect more faithfully their conservative teachings on matters of *fiqh*, the Himpunan Ulama Dayah Aceh (Ulama Association of Aceh Islamic Boarding Schools). They have also asserted their newfound influence in the ritual sphere, taking control of the main mosque in Banda Aceh, where their version of prayer ritual (involving the morning *qunut* prayer, a repeat of the Friday prayer, and more prayer cycles at certain times) is the rule.[26] They have succeeded in framing the legal agenda as the gradual extension of sharia, often over and against the much more hesitant stance taken by the university scholars. In addition, former GAM members, highly critical of sharia legislation for reasons explained earlier and close both to the governor and to the leading political party, the Partai Aceh (Aceh Party), have created their own council, the Majelis Ulama Nanggroe Aceh (Aceh Province Ulama Council).[27]

The line between traditionalist and reformist religious groups cross-cuts a second fault line that has both legal and political roots. Aceh is caught between enjoying autonomy in religious law matters and obeying dictates from the legally superior national Parliament and higher courts, specifically the Supreme Court and Constitutional Court. The enabling laws are themselves ambiguous: if the special autonomy law of 2001 grants Aceh's new Mahkamah Syariah (Sharia Courts) jurisdiction over "Islamic sharia as found within the system of national laws," subsuming the former under the latter, the Acehnese *qanun* of October 2002 grants these courts jurisdiction over matters of family law, commercial law, and *jinaya* (criminal law)—in other words, far beyond the scope of religious law "as found within the system of national laws." The Aceh appellate Syariah Court obeys the Supreme Court and the written national laws and tends to find common cause with the university scholars and reformist ulama. One leading appellate judge has told me that he would rather see a halt to further implementation of sharia, for example, but he does not wish to make his opinion public.

But if *qanun*s begin to conflict explicitly with national laws, this position and this silence may become harder to maintain, and the legal disputes may make more public both the structural-legal contradiction and the divisions between reformist and traditionalist ulama. The first test of this unclear legal structure threatened to occur on September 14, 2009, before newly elected deputies could take their seats, when the Acehnese Parliament endorsed a draft Islamic criminal code that included penalties of stoning to death for adulterers and caning of unmarried people caught engaging in sex or homosexual conduct. Local and national human rights groups spoke out against the law, Governor Irwandi Yusuf refused to sign it, and the chair of the Aceh MPU, Muslim Ibrahim, called for the draft bill to be revised. Indonesia's Constitutional Court said that the measure could be challenged as unconstitutional. By late 2012, the bill had been stripped of the controversial provisions by the Dinas Syariat Islam and sent back to Parliament. A constitutional showdown had been avoided but might arise in the future.

Muslim Ibrahim's positions on the bill reflect the difficulty in which some prominent ulama find themselves. On the one hand, he called for revisions to make the procedures for investigating and sentencing in adultery cases clearer (and thereby more difficult to carry out) and implied that this bill might not be the highest-priority item on the parliamentary agenda: "The important thing is to first fulfill the rights of Muslims." On the other hand, he could not oppose the bill on principle: "There is no Muslim who is opposed [to the law], especially as it is God's law. It's just a matter of time, whether to implement it now or in the future." [28] And after the bill became law, he said that the requirement of four witnesses to acts of adultery will mean convictions are almost impossible, but that "if it is scary, people will not commit the crime"[29] The governor's office has to walk the same fine line, not disputing the possibility of stoning, for example, but also signaling that Aceh may become the target of criticisms from the United Nations on grounds of human rights violations.[30]

In Aceh, actors engaging in public debate about new laws have to frame their positions in terms of sharia. For some actors, doing so is merely accepting the politically inevitable, but for others it is the morally and socially appropriate framework. In any case, the range of positions that they have taken attests to the capacity to evoke sharia with quite contrastive effects. Recall GAM's response to state-led efforts to "grant" sharia to Aceh: that sharia already was part of Aceh and hence needed no new legal rules. In 2000, even before Al Yasa' Abubakar began his tenure as the first head of the Aceh Dinas Syariat Islam, he argued along quite similar lines that Aceh had been sharia based before the Dutch wiped away the traces and that restoring older Acehnese institutions therefore fell under the rubric of instituting sharia. He proposed to begin by rebuilding the older system of village administration that featured a supravillage office, the *mukim*—not on the face of it a particularly Islamic institution.

Abubakar's subsequent public debates over the new laws centered on how to understand the issue of priorities among Islam's objectives, the *maqasid ash-shari'a*. In February 2007, at a conference held in the spacious hall of Banda Aceh's largest hotel, he was peppered with accusations that the laws passed so far had dealt with such lesser matters as drinking alcohol and meeting in secluded places with nonrelatives of the opposite sex and had ignored matters of greater importance. He countered with an argument from authenticity that it was the "wish of the Acehnese people to have Islamic law, not that of the central government," and that in any case because Islamic law in Aceh takes the legal form of *qanun*, and the *qanun* are passed by the local parliament and could be overturned by the Indonesian Supreme Court, they were laws like any other in Indonesia.[31]

But many in attendance at the conference did not see things this way. A lecturer at the Aceh State Islamic Institute agreed with Abubakar that human rights and gender equality were not in conflict with Islamic law because the five major objectives of Islamic law included the protection of the person. She argued that Muslims in Aceh needed to give highest priority to measures that protected lives, such as doing away with illegal logging, and not the measures passed so far. Other institute staff pointed to a poll that showed that the majority of Acehnese did not favor the implementation of Islamic law and that the new governor won because he did not favor its implementation. A lecturer at Universitas Syiah Kuala, the provincial university, said: "I was raised to obey God's commands, so I do not need the government to tell me what to do. I never asked for Islamic law in Aceh. Sexual disease and births out of wedlock are on the rise in Aceh since the implementation of Islamic law because whereas social control mechanisms previously stopped people from doing these things, now people wait for the government." Abubakar responded that it was the people's representatives in the provincial parliament who passed the laws: "If the people do not want it, then fine, we will leave it up to them."

A "focus group" discussion was held after the large session. Several speakers said that Islamic law "must be applied in contextual fashion" with priorities made clear in terms of the logic of the Qur'an's objectives (*maqasid*): emergency matters first, optional matters later on. One university lecturer and nongovernmental organization activist said: "When 40 percent of the people of North Aceh are poor, why is drinking alcohol the object of *qanun*?" Another pointed to environmental concerns as following into the top priority of "emergency" (*darurat*) because they endanger human lives. The former head of a district Religious Affairs Office in North Aceh said that the majority of cases that come to them involved child abuse, so it was a top priority item. Most speakers said that the state should not intervene in "private affairs." Abubakar responded to the objections by saying that the state had adopted Islamic law on the matters under debate—couples being found alone, drinking, and gambling—because people were starting to take matters into their own hands and administer justice in an illegal way. "The state needed to put things in order."

The debate turned not on whether Islam should serve as a norm or even the primary norm for life in Aceh, but on how far the state should go in turning norms into enforceable laws and whether it had correctly determined the priorities for Aceh. Both sides, Abubakar and those objecting to the laws, agreed that it mattered what the Acehnese thought—that legitimacy of Islamic law depended on local acceptance and perhaps even a history of a local call for its implementation.

Even some of the liberal ulama not in the public position occupied at the time by Abubakar (who subsequently left the post) support the general idea of implementing sharia in Aceh, critical as they may be of how it has been enforced. The relatively liberal scholar Hamid Sarong, dean of the School of Sharia at the State Islamic Institute, considers that the implementation of sharia developed out of a popular desire to have more effective law enforcement. "Before there was a plan to implement sharia in Aceh, people took the law into their own hands. In 1998–1999, the early reform period, there were several incidents where villagers found a couple together in *khalwat* [isolation] and could not marry them because one or both already were married, so they doused them in water and shaved their heads. The national government then passed the new laws. If the sharia laws were annulled, things would spin out of control again because national law has not functioned for a long time now; [before the laws] there was gambling and drinking everywhere."[32]

Hamid Sarong's position captures the difficulty of Aceh's status quo. The province has never had a clearly resolved legal status, nor has it enjoyed many years of continual peace. Is it surprising that post-Helsinki Aceh—left on war footing under the Dutch and never retaken after World War II, merged with North Sumatra and then given separate status but immediately plunged into the 1950s Darul Islam rebellion, torn by the massacres of 1965–1966 (which for some provided the opportunity to take revenge on former proponents of the Darul Islam), repressed politically and militarily by the New Order regime, bloodied increasingly through the 1990s, and then partially wiped out by the tsunami of late 2004—seems not to have returned to "normality"? Acehnese worry about law and order and protection from military repression, but also about finally claiming their right to shape their own future. To the extent that this future draws on the past imagined as the "Serambi Mecca," sharia represents standing up to Jakarta and standing for an authenticity based in some way or another on Islam.

In this brief tour of national and local debates, nowhere does sharia appear as a stable signifier. Domesticated nationally as Islamic law, longed for nostalgically via the Jakarta Charter, it has emerged here and there as a new sign of provincial or regional distinctiveness and authenticity. Other signifiers can fill this same slot; in South Sulawesi, Makassar's political leaders highlighted local forms of language and literature, whereas Bulukumba's leaders focused on the omnipresence of the Qur'an. Elsewhere in Indonesia, local *adat* councils formed to call for self-governance in the name of age-old traditions. Even within a sharia framework, the examples from Sulawesi and Aceh illustrate the many ways in which sharia can be imagined: as Arabic literacy, as practical mastery of Islamic rituals, as revivals of older political forms, as a way of life, as statutes, or as attention to the broader "objectives of sharia."

This variety tells us that sharia is above all a loose collection of signs differentiated by province, region, and city and difficult to capture in opinion polls or infer from election results. These signs are deeply situated in the history of struggles for independence against the Dutch, the ensuing struggles for autonomy against Jakarta, and the debates about the relative role of religion in the country's law and politics. In the era of reform and decentralization, signs of sharia do indeed enjoy renewed prominence, but they transmit complex and varied messages. They express the resurgence of local capacities to define and exploit ideas of authenticity, autonomy, and morality—ideas that have strong political, cultural, and often religious dimensions. They are part of a larger story, but that story is of an Indonesia in the process of redefining and relegitimizing its institutions, not an Indonesia captured by a uniform national religious frenzy.

9

Unfinished Business

Law Reform, Governance, and the Courts in Post-Suharto Indonesia

Tim Lindsey and Simon Butt

President Susilo Bambang Yudhoyono stressed his resolve to purge the "judicial mafia," calling on law-enforcement agencies to commit to the fight. "Remember, in the hands of corrupt law enforcers, anything bent can be straightened and the straight can be bent. I want judicial mafia practices to cease," said Yudhoyono at the State Palace. . . . Law-enforcement officials, whether in Jakarta or the regions, should not manipulate the law, he said. The President named eliminating corruption in the judiciary as one of his top priorities when announcing the government's first-100-day program in October.

—SRI MUNIGGAR SARASATI, COMMENTING ON THE SPEECH
PRESIDENT SUSILO BAMBANG YUDHOYONO MADE UPON
REELECTION IN 2009[1]

For most of Suharto's three-decade reign, there were virtually no effective checks on the exercise of state power: government was for the most part not done by law. A constitution formally bound the government and declared Indonesia to be a "law state" (*Rechtsstaat*), but no judicial institution had power to hold the government to account for breaching it.[2] In any event, by many accounts most judges were corrupt and lacked independence from government: their decisions were routinely ordered by government (sometimes by telephone) or purchased by litigants (often with court clerks acting as brokers).[3]

The result was a dysfunctional legal system that consistently failed citizens but served the Suharto government well, providing almost complete legal impunity for many state actors, in particular military perpetrators of human rights abuses.[4] Daniel Lev's damning account of the decrepitude of the Indonesian legal system by the end of the Orde Baru (New Order) suggests the magnitude of the problem that faced Suharto's successors after "the old man" resigned in May 1998:

Indonesia stands out for the extent to which its state was reduced to institutional shambles over a period of forty years. . . . In mid-1998, when

President Suharto resigned his office, not a single principal institution of the state remained reasonably healthy. Corruption, incompetence, mis-orientation, and organizational breakdown were characteristic. The courts, prosecution, and police were underfunded and self-funded. All had been subjugated by political authority since at least 1960 and allowed substantial leeway, within the terms of their subordination, to fend for themselves. Legal process had little integrity left, as was equally true of public policy.[5]

Despite the enormity of the task facing the post-Suharto Reformasi (Reformation) movement and, in particular, the advocates of law reform, Indonesia's legal system has since taken important steps toward developing a system of governance based on the rule of law or, as it is known in its Indonesian manifestation, *negara hukum* (literally "law state"). *Negara hukum* is, in general terms, the equivalent of the Dutch *Rechtsstaat*, and in theory both terms should be distinguished from the Anglo-American common-law notion of "rule of law."[6] Despite this distinction, the three terms are increasingly used interchangeably by Indonesian law reform advocates (particularly civil society organizations), and the common-law notion of "rule of law," with its links to representative democracy and separation of powers, is beginning to displace other meanings in common usage.

Negara hukum is identified as the basis of the state in Article 1(3) of the Indonesian Constitution,[7] but to our knowledge it has never been formally defined in Indonesia by regulation or by a court. It has, however, been variously articulated in a range of contexts to require legality—that is, that the state (including government officials and institutions, local governments, and the military) must itself comply with the law when performing its functions; that there must be an independent judiciary; and that fundamental human rights must be protected.[8] In addition, it has been found that the *negara hukum* principle requires the state to provide citizens with rights to legal aid, legal certainty, access to justice, a fair trial, and due process.[9]

This chapter seeks to assess how far Indonesia's legal system has come along its path from the "institutional shambles" of 1998 to the rule of law, focusing on the role of the Mahkamah Agung (Supreme Court). We consider reforms aimed at removing government control over the administration of the courts (which bears upon the "judicial independence" limb of the *negara hukum*); and the Supreme Court's task of reviewing *perda* (regional regulations) to ensure that they do not breach national-level laws (which relates to the "legality" limb of the *negara hukum*).

Toward an Independent Judiciary

Since the end of the New Order in 1998, the primary legal instrument with which government must comply—the Indonesian Constitution—has been significantly amended to provide for a liberal democratic polity with separation of powers (*trias politika*). The document now provides for an independent judiciary and a full catalog of internationally recognized human rights, drawn almost intact from the Universal Declaration of Human Rights.[10]

Pursuant to these amendments, the Mahkamah Konstitusi (Constitutional Court) was established in 2003 (Art. 24C of the Constitution). This new court has the task, among others, of enforcing the Constitution and implementing the *trias politika*. It does this by resolving disputes between state entities, determining impeachment, acting as a court of disputed returns, and, most important, reviewing national statutes (*undang-undang*) at the request of citizens and legal entities to determine whether the statutes comply with the Constitution (including, of course, its human rights provisions). It can invalidate noncompliant statutes if it considers that necessary. These tasks the Court has generally carried out competently, reliably, and impartially.[11] The Court has even identified several implied rights that Indonesia, as a "law state" (*negara hukum*), must provide to its citizens.[12] The Constitutional Court is thus now widely seen as an important check on the exercise of national legislative power and perhaps the most professional judicial institution in Indonesian legal history. However, its reach in review cases is limited: it lacks the power to test whether the many thousands of lower-level laws (including *perda*, regional regulations) comply with the Constitution and national statutes. This task is left to the Supreme Court. As we show later, the Supreme Court has thus far failed to perform this function effectively.

Important, too, has been a major reconfiguration of the organizational structure of Indonesia's other courts. In 2004, administrative, financial, and organizational control of the general, administrative, religious, and military courts was transferred to the Supreme Court pursuant to Law No. 35 of 1999. The executive branch—in particular the Department of Judicial Affairs— had previously controlled them.[13] In addition, the armed forces had authority over the Military Courts, and the Department of Religion over the Religious Courts. Before the 2004 reconfiguration of the organizational structure of the country's courts, the administration of the courts was often contested, typically ineffective, and always overwhelmingly dominated by the executive branch and its political interests.[14] Moreover, to ensure decisions that the

state favored, the executive is said to have frequently exploited judicial dependence on government for positions, pay, and promotion.[15]

As with the creation of the Constitutional Court, the reforms that gave the
Supreme Court sole authority over judicial administration were part of the
broad regulatory and institutional response to demands for an independent
judiciary stemming from the popular Reformasi movement that emerged in
1998. This movement was driven largely by civil society and in particular by
many of the nongovernmental organizations (NGOs) concerned with governance and law reform that had been quickly established as the New Order's
systematized legal and administrative repression of civil society evaporated.
These organizations' idea that Indonesia's judicial system required urgent and
radical overhaul soon became mainstream and bipartisan, endorsed by each
administration succeeding Suharto and included in each successive national
development plan. The idea led in 2009 to the much publicized (if also much
questioned) commitment by the newly reelected Yudhoyono administration
that appears at the start of this chapter: to put an end to "judicial mafia," a
popular term for institutionalized corruption and dysfunction entrenched in
the legal system and inherited from the New Order.

A major step in the reconfiguration of the judiciary to respond to these
demands for reform was the amendment in 2001 of Article 24 of the Constitution. This provision was originally a bland grant of power to government
to deal with the judiciary as it saw fit.[16] It made no mention of justice, for
example, or of judicial independence. In its amended form, however, Article
24 is now a clear statement of the judiciary's independence from government
as well as formal recognition of the different branches of the judiciary. As
amended, this article states that

1. The judicial power is the independent power to maintain a system of
   courts with the objective of upholding law and justice.
2. The judicial power is exercised by a Supreme Court and the general
   courts, religious courts, military courts, administrative courts below it,
   and by a Constitutional Court.

The new principles in Article 24 are set out again in the Law on the Judiciary, Law No. 4 of 2004, which requires judicial independence in a number
of its provisions. They are further implemented through the cascading chain
of regulation that is typical of legal administration in Indonesia.[17] The changes these regulations introduced were intended to remove judges' dependence

on government favor for pay, promotion, continuing employment, and favorable transfers.[18] Together they are usually referred to generically as the "one-roof" (*satu atap*) reforms, a reference to the fact that under the New Order the courts were housed beneath two roofs—that is, under both the Supreme Court and under the executive—but are now principally under the sole authority of the Supreme Court.

The reforms were not just structural, however. The leadership of Chief Justice Bagir Manan (2001–2008) saw the Supreme Court embark on an unprecedented program of internal reform. This process involved new partnerships with civil society, including, for example, Lembaga Kajian dan Advokasi untuk Independensi Peradilan (LeIP, Institute for Study and Advocacy for Judicial Independence) a leading judicial reform NGO.[19] The idealistic young lawyers of LeIP, led by Rifqi Assegaf, helped the Court draft ambitious Judicial Reform Blueprints, which, although imperfectly and incompletely implemented, have now become a central part of the Court's routine administration.

It is clear that the raft of reforms resulting from the implementation of the *satu atap* restructuring through the Blueprints has begun to create a more open judicial culture in the Supreme Court. It also appears to have begun to build a greater degree of judicial independence—from government at least, in the sense that the central government can no longer direct Supreme Court decisions and indeed now finds the Court quite willing to decide against it, a very rare occurrence under Suharto.[20]

Unfinished Business

All these reforms are the result of a genuine demand that something at last be done about the desuetude of the Indonesian judicial system, entrenched since at least the late 1950s.[21] These demands were supported by many Indonesians, most obviously in civil society, but also in small and determined groups of reform-minded leaders within government and the courts themselves. The reforms have now begun to trigger positive, albeit very slow, change to Indonesia's legal system but are often overlooked or discounted in assessments of Indonesia's post-Suharto Reformasi. This has been in part because legal system reform is usually an inherently complex and slow process in any country, regardless of the type of system involved.[22] It is also overlooked because the changes that have taken place within the Indonesian judiciary are often not immediately apparent to the public observing the day-to-day activity of the courts through the lens of the media and local politics. Controversial political cases and corruption scandals are rarely an accurate measure of the complex business of court reform.

The judicial reforms as a whole are more often dismissed, however, simply because many have, in fact, failed despite the best efforts of reformers within civil society, the courts, and government. Other reforms have had only very limited impact, and some have spawned new problems. Despite genuine attempts to transform the Indonesian Supreme Court, both from within that institution and without, many of the key impediments to an effective *negara hukum*, whether direct or indirect, can sadly still be traced to it. In other words, Indonesia's court reforms have been significant, but so too are the obstacles that still confront them—perhaps even more so than the reforms.

In this chapter, we seek to identify some key impediments remaining to judicial reform and to offer an assessment of the trajectory of Indonesia's legal system since 1998. In the next section, we deal with direct impediments, showing that judicial illegality (and, in particular, corruption) survives in most courts (with a few honorable exceptions)[23] and hampers progress toward the rule of law. We argue that this continued judicial illegality is to a large extent the result of successful resistance to reforms aimed at improving external judicial accountability. This resistance has been led by the Supreme Court, which, although willing to undertake a limited and gradual internal reform process, has seen external accountability mechanisms as threatening and has "pushed back" aggressively against them. This attitude has resulted in particular in the effective emasculation of the Komisi Yudisial (Judicial Commission), a new body established in 2005 and entrusted with detecting impropriety among Indonesia's judges as a counterbalance to the increase in judicial autonomy created by the *satu atap* reforms. The result is that the Supreme Court is still often unable to perform competently and honestly the pivotal role allocated to it: impartially adjudicating disputes not only between citizens, but also between citizens and the state, and between state institutions themselves, including the various tiers and arms of government.

In the second half of this chapter, we discuss another key obstacle to reform of the Indonesian legal system that we argue is also a result of judicial dysfunction, albeit indirectly: decentralization and the legal chaos that has followed in its wake. Decentralization has clearly fulfilled aims of enhancing democracy and bringing government closer to the people.[24] Indonesia has by most accounts now transformed from one of Southeast Asia's most repressive and centralized political systems to its most decentralized, open, and electorally democratic.[25] Indonesians have voted in more free, fair, and highly competitive elections and more often than citizens of nearly any other democracy since 2004.[26] Decentralization has not, however, always improved the quality of governance for many Indonesians: closer government does not necessarily mean better government. Rather, as this chapter seeks to show, it has given broad-ranging lawmaking powers to many hundreds of lawmaking institutions and individuals, most lacking lawmaking expertise and experience, let alone training. The result is the production of many thousands of laws, a significant proportion of which may be ill-directed, inconsistent or unnecessary, and, in some cases, unjustifiably burdensome and even nonsensical. Many of these laws also exceed the lawmaking powers of those purporting to enact them. No matter how redundant, repugnant, or illegal these local laws may be, however, many are virtually impossible to remove from the books.[27]

Again, as this chapter explains, the latter problem is attributable, in part at least, to the Supreme Court and its failure to perform its functions adequately—in this instance, to review the legality of local laws against standards and principles established in national law. In particular, the Supreme Court has flatly refused to conduct some reviews, imposing an overly restrictive limitation period on the lodgment of petitions, and in other cases it has allowed questionable local laws to stand without providing any real justification for its decisions. These behaviors are, we argue, a further example of how the Supreme Court's continued dysfunction impedes the realization of the rule of law in Indonesia. In particular, we argue that in the *perda* (regional regulations) review cases the Supreme Court has failed to adequately referee disputes over the competing jurisdictions of various tiers of government arising out of decentralization and has failed to clarify what the "law" is, despite being asked to do so, thus creating confusion and uncertainty. Citizens and governments alike can hardly be expected to comply with the law if one of the highest courts in the land consistently fails to declare the relevant law in important disputes involving the government.

These failures obviously have the potential to inflict enormous damage on Indonesian governance, and they mean that despite reform of Indonesia's legal system the business of creating an open, transparent, clean, and effective judiciary remains unfinished. The centrality of the courts in resolving disputes involving the state and in interpreting and applying the law means that continuing weakness in the courts affects the entire legal system and hampers the progress of Reformasi more broadly. Reform of the Supreme Court as the apex of the various branches of Indonesia's judicature is especially vital to Indonesia's prospects of becoming a properly functioning rather than aspirational rule-of-law state, which, in turn, means that Indonesia still has a long way to go to achieve the *negara hukum* that so many thought they had won twelve years ago.

Lawless Judges

With respect, first, to the problem of judicial corruption, numerous surveys indicate that despite post-Suharto judicial reform, Indonesia's courts are still perceived to be among the most corrupt institutions in the country.[28] Some judges have, in fact, admitted to extorting money from litigants using an auctionlike process in which parties bid for a favorable judgment.[29] It is widely believed that judicial corruption remains institutionalized, particularly in first-instance courts. Lower-ranked judges who accept bribes are still expected to pass a proportion of the spoils up the chain to their various superiors.

Low judicial salaries and operational budgets have long been identified as triggers for judges to seek additional sources of finance and income, but despite substantial increases in judicial salaries in Indonesia in recent years, corruption levels have by most accounts not decreased correspondingly. There is, of course, a degree of naïveté in thinking that an already corrupt judge would suddenly be persuaded to righteousness by a windfall salary increase, and many therefore dismiss the salary increases as a "reward" for the corrupt that will likely only enhance their sense of impunity.[30]

We acknowledge that most claims about the extent of judicial corruption in Indonesia are based on anecdotal accounts, commonly revealed in media reports and informal discussions with lawyers and law reform activists, rather than on firm empirical data.[31] There are obvious dangers in relying on such accounts, particularly from media sources,[32] but in the face of overwhelming public perception and ever-increasing anecdotal evidence and with little to indicate the contrary, we proceed on the assumption that they are largely accurate.

As mentioned, the problems of institutionalized corruption in the judiciary are closely associated in public perception with the Supreme Court, which is commonly assumed, at least in legal circles, to be one of the most corrupt judicial institutions in Indonesia. No matter how impartial, competent, or otherwise professional adjudication provided by lower-level courts may be, it is assumed that a manipulated outcome is likely in the Supreme Court, the final avenue of appeal in all but constitutional cases.[33] These perceptions are aggravated by the fact that the Supreme Court has a longstanding and deeply entrenched culture of guarding its own and resisting outside scrutiny.[34] Although most judges in the Supreme Court now publicly accept the need for reform and for presenting their institution as more open and transparent, and although some measures to achieve these goals have been undertaken (for example, by making more decisions freely available to the public),[35] the Court remains intransigent in its hostility to external attempts to hold individual judges to account for apparent misconduct.

There are many examples of this resistance, but one conspicuous recent case involved the Court's response to the Judicial Commission when the commission began investigating Supreme Court judges soon after the former's establishment in 2005. Most countries around the world have established institutions (usually judicial commissions or judicial councils) that attempt to strengthen judicial accountability, including by holding judges to account for impropriety.[36] Some of the targeted judges brought a case before the Constitutional Court seeking to strike down Judicial Commission Law provisions that allowed the Commission to supervise the Supreme Court's performance by analyzing its decisions. These judges argued that Judicial Commission scrutiny might cause them to decide cases differently than the way they usually would or would otherwise put undue pressure on them and might therefore compromise the independence that the amended Constitution and the new *satu atap* model now required of them. The Constitutional Court agreed, prohibiting the Judicial Commission from reviewing Supreme Court or Constitutional Court decisions—and perhaps even those of other Indonesian courts.[37] As mentioned, the result of this decision was to remove the primary accountability mechanism put in place to counterbalance the greatly increased autonomy the *satu atap* reforms brought to the Supreme Court and the courts below it. The decision also left the Judicial Commission able to do very little beyond suggesting new appointments to the Supreme Court.

The result is that detecting and punishing judicial impropriety are now, in a formal sense, almost exclusively a matter for the Supreme Court, but the Court has virtually no incentive to actively pursue allegations of judicial corruption among its own ranks. After all, corruption brings significant financial benefits to Supreme Court judges personally and provides funds arguably critical to the running of the Supreme Court and the courts for which it is responsible.

Even if the Supreme Court were inclined or pressured to pursue particular allegations, corruption is by its very nature a difficult crime to detect, and the Court has few investigatory powers and little experience in this area. Responsibility for dealing with judicial conduct in Indonesia has accordingly shifted largely from the formal sector to the informal. Most revelations of judicial misbehavior in recent years have thus come not from the courts or the Judicial Commission or from the police or public prosecution service or even from the two agencies that have reported large numbers of public complaints about judicial corruption, the Komisi Pemberantasan Korupsi (Corruption Eradication Commission)[38] and the Ombudsman.[39] Rather, the most active judicial "watchdog" is still civil society and, in particular, the media and those same NGOs that were in the vanguard of the legal and governance Reformasi movement a decade or so ago—such as LeIP, Pusat Studi Hukum dan Kebijaksanaan Indonesia (Center for Indonesian Law and Policy Studies), Yayasan Lembaga Bantuan Hukum Indonesia (Indonesian Legal Aid Institute Foundation), Indonesia Corruption Watch, Masyarakat Transparensi Indonesia (Indonesia Transparency Society), and the like.

Unfortunately, even when judicial impropriety is detected by either formal or informal means, as it sometimes is, there is little prospect that offenders will be punished. If a judge has committed a criminal offense, he or she will be tried before a court from which appeal will inevitably reach the Supreme Court, and so decisions have generally favored fellow members of the bench. Even in the highly publicized "Endin and the Three Judges" case,[40] where Endin, a *calo* or go-between, gave evidence that he had bribed three Supreme Court judges, the courts found in favor of the judges, using poorly justified and spurious technical arguments to defeat the action in a pretrial hearing (*pra-peradilan*), and then even dissolved the government's Tim Gabungan Pemberantasan Tindak Pidana Korupsi (Joint Anticorruption Team), which was prosecuting the case. Endin himself was convicted in another proceeding of criminally defaming the judges by making the original allegations of corruption against them.[41] For obvious reasons, internal Supreme Court mechanisms are even less likely to result in punishment of judges than would a trial, and even if punishment does ensue, it is likely to be relatively light—a transfer or suspension, for example.

The result is that there are now no apparent disincentives for corruption in the Supreme Court other than "shaming" by the media and NGOs, and shaming in this context is a limited sanction, the effect of which will always be relative to the thickness of the judicial hide, individual or collective. This lack of disincentives matters because corrupt judges are rational individuals, disinclined to change their behavior unless their improprieties are likely to be detected and punished in a way that might cause them significant damage.[42] Being rational, corrupt judges will therefore continue to prioritize "wet" (*basah*) cases—for example, commercial cases or major criminal or corruption cases, where the personal or financial stakes are high, and opportunities for bribery better—over "dry" cases, such as administrative disputes involving branches of the bureaucracy, or petty crimes, for example.

Judicial corruption has significant implications beyond the manipulation of individual cases, however. Corrupt judiciaries cannot be relied on to consistently enforce any type of laws—including those that purport to restrict government power. When judges perpetuate or legitimize the illegality of the actions of parties to litigation by not properly applying, interpreting, enforcing, or upholding the law, they contribute, of course, to the erosion of the rule of law. This erosion is all the greater when the parties are governments or state officials, and the courts are, in effect, providing governments with immunity for illegal acts.

Regardless of the rationale for, or even the nature of, government actors' illegality, if the judiciary fails to enforce the law against state officials, whether judges or others, then there is little else to prevent the state acting illegally, save, as mentioned, "shaming" through the media or academic critique. Such shaming strategies can be risky, however, if the state actor can wield political or physical power or threats, as most can to some extent at least. During the New Order period, for example, journalists were routinely threatened and publications shut down for criticizing the government. Even after the fall of Suharto, and despite a general opening up of the media and more permissive stance toward criticism of the state, some critics have faced threats of civil and criminal defamation litigation.

Without an effective judiciary, government in Indonesia can proceed largely unrestrained by law, and, as we show in the next section, government in Indonesia now means more than just "Jakarta." It reaches down to the local level, and it is at this level that the failure of the Supreme Court—the institution charged with the responsibility for reviewing local laws—to reform itself sufficiently to carry out its curial responsibilities effectively, predictably, and transparently is beginning to have a hugely damaging effect on the rule of law.

Decentralization: The Rule of What Law?

Regional autonomy radically changed Indonesia's legal landscape.[43] Under Suharto, lawmaking authority was, like the state itself, highly centralized. The national legislature produced broadly worded and sometimes vague statutes that typically left the detail to the vast bulk of regulation emanating from the national executive.[44]

With the diffusion of government power following Suharto's departure came a proliferation of lawmaking bodies and the production of a vast mass of new regulation at lower levels of government. Provinces (*propinsi*), districts or regencies (*kabupaten*), and municipalities (*kota*) all now have the widest possible autonomy (*otonomi seluas-luasnya*) to make their own policies and local laws, usually referred to as *perda* (from *peraturan daerah*, regional regulations), on any issue not expressly reserved for the national government.[45] Even villages have formal powers to pass laws on some issues. By 2010, there were thirty-four provinces and almost five hundred municipalities and districts spread across Indonesia.[46] Each tier of government now has its own legislature and executive, both equipped with these broad lawmaking powers to issue *perda*.[47] Decentralization has thus spawned more than one thousand lawmaking institutions and individuals. By 2006, it was claimed that local lawmakers had issued around twelve thousand *perda* altogether.[48] Yet despite the efforts of the World Bank (which, at time of writing, had uploaded almost three thousand *perda* to a Web site, www.perdaonline.org), estimating the number of enacted *perda* is virtually impossible: there is no central repository. If each lawmaking institution or individual passes more than one *perda* per year, as invariably they do, the actual numbers are likely to be much higher than this estimate—probably several times over.

On one view, this dispersion of lawmaking power and the multitude of new laws that it has produced are highly desirable. After all, one of the main purposes of regional autonomy was to give power to the regions to regulate their own affairs and to bring government "closer to the people" so that it could be more responsive to citizens' needs.[49] These expectations have, it appears, been met by some local governments, which have drawn praise for issuing *perda* providing impressive yet affordable public services or setting meaningful environmental standards, for instance.[50] By other accounts, however, many local legislative bodies have fallen far short of these expectations.[51] Many complaints relate to *perda* that seek to impose conservative religious or traditional norms, such as the controversial Islamizing *perda syariah* (sharia), although we do not consider these regulations further in this chapter.[52] More common still are complaints that lawmakers have used their lawmaking powers primarily to issue *perda* that impose new and often excessive taxes (*pajak*) and user charges (*retribusi*) upon citizens, businesses, and investors.[53] It is also of real concern that officials without legal or drafting experience are often given the task of conceiving and wording *perda*. The result has been *perda* that are so unclear as to be unworkable, are unnecessary, contradict other local laws or national laws, or are simply oppressive and unreasonable. According to a central Finance Department official, "What [has happened] is a type of euphoria, where the region appears no longer to observe the applicable rules, including by enacting regulations that regulate issues outside of their jurisdiction."[54]

If even a small proportion of *perda* issued by local lawmaking bodies suffer one or more of these reported flaws, then "problematic" *perda* might number in the hundreds or even thousands. If, as it is commonly suspected, the proportion is higher, then regional autonomy is creating an unworkable mass of law. The result inevitably is that the original governance objectives of the decentralization process are being lost in a web of regulation that is overlapping, redundant, clunky, and sometimes plain unfair.

The significance for legal Reformasi more generally of the limited progress made in judicial reform described earlier in this chapter becomes apparent when the obvious question arising from our account of decentralization is articulated: What can be done about inappropriate *perda*?

Reviewing *Perda*

There are currently two mechanisms for the review of *perda*. One involves the executive branch, but the other (and in our view the more important) involves the Supreme Court. Both mechanisms are unfortunately flawed for reasons that we describe here, but the Supreme Court's continuing dysfunction means that it has failed almost completely as a means of checking local government regulatory incoherence and misbehavior. The result is that once *perda* are enacted, citizens can do virtually nothing to challenge those that they believe breach their constitutional or other legal rights, which, in turn, means that there are very few means by which the poor governance outcomes created by the decentralization reforms can be reversed.

We turn now to the first review mechanism, which we call "bureaucratic review." Provincial lawmakers must send their *perda* to the Ministry of Home Affairs within seven days of enactment. The ministry then reviews the *perda*, often with the assistance of the Ministry of Finance. It does so by reference to two criteria—the "public interest" (*kepentingan umum*) and consistency with "higher laws" (*peraturan perundang-undangan yang lebih tinggi*)—and can invalidate *perda* that fail to satisfy these criteria.[55] Similar mechanisms exist for the review of district and city *perda* by provincial government officials.[56] Several thousand *perda* have so far been reviewed through this process, and several hundred have been revoked, virtually all of which sought to impose an illegal tax or user charge prohibited by a national law.[57] Many *perda*, however, bypass the bureaucratic review mechanism altogether, in three ways. First, some local governments have avoided having their *perda* reviewed by simply not sending them to the ministry.[58] Second, some *perda* continue in force by default. The central government's right of review expires sixty days after the regulation is sent for review. If it does not invalidate the *perda* within this time, then the *perda* will come into force automatically.[59] According to some reports, many *perda* slip through simply because the central government has not allocated sufficient resources to review all the *perda* it receives.[60] Third, some local governments are said to have defiantly refused to rescind *perda* that the central government has invalidated.[61]

The other external mechanism for the review of *perda* is "judicial review" conducted by the Supreme Court. This avenue is the only one available to local legislatures and executives to challenge the central government's revocation of their *perda*.[62] It is also the sole means by which citizens can challenge *perda* that they believe do not comply with national legislation.[63] A reading of the sixteen Supreme Court *perda* review decisions available to us[64] reveals that, like the Ministry of Home Affairs, the Supreme Court has invalidated very few types of non-revenue-raising *perda*.[65] More significantly, however, this reading also uncovers two trends that undermine the Supreme Court's credibility in adjudicating jurisdictional matters between national and local governments—a function that, as we explain later, is essential for a working rule-of-law system in Indonesia.

The first trend, clear from several cases, is that the Supreme Court strictly follows a 180-day limitation period set by internal regulations the Court issued to govern lodgment procedures in review cases.[66] By so doing, the Court has consistently refused to hear cases lodged more than 180 days after the contested *perda* was enacted. In such cases, it simply dismisses the application for review without even considering the merits and, in particular, the presence of flaws in the *perda*. The Court surely should not avoid hearing these review cases on the basis of a lower-order procedural regulation, particularly when the right to review is provided by the Constitution itself, which does not impose time limits for the lodgment of reviews. Rather, the Court should recognize the importance of its function in maintaining Indonesia's legal order and adopt a less formalistic and restrictive approach. Its failure to do so suggests it does not wish to deal with *perda* review cases, perhaps because they involve complex issues, are politically controversial, and are usually "dry"—that is, they are unlikely to be a significant source of rents for the judges.

As things now stand, local governments can quite easily avoid a Supreme Court review altogether. Local governments aware of the limitation period (as most are) might pass a controversial *perda* but put off implementing or enforcing it for 180 days in order to deliberately render it unreviewable. In other cases, citizens might not become aware of the injurious effect of a *perda* until more than 180 days after its enactment. Even at the national level, access to legal information—such as statutes, government regulations, and the like—has long been extremely problematic, and there is evidence that it is worse still at the local level.[67] It is thus certainly conceivable that citizens might not even be able to obtain laws made by their local parliaments or executives within 180 days of their enactment.

Also of considerable concern is the second trend identified. In several decisions, the Supreme Court has upheld *perda* without categorizing the subject matter and scope of the *perda* in question or considering the scope of higher-level national laws that potentially cover the same or similar subject matter.[68] In such decisions, the Supreme Court has simply declared that the *perda*'s subject matter, being a local political matter, falls within the jurisdiction of the local government; the Court thus entirely ignores the issues of potential clash with higher-level laws.

A conspicuous example of this type of decision was the Supreme Court's review of a notorious Tangerang City *perda* that, among other things, purported to allow "public-order officials" to detain persons on suspicion of prostitution.[69] In 2007, this *perda* was used as the legal basis to detain a number of people, including Lilies Lindawati, a pregnant woman who claimed to be waiting for her husband but who was suspected on the flimsy grounds that she was alone on the street after dark, was wearing makeup but no head scarf, and had lipstick in her bag. This incident drew domestic and international media attention.[70] According to press reports, the public advocate representing Ms. Lindawati (and two other women who had been detained under the same *perda*) put forward several arguments for the *perda*'s invalidity, including that the local government lacked jurisdiction to make the *perda*, that the law contradicted higher-level laws, and that it breached international antidiscrimination laws. We have not been able to obtain a copy of the Supreme Court's decision. Indeed, at the time of writing (several years later), the Court was yet, to our knowledge, to formally issue the decision. Supreme Court spokesperson Djoko Sarwoko instead simply "announced" it at a press conference. In a sparse statement reminiscent of reasoning employed in other "second-trend" review cases, Sarwoko simply declared that the Court had held that the *perda*'s subject matter was a "political matter" and was therefore within the power of the Tangerang City authorities. In other words, the Court held that the *perda* was "a political product of the executive and legislature" and therefore was formally valid and outside the jurisdiction of the Supreme Court, but without explaining why this could be so.[71] No mention was made of the basic question of whether the *perda* conflicted with higher-level laws.

The lawmaking practices of many local governments, and the failure of the Supreme Court, and the Ministry of Home Affairs to invalidate defective *perda* that contradict higher laws are undermining the rule of law in Indonesia in important ways. For one thing, local governments are not being constrained by law in their lawmaking—that is, by the jurisdictional limits imposed by the 1999[72] and 2004 Autonomy Laws. Local governments have thus been able to pass many thousands of poorly drafted laws purporting to regulate almost any subject matter, regardless of their perversity, their internal structural and drafting flaws, their potential injuriousness to citizens or business, the detriment to local and national economies or to standards of public services, or their inconsistency with higher-level laws—even those that purport to provide for basic human rights. It is only when these local laws seek to raise revenue for local governments that local legislators face constraints.

The implications for rule of law of the Supreme Court's recusance in the review of *perda* local legislation are more far-reaching still. It should be understood that despite common perceptions and claims to the contrary,[73] the central government has lost no formal lawmaking power through decentralization. As mentioned, Article 10(3) of the 2004 Autonomy Law reserves several areas as the exclusive domain of the central government, and Article 10(5) declares that the central government retains power to legislate in all areas not mentioned in Article 10(3).[74] Legally speaking, then, the central government can continue to regulate any matter over which regional governments also have jurisdiction. In other words, local governments have no exclusive lawmaking jurisdiction. Rather, they have been given a limited list of powers that they share with the central government and in respect of which the central government retains overriding power because most types of national laws formally override local laws that are inconsistent with them. A "hierarchy of laws" (*tata urutan peraturan perundang-undangan*),[75] the binding cornerstone of Indonesia's legal order, ranks the relative precedence or weight of *perda* below that of a plethora of national laws, including the Constitution, statutes, government regulations, and presidential regulations. Local laws, therefore, will have legal force, at least formally, only if, when passed, they do not contradict a higher law on the hierarchy; and once passed, a *perda* is susceptible to being overridden by a statute, government regulation, or presidential regulation.

Given that the national government has issued a very large number of laws regulating many areas of Indonesian social, cultural, political, and economic life over the decades since independence in 1945, it is difficult to see what formal "space" is left for local laws beyond establishing and regulating particular local institutions and government services. In other words, it is highly likely that a large proportion of *perda* are, in fact, formally invalid because they attempt to regulate an issue that has already been regulated in a national-level law that formally trumps it. There may be an argument that certain powers have been delegated to the local level, either implicitly or expressly,[76] but this argument will not save a *perda* that directly conflicts with a higher-level national law. It seems reasonable to surmise that many *perda* either replicate or contradict national laws and are therefore superfluous because of the contradiction, hence irrelevant or invalid. But the absence of an effective review process means that there is a mass of local laws on the books that arguably have no little formal legal weight—that perhaps are not laws at all in a formal sense. No institution, not even the Supreme Court, is so far capable of cleaning up this legal debris or willing to do so.

The consequent unimpeded proliferation of these problematic local laws is now creating widespread legal confusion. The willingness of both the executive and the Supreme Court to allow *perda* to be implemented without assessing whether they fit within the existing legal framework leaves citizens, institutions, and businesses uncertain as to the laws with which they must comply and those that they can safely ignore. Even before regional autonomy, Indonesia's laws and its legal system were already largely dysfunctional and often not deserving of much respect from citizens and governments alike. As the number of such laws rises, we are concerned that law is at risk of becoming increasingly irrelevant in Indonesia, with predictable consequences for governance and the rule of law.

Cleaning Up the Legal Debris?

The courts in post-Suharto democratic and constitutionalist Indonesia are, in principle, the forum where intractable disputes between citizens, between citizens and the state, and between different parts of the state should ultimately be resolved. They are also where the meaning of laws, the powers and functions of private and public institutions, and the nature and extent of rights should be determined. In other words, under Indonesia's new system of separation of powers, the power to define and shape the legal relationship between state and citizens is formally in the hands of the courts— in particular the Constitutional Court and the Supreme Court.

The Indonesian courts are thus in a position of greater power and autonomy than they have been at any time in the past four decades at least. In theory, the judiciary is now a key arbiter of the post-Suharto Reformasi process that has sought to roll back the overwhelming power of the authoritarian state built under Suharto's New Order and replace it with a more open, transparent system of governance in which individual rights have greater currency and the powers of the executive and the legislature are hemmed in by institutionalized democratic checks and balances.[77] If, however, the courts are themselves dysfunctional or lawless, then none of this can happen, or at least it cannot happen in a predictable, rational, and fair fashion: a properly functioning judiciary is essential to ensure that government operates by law.

Governments everywhere push the boundaries of legality, and in a properly functioning separation of powers system it often falls to the judiciary to determine formally whether an act is illegal and, if so, to remedy it. Most executives and legislatures, in fact, inherently seek to expand their power through regulation and administrative action and simply by doing so inevitably test the limits of their formal authority. In some circumstances, governments may breach the law blatantly, deliberately, and with some form of ulterior intent—such as to remove political rivals or dissidents, to secure personal benefits from public resources, or to cover up military human rights abuses.[78] In other circumstances, the legality or illegality of state action is far less clear-cut. Well-intentioned governments might test existing rules in an attempt to provide benefits to citizens or improvements to governance systems.[79] In the case of Indonesian decentralization, the sheer multiplicity of new organs of government and their enthusiasm for passing laws means that all these factors are in play simultaneously. The result is that regulating the substance of *perda*—"cleaning up the legal debris"—is fast becoming a task that is critical to the future of governance in Indonesia and one that the Constitutional Court has on several occasions suggested that it would be willing to undertake if it were granted the power to review lower-level laws—a power that is currently the monopoly of the Supreme Court. Some Constitutional Court judges have even openly speculated on ways they might reinterpret the Court's jurisdiction to authorize the exercise of just such a power, despite the apparently clear words of the Constitution that limit the Constitutional Court to reviewing statutes against the Constitution. Adding this power would, of course, dramatically increase the Constitutional Court's legal and political importance in Indonesia and correspondingly diminish that of the Supreme Court.

The Supreme Court's inability to reform and rid itself of a defensive, involuted culture that protects institutionalized corruption, prioritizes rent seeking, and does not sufficiently value curial professionalism has contributed to its failure to deal with *perda* in the way contemplated by the laws regulating both the judicial system and decentralization. If the Supreme Court cannot rise quickly enough to the challenge of its new post-Suharto role as a key arbiter of legality in Indonesia, then it puts at risk both the future of Reformasi and the rule-of-law aspirations it embodies. The Supreme Court may again find itself relegated to the margins of public life it occupied under Suharto, with its hopes frustrated in achieving the respect and standing that should be its due as the peak appeal court of a new and vibrant democracy.

Abbreviations: Ar. = Arabic; In. = Indonesian; Jav. = Javanese; Mal. = Malaysian.

ADAT (In.; Mal.; Ar. ʿADA): Indigenous traditions often respected or tolerated in societies.

ʿALIM, pl. ʾULAMAʾ (Ar.): Learned person, a Muslim scholar.

BUGIS: An ethnic/religious group in Indonesia.

FATWA, pl. FATAWA (Ar.): Judicial opinion voiced by a Muslim scholar, known specifically as a mufti.

FIQH (Ar.): Islamic jurisprudence.

HADITH, pl. AHADITH (Ar.): Tradition related or exemplified by the Prophet.

IMAM (Ar.): Leader, most often of communal prayers.

KAFIR, pl. KUFFAR (Ar.): Unbeliever.

KAMPUNG (Mal.): Village, ward.

KLENTENG: Chinese temples in Indonesia.

KYAI (Jav.): Respected Islamic scholar.

MALIKI (Ar.): Member of the juridical school attributed to Malik b. Anas (711–795).

PANCASILA (In.): Five Principles, forming the Indonesian state philosophy.

PERDA (In.): Regional law; *peraturan daerah* = regional regulations.

PESANTREN (Jav.): Boarding school for religious instruction.

PURA (BALINESE): Temples; derives from Sanskrit.

REFORMASI (In.): Reformation movement led by students beginning in 1998.

SANTRI (Jav.): Student of religion.

SHAFI'I (Ar.): Member of the juridical school attributed to Muhammad b. Idris al-Shafi'i (767–820).

SHARI'A (Ar.): Holy Law as revealed to Muhammad and interpreted by the ulama.

SUFISM (Ar.): Muslim mysticism.

SUNNI (Ar.): Member of the orthodox community.

SURA (Ar.): Chapter of the Qur'an.

'ULAMA' (Ar.): Religious scholars. See '*alim*.

UMMA, pl. UMAM (Ar.): Community, nation.

WAHHABI (Ar.): Follower of the teachings of the Wahhabiya.

WAHHABIYYA (Ar.): Pietist movement founded in Arabia by Muhammad b. 'Abd al-Wahhab (1703–87).

ZAKAT (Ar.): Alms.

1. Indonesian Democracy in Theoretical Perspective

1.   However, the distinguished anthropologist Robert W. Hefner has of course written
     an extremely valuable book on the context in which the democratization attempt in
     Indonesia began. See Robert W. Hefner, *Civil Islam: Muslims and Democratization in
     Indonesia* (Princeton, N.J.: Princeton University Press, 2000). An excellent volume
     that deserves to reach a wider audience is Edward Aspinall and Marcus Mietzner,
     eds., *Problems of Democratization in Indonesia: Elections, Institutions, and Society*, In-
     donesia Update Series (Singapore: Institute of Southeast Asian Studies, 2010). As
     is clear from the description of the contributors to our volume, most of them have
     written major works on aspects of democratization in Indonesia, but as a group we
     felt that we should combine our efforts to address the theme of democratic transition
     and consolidation. There are, of course, many books on Turkey, but their central
     focus is often more on issues such as modernization, the Atatürkist legacy, *laïcité*,
     the role of the military, and, most recently, the role of the Adalet ve Kalkınma Partisi
     (Justice and Development Party) than on democratic transition and consolidation.
     Two volumes that relate to the issue of democracy in a Muslim country have joined
     this volume in a miniseries: Ahmet Kuru and Alfred Stepan, eds., *Democracy, Islam,
     and Secularism in Turkey* (New York: Columbia University Press, 2012), and Ma-
     madou Diouf, ed., *Tolerance, Democracy, and Sufis in Senegal* (New York: Columbia
     University Press, 2013). However, neither of these volumes is as centrally concerned
     with democratic transition and consolidation as is this volume.

2. For the post-1945 Dutch challenge and secessionist movements, see Merle Ricklefs, *A History of Modern Indonesia Since c. 1200*, 4th ed. (Stanford, Calif.: Stanford University Press, 2008), especially chap. 5A.

3. In current international dollars. See World Bank, *Global Economic Prospects 2010: Crisis, Finance, and Growth* (Washington, D.C.: World Bank, 2010), at http://siteresources.worldbank.org/INTGEP2010/Resources/GEP2010-Full-Report.pdf, accessed November 1, 2012.

4. For Indonesia's annual per capita growth rate percentages, see the World Bank databank at http://data.worldbank.org/indicator/NY.GDP.PCAP.KD.ZG, accessed November 1, 2012 .

5. See Freedom House's annual *Freedom in the World* reports at http://www.freedomhouse.org/report/freedom-world/2012/indonesia (or substitute India), accessed November 1, 2012. Polity IV numbers are available at http://www.systemicpeace.org/polity/polity4.htm, accessed November 1, 2012.

6. See Berni Moestafa, "Indonesia in Place Among BRIC Nations, Templeton Says" (Update 1), *Bloomberg Business Week*, January 28, 2010, at http://www.businessweek.com/news/2010-01-28/indonesia-in-place-among-bric-nations-templeton-says-update1-.html, accessed December 22, 2010.

7. Juan J. Linz and Alfred Stepan, *Problems of Democratic Transition and Consolidation: Southern Europe, South America, and Post-Communist Europe* (Baltimore: Johns Hopkins University Press, 1996), esp. part I.

8. These amendments stipulated that *(a)* members of Parliament and regional legislatures be directly elected; *(b)* a new upper house, also directly elected, Dewan Pemerintahan Daerah (Regional Representative Council), be created; *(c)* the president and vice president be directly elected and their terms limited to 2 five-year terms; *(d)* a constitutional court be established for judicial review; and *(e)* human and political rights be strengthened.

9. John Rawls, *Political Liberalism* (New York: Columbia University Press, 1996), xviii, 133–172.

10. For "social imaginaries," see *Charles Taylor, Modern Social Imaginaries* (Durham, N.C.: Duke University Press, 2004). For Taylor's discussion of the idea of human "flourishing," see Charles Taylor, *The Secular Age* (Cambridge, Mass.: Harvard University Press, 2007).

11. Gramsci's concept of a series of "moats" that protect nondemocratic regimes can also be used to help buttress a democratic regime. See Antonio Gramsci, *Selections from the Prison Notebooks* (New York: International, 1971), 238.

12. For the "twin toleration" argument that democracy needs the toleration of democracy by religion and the toleration of religion by democratic leaders, see Alfred Stepan, "The World's Religious Systems and Democracy: Crafting the 'Twin Tolerations,'" in *Arguing Comparative Politics*, 213–253 (New York: Oxford University Press, 2001), esp. 215–217.

13. On the Immanent Frame blog run by the Social Science Research Council, see Alfred Stepan, "Contrasting Progress on Democracy in Tunisia and Egypt," at http://blogs.ssrc.org/tif/2011/04/21/contrasting-progress-on-democracy-in-tuni-

sia-and-egypt/, accessed March 30, 2012. See also Alfred Stepan, "Tunisia's Twin Tolerations— Friendly Democratic Transition," *Journal of Democracy* 23 (2) (April 2012): 89–103. The Freedom House blog post by Alfred Stepan after his return from a Freedom House–sponsored mission to Tunisia and Egypt in March 2011 contrasts military responses in the two countries. See Alfred Stepan, "The Recurrent Temptation to Abdicate to the Military in Egypt," at http://blog.freedom-house.org/weblog/2012/01/two-perspectives-on-egypts-transition.html#The%20 Recurrent, accessed March 30, 2012.

14. For much greater detail on the pro-democratic activities of these and other key Islamic actors and especially on their abilities to create important alliances with activists of other religions and with secular actors, see Mirjam Künkler's dissertation, "Democratization, Islamic Thought, and Social Movements: Coalitional Success in Indonesia and Failure in Iran," Columbia University, 2008. Also see Künkler's essay in this volume, "How Pluralist Democracy Became the Consensual Discourse Among Secular and Nonsecular Muslims" (chapter 3).

15. See Abdolkarim Soroush, *Reason, Freedom, and Democracy in Islam* (Oxford: Oxford University Press, 2000).

16. The latter number is based on vote share for the Partai Keadilan Sejahtera (PKS, Prosperous Justice Party), the Partai Bulan Bintang (Crescent Star Party), and the Partai Pesatuan Pembangunan (United Development Party). PKS still supports the incorporation of sharia into public life, but after 1999 it no longer advocated using the state as the primary mechanism for its implementation.

17. A note on Indonesia's religious landscape: 86.1 percent of the population are Sunni Muslim, 5.7 percent Protestant Christian, 3 percent Catholic Christian, 1.8 percent Hindu, and 1 percent Buddhist. Within the Muslim community, 65 percent (65–70 million people) are followers of NU and Muhammadiyah.

18. See Alfred Stepan, "The Contribution by Muslims to the Multiple Secularism of Modern Democracies," in *The Boundaries of Toleration*, edited by Alfred Stepan and Charles Taylor, page nos. not yet available (New York: Columbia University Press, 2013).

19. For Linz and Stepan, "behaviorally, democracy becomes the only game in town when no significant political groups attempt to overthrow the democratic regime or secede from the state." See Linz and Stepan, *Problems of Democratic Transition and Consolidation*, 5.

20. Marcus Mietzner, *Military Politics, Islam, and the State in Indonesia: From Turbulent Transition to Democratic Consolidation* (Singapore: Institute of Southeast Asian Studies, 2009). See also the review of Mietzner's book in "The Burmese Road to Ruin," *The Economist*, August 13, 2009, at http://www.economist.com/node/14210809, accessed November 1, 2012.

21. Personal discussion between Alfred Stepan and the Indonesian minister of defense Juwono Sudarsono, Jakarta, September 25, 2009.

22. For the substantially more constraining role of the military in Brazil, Chile, and Portugal, see Linz and Stepan, *Problems of Democratic Transition and Consolidation*, esp. chaps. 7, 11, and 13.

23. Examples of the few residual prerogatives are the army's territorial command structure, which still remains intact, and the army's de facto impunity from legal trials in regard to human rights abuses.

24. See Arifah Rahmawati and Najib Azca, *Police Reform from Below: Examples from Indonesia's Transition to Democracy* (Stockholm: Institute for Democracy and Electoral Assistance, n.d.), at http://www.idea.int/publications/dchs/upload/dchs_vol2_sec2_2.pdf, accessed November 1, 2012.

25. Alfred Stepan and Juan J. Linz went to Indonesia in August 1999 shortly after the fall of Suharto to participate in a conference about constitutional futures for a democratic Indonesia. Upon arrival, they were unexpectedly met at the Jakarta airport by military officials who told them to go with them to military headquarters. Once Stepan and Linz were there, leading officials from the military discussed their extreme reservations about federalism and their concerns about Stepan and Linz's conference paper, which discussed at length federalism as a possible formula for managing large diverse countries such as India and Indonesia.

26. "Observations on Indonesia's Fiscal Decentralization from a Panel of International Experts," n.d., at http://siteresources.worldbank.org/INTINDONESIA/Resources/Decentralization/Panel_thoughts_on_IndonesiaII.pdf, accessed November 1, 2012. The Expert Panel consisted of Richard Bird (University of Toronto), Roy Bahl, Jorge Martinez (Georgia State University), Roy Kelly (Duke University), and Dana Weist and Bert Hofman (World Bank). The panel also highlighted the "brand new inter-governmental fiscal system [that] was put in place—all of this without major disruption in government services. Over time, the regional share in spending is likely to rise to 45–50 percent, making Indonesia one of the most decentralized countries in the world—and much more decentralized than would be expected on the basis of the country's structural characteristics."

27. Ricklefs, *A History of Modern Indonesia Since c. 1200*, 388.

28. See chapter 7, "Federacy: A Formula for Democratically Managing Multinational Societies in Unitary States," in Alfred Stepan, Juan J. Linz, and Yogendra Yadav, *Crafting State-Nations: India and Other Multinational Democracies* (Baltimore: Johns Hopkins University Press, 2011).

29. In addition to Aspinall's chapter in this volume, see his invaluable book on Aceh: Edward Aspinall, *Islam and Nation: Separatist Rebellion in Aceh, Indonesia* (Stanford, Calif.: Stanford University Press, 2009).

30. World Bank, *World Development Indicators* (Washington, D.C.: World Bank, updated annually), at http://data.worldbank.org/indicator (search by year), accessed November 4, 2010.

31. For Pakistan and Indonesia, see the indispensible volume that reviews madrasas in eight different countries: Robert W. Hefner and Muhammad Zaman, eds., *Schooling Islam: The Culture and Politics of Modern Muslim Education* (Princeton, N.J.: Princeton University Press, 2007), 85–86.

32. See David Dainow, "Montreal Jewish Court of Arbitration," *Bulletin of the National Conference of Jewish Charities* 6 (1) (August 1915): 6–7.

33. Many Catholics around the world similarly seek marriage annulment from the Vatican just as much as a civil divorce because civil divorce is not sufficient in making Catholic remarriage possible. From a Catholic point of view, all those divorced by civil law who wish to remarry in the Catholic faith are bigamists until their previous marriage has been lawfully annulled by the Vatican. To annul the marriage, Catholic councils collect evidence, hear the case, and send the annulment for certification to the Vatican, which makes the final decision. Therefore, regarding Catholic marriage, too, in most countries a situation of de facto legal pluralism exists where Catholic canon is made use of in addition to state law. Here, too, this coexistence of religious and state law can be rights enhancing while not being state eroding.

34. This is a central finding of a study of the breakdown of democracy in twelve different European and Latin American countries: Juan J. Linz and Alfred Stepan, eds., *The Breakdown of Democratic Regimes* (Baltimore: Johns Hopkins University Press, 1978), esp. viii–x.

35. Article 7(1) of Law No. 10 of 2004 on Lawmaking.

36. Daniel Kaufman, Aart Kraay, and Massimo Mastruzzi, *Governance Matters VIII: Aggregate and Individual Governance Indicators:1996–2008*, World Bank Policy Research Working Paper no. 4978 (Washington, D.C.: World Bank, June 29, 2009).

37. See Transparency International, *Corruption Perceptions Index 2011* (Berlin: Transparency International, 2011), at http://www.transparency.org/policy_research/surveys_indices/cpi/2011/results, accessed November 1, 2012.

38. For an excellent review of these events, see Donald K. Emmerson, *Exit Sri Mulyani: Corruption and Reform in Indonesia* (N.p.: East Asia Reform, 2010).

39. Ever since the Surat Keputusan Bersama Menteri Agama dan Menteri Dalam Negeri No. 1 (Regulation on Building Houses of Worship), a joint decree by the Ministry of the Interior and the Ministry of Religious Affairs, was issued in 1969, it has been extremely difficult to obtain the permission to build churches. Many Sunday services of smaller Christian groups are therefore held in school halls, hotels, or rented premises.

40. Article 29 reads "(1) The State shall be based upon the belief in the One and Only God. (2) The State guarantees all persons the freedom of worship, each according to his/her own religion or belief." In 1999, the guarantee of religious freedom was reinforced by the enactment of Law No. 39 on Human Rights, which provides that every individual is at liberty to follow his or her religion and to perform religious services in manners relevant to his or her religion.

2. Indonesian Democracy: From Transition to Consolidation

1. Juan J. Linz and Alfred Stepan, *Problems of Democratic Transition and Consolidation: Southern Europe, South America, and Post-Communist Europe* (Baltimore: Johns Hopkins University Press, 1996), 3.

2. Ibid., 5–6.

3. In Freedom House's annual rankings, Indonesia moved from Not Free to Partially Free after the 1999 elections. It became Free in 2006 and has remained so since then. Today's rankings are: Political Rights, 2, and Civil Liberties, 3, meaning Free. See http://www.freedomhouse.org, accessed May 2, 2013.

4. R. William Liddle, "Indonesia's Democratic Transition: Playing by the Rules," in Andrew Reynolds, ed., *The Architecture of Democracy*, 373–399 (Oxford: Oxford University Press, 2002).

5. The Piagam Jakarta (Jakarta Charter) was an addendum to the preamble of the 1945 Constitution, seven words stating that Indonesian Muslims, in addition to believing in God, were obliged to follow sharia. The charter was a famous compromise adopted by a committee of nine nationalist and Muslim leaders on June 22, 1945, in the dying days of the Japanese occupation. It quickly met opposition from eastern Indonesian Christians and others. The Muslim leaders then agreed to strike the seven words, leaving just the statement that all Indonesians believe in "the oneness of God" ("ketuhanan yang maha esa") in the Constitution as adopted on August 18. See Merle Ricklefs, *A History of Modern Indonesia Since c. 1200* (Stanford, Calif.: Stanford University Press, 2001), 258, 262.

6. Under Indonesia's unique threshold law in effect for the 1999 and 2004 elections, a party receiving less than 2 percent of the national vote in 1999 (or 2004) could hold seats in the 1999–2004 (or 2004–2009) Parliament but was not allowed to contest the 2004 election. The solution, adopted by several parties, was to change their name enough to satisfy the national election commission but not so much as to confuse the voters. In 2008, the law was changed so that parties receiving less than 2.5 percent of the total number of parliamentary seats in 2009 (or 3 percent of the popular vote) do not hold seats in the 2009–2014 Parliament. The new law is consistent with international practice.

7. Secular parties, led by President Susilo Bambang Yudhoyono's Partai Demokrat (Democrat Party) with 21 percent, swept the 2009 parliamentary elections with a total of 70 percent of the vote. Among Islamist parties, only PKS (8 percent of vote) and PPP (5 percent of vote) reached the threshold for parliamentary seats.

8. The best analyses of Jemaah Islamiyah are those by the International Crisis Group coordinated by Sidney Jones, a contributor to this volume. See in particular International Crisis Group (ICG), *Jemaah Islamiyah in South East Asia: Damaged but Still Dangerous*, Asia Report no. 63 (Brussels: ICG, 2003). For more recent evaluations, see ICG, *Indonesia: Jemaah Islamiyah's Current Status*, Asia Briefing no. 63 (Brussels: ICG, 2007); and ICG, *Indonesia: Noordin Top's Support Base*, Asia Briefing no. 95 (Brussels: ICG, 2009).

9. Greg Fealy, "Hizbut Tahrir in Indonesia: Seeking a 'Total' Islamic Identity," in Shahram Akbarzadeh and Fethi Mansouri, eds., *Islam and Political Violence: Muslim Diaspora and Radicalism in the West*, 151–164 (London: Tauris, 2007).

10. Authors' interview with Ismail Yusanto, HTI spokesperson, Jakarta, September 20, 2008. The interview was cut short so that Yusanto could attend a meeting with other Islamist groups to plan lobbying strategy concerning the antipornography bill.

11. ICG, *Indonesia: Implications of the Ahmadiyah Decree*, Asia Briefing no. 78 (Brussels: ICG, 2008).

12. Blair King, "Empowering the Presidency: Interests and Perceptions in Indonesia's Constitutional Reforms, 1999–2002," Ph.D. diss., Ohio State University, 2004.

13. Chapter 3 of King's "Empowering the Presidency" is the best account of PDIP's attempts under conservative leadership to limit the extent of constitutional reform between 1999 and 2002.

14. Salim Said, *Legitimizing Military Rule: Indonesian Armed Forces, 1958–2000* (Jakarta: Sinar Harapan, 2006).

15. Human Rights Watch, *Unkept Promise: Failure to End Military Business Activity in Indonesia* (New York: Human Rights Watch, 2010).

16. "Hingga kini gerakan ABS belum ditemukan" (Until Now the "Anybody but Susilo" Movement Can't Be Found), February 2, 2009, at http://www.vivanews.com, accessed February 5, 2009.

17. Edward Aspinall, *Islam and Nation: Separatist Rebellion in Aceh, Indonesia* (Stanford, Calif.: Stanford University Press, 2009).

18. "Aceh Party Wins Election, Without Celebration," *Jakarta Post*, May 19, 2009.

19. For a nuanced treatment focusing on conflicting loyalties to state and nation since Dutch colonial times, see Donald K. Emmerson, "What Is Indonesia?" in John Bresnan, ed., *Indonesia: The Great Transition*, 7–74 (Lanham, Md.: Rowman and Littlefield, 2005).

20. All three points of view are represented in Maribeth Erb and Priyambudi Sulistiyanto, *Deepening Democracy in Indonesia? Direct Elections for Local Leaders (Pilkada)* (Singapore: Institute of Southeast Asian Studies, 2009).

21. Authors' interview with Eko Subowo, director of capacity building and regional performance evaluation, Ministry of Home Affairs, Jakarta, September 2008.

22. Saiful Mujani founded and is executive director of LSI, and R. William Liddle is a member of its board of directors. LSI's website is lsi.or.id. The data reported on in the text are from Saiful Mujani, *Masalah konsolidasi demokrasi dan pemilu 2009* (The Problem of the Consolidation of Democracy and the 2009 Elections) (Jakarta: Lembaga Survei Indonesia, 2009).

23. The questions were worded as follows: "In your opinion, how is the freedom to speak or have an opinion [to form or join an organization] under the present government compared to the previous Suharto New Order government? Is it much better, better, the same, worse, or much worse now?" "Much better" and "better" were coded as support for the current government; "worse" and "much worse" were coded as support for the Suharto government.

24. Mohammad Zulfan Tadjoeddin, *Anatomy of Social Violence in the Context of Transition: The Case of Indonesia 1990–2001* (Jakarta: United Nations Support Facility for Indonesian Recovery, 2002), 58, 30.

25. Jacques Bertrand, "Ethnic Conflicts in Indonesia: National Models, Critical Junctures, and the Timing of Violence," *Journal of East Asian Studies* 8 (2008), 441.

26. Patrick Barron, Kai Kaiser, and Menno Pradhan, "Understanding Variations in Local Conflict: Evidence and Implications from Indonesia," *World Development* 37

(2009): 698–713. See also Ashutosh Varshney, "Analyzing Collective Violence in Indonesia: An Overview," *Journal of East Asian Studies* 8 (2008): 341–359. One of Varshney's conclusions is that "the scale of ethnocommunal violence in Indonesia does appear to be enormous" (346).

27. Authors' interviews with nongovernmental organization activists in Medan, Jakarta, and Surabaya in March and April 2008. See also Eric Bjornlund, R. William Liddle, and Blair King, *Indonesia: Democracy and Governance Assessment: Final Report* (Bethesda, Md.: Democracy International, 2008).

28. Stephen Sherlock, *The Indonesian Parliament After Two Elections: What Has Really Changed?* Centre for Democratic Institutions Policy Papers on Political Governance (Canberra: Centre for Democratic Institutions, Australian National University, 2007).

29. Only 29 percent of Indonesian voters strongly agree or somewhat agree that they have the ability to participate in politics. In Asia, this number compares unfavorably with that for Thailand (76 percent) but is only slightly lower than for Taiwan (35 percent), about the same as for Korea (28 percent) and the Philippines (27 percent), and higher than for Japan (19 percent). See Saiful Mujani, "The State of Indonesian Democratic Governance: A Popular Assessment," unpublished manuscript, 2008.

30. R. William Liddle and Saiful Mujani, "Indonesia in 2005: A New Multiparty Presidential Democracy," *Asian Survey* 46 (2006):132–139.

31. A valuable collection of articles on this topic is Tim Lindsey, ed., *Indonesia: Law and Society*, 2nd ed. (Annandale, Australia: Federation Press, 2008). See also Lindsey and Simon Butt's essay in this volume, chapter 9.

32. Daniel Kaufmann, Aart Kraay, and Massimo Mastruzzi, *Governance Matters VIII: Aggregate and Individual Governance Indicators, 1996–2008*, World Bank Policy Research Working Paper no. 4978 (Washington, D.C.: World Bank, June 29, 2009), at http://ssrn.com/abstract=1424591, accessed October 28, 2012. The Indonesian data on rule of law are in appendix C, p. 93.

33. Lembaga Survei Indonesia (LSI), *Prospek kepemimpinan nasional: Evaluasi publik tiga tahun presiden* (The Prospect for National Leadership: Public Evaluation of the President's Three Years) (Jakarta: LSI, 2007).

34. Linz and Stepan, *Problems of Democratic Transition and Consolidation*, 11.

35. Rizal Mallarangeng, *Mendobrak sentralisme ekonomi* (Battering Down Economic Centralism) (Jakarta: KPG–Freedom Institute, 2002).

36. Indonesia ranks 111 out of 180 on Transparency International's Corruption Perception Index. Other countries ranked at 111 are Algeria, Djibouti, Egypt, Kiribati, Mali, Sao Tome and Principe, the Solomon Islands, and Togo. See http://www.transparency.org/policy_research/surveys_indices/cpi/2009/cpi_2009_table, accessed January 31, 2010.

37. LSI, *Prospek kepemimpinan nasional*.

38. The Economic Freedom Network is sponsored by the Canada-based economically liberal Fraser Institute. The key ingredients of economic freedom, operationalized in forty-two variables, are "personal choice, voluntary exchange coordinated

by markets, freedom to enter in and compete in markets, and protection of persons and their property from aggression by others." See http://freetheworld.com, accessed February 16, 2009.

39. Richard Robison and Vedi Hadiz, *Reorganising Power in Indonesia: The Politics of Oligarchy in an Age of Markets* (London: RoutledgeCurzon, 2004).

3. How Pluralist Democracy Became the Consensual Discourse Among Secular and Nonsecular Muslims in Indonesia

1. The NU has an estimated 35 to 40 million followers and is one of the largest Islamic organizations in the world. A 2002 survey found that more than 50 percent of Indonesian respondents identified themselves as part of or close to NU.

2. Starting in 1935, Zainal Abidin Ahmad (1911–1983) was the editor of the magazine *Pandji Islam*, which featured the debates between Sukarno and Mohammad Natsir on the nature of the state. Zainal later became president of the prestigious Perguruan Tinggi Ilmu al-Qur'an (Institute of Qur'anic Science) in Jakarta. A lifelong academic deeply interested in political philosophy, he wrote his most elaborate work, *Membentuk negara Islam* (Building an Islamic State) (Jakarta: Widjaya, 1956), discussed here, as a vision of a state that reconciles religion and democracy.

3. Zainal, *Membentuk negara Islam*.

4. Zainal Abidin Ahamad, extract number 12-2 in Greg Fealy, "Islam, State, and Governance," in Greg Fealy and Virginia Hooker, eds., *Voices of Islam in Southeast Asia: A Contemporary Sourcebook* (Singapore: Institute of Southeast Asian Studies, 2006), 214.

5. Zainal, *Membentuk negara Islam*, 177, my translation.

6. Haji Abdul Malik Karim Amrullah, "Address to the Konstituante 1957," in *Debat dasar negara Islam dan Pancasila: Konstituante 1957* (Debate on Islamic and Pancasila-Based State: Constitutional Assembly) (Jakarta: Pustaka Panjimas, 2001), 98.

7. For a very thorough discussion of when and how "promoting the good and preventing evil" and "commanding right and forbidding wrong" have been invoked by Muslim thinkers in a variety of historical and geographical contexts, see Michael Cook, *Commanding Right and Forbidding Wrong in Islamic Thought* (Cambridge: Cambridge University Press, 2001). For notions of *maslahat*, which took on particular significance in questions of government in postrevolutionary Iran, see, for instance, Felicitas Opwis, "Islamic Law and Legal Change: The Concept of *Maslaha* in Classical and Contemporary Islamic Legal Theory," and Said Amir Arjomand, "Shari'a and Constitution in Iran: A Historical Perspective," both in Abbas Amanat and Frank Griffel, eds., *Shari'a: Islamic Law in the Contemporary Context*, 62–83 and 156–165 (Stanford, Calif.: Stanford University Press, 2007).

8. In 1952, Chasbullah was the main protagonist behind NU's decision to break off from Masyumi. A faction around Mohammad Natsir had succeeded in persuading Masyumi delegates to limit the power of the NU-dominated Majelis Syuro (Advisory

Council) within Masyumi, of which Chasbullah himself had been the chairman. This decision to limit the council's power, made at the 1949 Annual Convention of Masyumi in Yogyakarta, created the first instance of tensions between NU and Muslim modernists. At the forefront of this intra-Masyumi disagreement was the distribution of cabinet posts, of which NU, according to internal Masyumi decision making, should not receive any. In particular, this meant that NU would lose its preeminence in the Department for Muslim Affairs in the Ministry of Religion and thus an important source of patronage. By separating from Masyumi, NU succeeded in retaining control over the Department for Muslim Affairs. As the 1955 elections showed, NU did probably account for nearly half of Masyumi's pre-1952 strength, and Masyumi's decision not to allocate any cabinet posts to NU seems inappropriate in hindsight. NU received 18 percent of the vote in 1955, Masyumi 20 percent.

9. The Mutazilite school was the dominant theological school in the ninth and tenth centuries that, crudely put, facilitated a synthesis between reason and revelation. The school employed rationalism in the service of scripture and theology.

10. It is not clear whether the regime placed Nasution in this strategic position as rector of the IAIN Jakarta in full knowledge of the likely ramifications. Nevertheless, once Nasution proposed the thorough curriculum reforms, he had the support of Mukti Ali, the minister of religious affairs at the time and a graduate of McGill University, and Mulyanto Sumardi, for a time the director of the Department of Religious Affairs, and an Ed.D. graduate of Columbia University's Teacher's College (with a dissertation on the Indonesian language titled "A Sector Analysis of Modern Written Indonesian").

11. Nasution's renovation of the education offered in the IAIN was matched in its profundity only by the work of Azyumardi Azra in the 1990s, who significantly expanded instruction in the sciences and transformed the IAIN into a university, from then on called the Universitas Islam Negeri (State Islamic University).

12. Quoted in *Refleksi pembaharuan pemikiran Islam: 70 tahun Harun Nasution* (Renewed Reflections of Islamic Thought) (Jakarta: Pasar Minggu, 1989), 47, my translation.

13. One of the most important twentieth-century Islamic scholars, Fazlur Rahman, is particularly known for his acknowledgment of the contextual revelation of the Qur'an.

14. The full thesis title was "Ibn Taimiya on Kalam and Falsafah: A Problem of Reason and Revelation in Islam."

15. In the 1950s and early 1960s, the HMI was closely associated with the ideas of the Masyumi. The HMI was the driving force behind student movements in the 1960s and 1970s and attracted an extensive membership, establishing chapters in almost every university. By the 1980s, the Islamic student association had an estimated membership of 150,000. In addition, it is estimated that once the regime opened up to allow more (highly qualified) modernist Muslims in the state bureaucracy and political office, the majority of the civil servants came from an HMI background. Edward Aspinall cites figures from the magazine *Umat* to the effect that 250 of 500 members of the Dewan Perwakilan Rakyat (People's Representa-

tive Council) in 1997 were HMI members. See Edward Aspinall, "Opposition and Elite Conflict in the Fall of Soeharto," in Geoff Forrester and R. J. May, eds., *The Fall of Soeharto* (Bathurst, U.K.: Craford House, 1998), 133.

16. See Martin van Bruinessen, "Nurcholish Madjid, Indonesian Muslim Intellectual," *ISIM Review* 17 (2006): 22–23, and Adam Schwarz, *A Nation in Waiting: Indonesia's Search for Stability*, 3rd printing (Singapore: Talisman, 2004), 358–363.

17. See van Bruinessen, "Nurcholish Madjid."

18. From translated extract number 12-5 in Fealy, "Islam, State, and Governance," 222.

19. In the translation by Yusuf Ali, one of the three major translations of the Qur'an in English: "The Religion before Allah is Islam (submission to His Will): Nor did the People of the Book dissent there from except through envy of each other, after knowledge had come to them. But if any deny the Signs of Allah, Allah is swift in calling to account."

20. See Andi Faisal Bakti, "Islam and Modernity: Nurcholish Madjid's Interpretation of Civil Society, Pluralism, Secularization, and Democracy," *Asian Journal of Social Sciences* 33 (3) (2005), 493.

21. Translated by Yusuf Ali.

22. See Komaruddin Hidayat's discussion of this aspect of Madjid's theology in "Contemporary Liberal Islam in Indonesia, Pluralism, and the Secular State," in Chaider S. Bamualim, ed., *A Portrait of Contemporary Indonesian Islam*, 53–66 (Jakarta: Sankt Augustin, 2005). Hidayat writes, "Islam, as said by Cak Nur [Nurcholish Madjid], is a generic value that can be Christian, Hindu, Buddhist, Konghucu, Jewish or Tao and may even be found in Marxist philosophy. . . . Each religion, he says, is a vehicle, *wasila*, the means by which to reach the main goal: self-surrender to the All-Mighty" (58).

23. Van Bruinessen, "Nurcholish Madjid," 22.

24. From the translated extract in Fealy, "Islam, State, and Governance," 204–206. See also Olaf Schumann, "Offentliche Verantwortung der Religionsgemeinschaften in Indonesien, dem Land der Pancasila" (Public Responsibility of Religious Communities in Indonesia, the Country of Pancasila), in Christine Lienemann-Perrin and Wolfgang Lienemann, eds., *Kirche und Offentlichkeit in Transformationsgesellschaften* (Church and Public in Transitional Societies), 359–402 (Stuttgart: Kohlhammer, 2006).

25. Nurcholish Madjid, "The Necessity of Renewing Islamic Thought and Reinvigorating Religious Understanding," in Charles Kurzman, ed., *Liberal Islam: A Sourcebook* (New York: Oxford University Press, 1998), 286.

26. See Fauzan Saleh, *Modern Trends in Islamic Theological Discourse in 20th Century Indonesia: A Critical Survey* (The Hague: Brill, 2001).

27. Roem had taken part in the negotiations for Indonesian independence and had served as minister of the interior and minister of foreign affairs in several cabinets from 1945 to 1953. Parts of the correspondence are reprinted in Fealy and Hooker, eds., *Voices in Southeast Asian Islam*, 226–299. For a short commentary on the exchange, see also van Bruinessen, "Nurcholish Madjid," 22.

28. Madjid, "The Necessity of Renewing Islamic Thought," 294.

29. Kamaruzzaman Bustamam-Ahmad, "Tracing the Roots of Indonesian Muslim Intellectuals: A Bibliographical Survey," *Kyoto Review of Southeast Asia* 8 (March 2007), 5.

30. Both Nurcholish Madjid's *Islam kemodernan dan Keindonesiaan* (Islam, Modernity, and Indonesianness) (1999) and M. Dawam Rahardjo's *Intelektual intelegensia dan perilaku politik* (Intellectuals, Intelligentsia, and Political Behavior) (1993) were published by Mizan, as was the work of other thinkers discussed here, such as Harun Nasution's *Islam rasional* (Rational Islam) (1999), M. Amien Rais's *Cakrawala Islam* (Islamic Horizon) (1995), and Syafii Maarif's *Peta bumi intelektualisme Islam Indonesia* (A Map of Indonesian Islamic Intellectualism) (1995).

31. Kamaruzzaman Bustamam-Ahmad notes that young Muslim intellectuals such as Saiful Mujani, Budhy Munawar-Rachman, Ihsan Ali-Fauzi, Arief Subhan, Nasrullah Ali-Fauzi, Agus Wachid, Edy A. Efendy, Dewi Nurjulianti, and Nurul Agustina were products of the Philosophy and Religion Study Circle and Institute for Social and Economic Research, Education, and Information networks and later became major thinkers in their own disciplines. See Bustamam-Ahmad, "Tracing the Roots of Indonesian Muslim Intellectuals."

32. Greg Fealy notes that Siddiq played a major role in coordinating the pogrom against Communist Party members and sympathizers carried out by NU death squads in East Java in 1965–1966. See Greg Fealy, "Ahmad Siddiq," in *Encyclopedia of Islam*, 3rd ed., part 1, 75–76 (The Hague: Brill, 2007).

33. The group became known as the "Tim Tujuh," the seven young NU cadres who decided in 1983–1984 for a renewal of NU thought.

34. Siddiq remained NU's president until his death on January 23, 1989; Aburrahman Wahid held the chairmanship until he assumed the country's presidency in 1999.

35. See Fealy, "Ahmad Siddiq."

36. Abdurrahman Wahid, "Baik belum tentu bermanfaat" (The Good Is Not Necessarily Beneficial), *Tempo*, November 1, 1980, 61, translation in Greg Barton, "The Liberal, Progressive Roots of Abdurrahman Wahid's Thought," in Greg Barton and Greg Fealy, eds., *Nahdlatul Ulama, Traditional Islam, and Modernity in Indonesia* (Clayton, Australia: Monash Asia Institute, 1996), 213.

37. From Abdurrahman Wahid, "Dinamisasi dan modernisasi pesantren" (Dynamization and Modernization of Islamic Schools) (1981), quoted and translated in Barton, "The Liberal, Progressive Roots of Abdurrahman Wahid's Thought," 211.

38. See the chapter on Wahid in John L. Esposito and John O. Voll, *Makers of Contemporary Islam*, 199–216 (Oxford: Oxford University Press, 2001).

39. Abdurrahman Wahid, "Kyai ikhlas dan ko-edukasi" (Coeducation and the Sincere Kiai), *Tempo*, July 19, 1980, 33, translated in Barton, "The Liberal, Progressive Roots of Abdurrahman Wahid's Thought," 216.

40. Abdurrahman Wahid, "Menjadikan Hukum Islam sebagai Penunjang Pembangunan," *Prisma* 4 (August 1975): 53–62, translated as "Making Islamic Law Conducive to Development," *Prisma* 1 (November 1975): 87–94; also translated in Barton, "The Liberal, Progressive Roots of Abdurrahman Wahid's Thought," 202.

41. Wahid, "Menjadikan Hukum Islam," 62, as translated in Barton, "The Liberal, Progressive Roots of Abdurrahman Wahid's Thought," 207.

42. Edward Aspinall, *Political Opposition and the Transition from Authoritarian Rule: The Case of Indonesia* (Stanford, Calif.: Stanford University Press, 2005), 72.

43. Maintaining interreligious and intercommunal peace as a fundamentally Islamic value was certainly of great concern to Wahid. Other NU members may have had NU's future in mind more than intercommunal peace when deciding for the acceptance of Pancasila as the sole foundation of the state.

44. Compare Wahid's viewpoint with that of Abshar-Abdallah, who believes that universal religious values should contribute to creating and informing public values, but religious practice should be fundamentally private.

45. Abdurrahman Wahid, "Indonesia's Mild Secularism," *SAIS Review* 21, no. 2 (Summer–Fall 2001), 28.

4. Christian and Muslim Minorities in Indonesia: State Policies and Majority Islamic Organizations

1. I discuss some of the sources and practices of tolerance in Java in my book *Javanese Ethics and World-View: The Javanese Idea of the Good Life* (Jakarta: KDT, 1997), first published in German.

2. Because these traumatic events are a crucial point in Christian–Muslim relations in Indonesia, they should not be politely glossed over, as happens so often in "interreligious dialogues"; on the contrary, they should be faced squarely but unemotionally and realistically, even if a completely satisfying solution may be some time away. A list by the Forum Komunikasi Kristiani (Christian Forum for Communication) names 938 churches (up to June 1, 2004) that had been closed by violent attacks since 1945, many of them destroyed or burned down: 2 churches during Sukarno's presidency; 456 under Suharto, most of them after 1990; and the rest under the following three presidents. Even not counting the approximately 250 churches that were destroyed during the civil wars in Sulawesi and the Maluku Islands, some of which, as Sidney Jones makes clear, involved military or police complicity (where also mosques were destroyed), we still can count 688 churches that have been attacked.

3. The situation in the Maluku Islands in the sixteenth and seventeenth centuries is described in Adolf Heuken, *Be My Witness to the Ends of the Earth: The Catholic Church in Indonesia Before the 19th Century* (Jakarta: Cipta Loka Caraka, 2002).

4. One can only speculate about the deeper reasons for the climate of communal violence surrounding the democratic transition. Under President Suharto, people were not allowed to voice their grievances; they often felt themselves to be "victims of development"—for example, because they were driven from their land in favor of a government project with insufficient compensation, which often evaporated before reaching its rightful receivers. Complaining would have exposed them to accusations of being Communist, which since 1965 has been the same as being threatened with death. Thus, these "development victims" have had to accept and keep silent. Communal conflicts, too, were silenced and thus could not

be resolved. Feelings of being the victim of injustice steadily accumulated. People were disappointed and felt isolated and abused, and their anger grew. After the democratic opening following the fall of President Suharto, their anger burst to the surface. They now remembered all the injustices of occurring over more than thirty years. In addition, rapid modernization, with its breakdown of traditional social structures, made a plural society unstable. In other words, we have just begun to realize how big a task it is to unite such a number of different social components within the boundaries of a national state in such a way that they all feel at home, can evolve a positive commitment to each other as members of the same nation, and are reconfirmed in their respective social identities.

5. The term *Islamists* is misleading; by it, I mean not ideologues or fanatics, but, according to the Indonesian use of the word *Islam* in a political context, those who define their political participation according to Islamic ideas and pursue them through Islam-based parties.

6. Religiously motivated terror had been obvious since 1999 but was played down and never seriously investigated by either the state or Islamic authorities. The first bomb in a religiously motivated attack exploded in April 1999 at Istiqlal Mosque; the people hired to place the bombs were easily caught, but, strangely enough, information on whoever gave them the bombs and paid them never came to light—although the media reported that the house in western Jakarta where the transactions were made was quickly identified. The first climax of religiously motivated terrorism was, of course, the Christmas bombings of 2000, which, as I mentioned, were not investigated seriously. Only Bali changed the situation.

5. Veto Player No More?

1. Scott Mainwaring, *Transitions to Democracy and Democratic Consolidation: Theoretical and Comparative Issues*, Working Paper no. 130 (Notre Dame, Ind.: Kellogg Institute for International Studies, University of Notre Dame, 1989), 17.

2. Richard Gunther, "Opening a Dialogue on Institutional Choice in Indonesia: Presidential, Parliamentary, and Semipresidential Systems," in R. William Liddle, ed., *Crafting Indonesian Democracy* (Bandung, Indonesia: Mizan, 2001), 151.

3. Larry Diamond, "Elections Without Democracy: Thinking About Hybrid Regimes," *Journal of Democracy* 13 (2) (2002), 31.

4. Bertlesmann Stiftung, *Bertelsmann Transformation Index 2008—Indonesia Country Report* (Gütersloh, Germany: Bertelsmann Stiftung, 2008), 5, 11, 29, 31.

5. George Tsebelis, *Veto Players: How Political Institutions Work* (Princeton, N.J.: Princeton University Press, 2002), 19.

6. Ulf Sundhaussen, *The Road to Power: Indonesian Military Politics, 1945–1967* (Kuala Lumpur: Oxford University Press, 1982); Salim Said, *Genesis of Power: General Sudirman and the Indonesian Military in Politics, 1945–49* (Jakarta: Pustaka Sinar Harapan; Singapore: Institute of Southeast Asian Studies, 1992).

7. Marcus Mietzner, *Military Politics, Islam, and the State in Indonesia: From Turbulent Transition to Democratic Consolidation* (Singapore: Institute of Southeast Asian Studies, 2009), 37–67.

8. Ian McFarling, *The Dual Function of the Indonesian Armed Forces: Military Politics in Indonesia* (Canberra: Australian Defence Studies Centre, 1996), 37.

9. George McTurnan Kahin, *Nationalism and Revolution in Indonesia* (Ithaca, N.Y.: Cornell University Press, 1952).

10. The end of the war also terminated the tenure of many military emergency administrators across the archipelago. In the areas in which fighting between the Dutch and the Indonesian army took place (mostly on Java and Sumatra), military officers had acted as de facto heads of local government because civilian officials had been captured or had fled. With the war over, the military no longer fulfilled these functions.

11. Sundhaussen, *The Road to Power*, 65.

12. Most important, the regional rebellions between 1956 and 1958 as well as the ongoing Islamist insurgencies in West Java, Aceh, and South Sulawesi catapulted the military back into the very position of emergency administrators that it had reluctantly vacated after 1945.

13. Herbert Feith, "Dynamics of Guided Democracy," in Ruth McVey, ed., *Indonesia*, 2d rev. ed., 309–409 (New Haven, Conn.: HRAF Press, 1967).

14. Jamie Mackie, "Inevitable or Avoidable? Interpretations of the Collapse of Parliamentary Democracy," in David Bourchier and John Legge, eds., *Democracy in Indonesia: 1950s and 1990s*, 26–38 (Clayton, Australia: Monash University, 1994).

15. See Amos Perlmutter, *The Military and Politics in Modern Times* (New Haven, Conn.: Yale University Press, 1977), and Eric A. Nordlinger, *Soldiers in Politics: Military Coups and Governments* (Englewood Cliffs, N.J.: Prentice-Hall, 1977).

16. What exactly happened on September 30, 1965, remains unclear and will probably never be completely revealed. But it seems plausible that a small group of PKI officials and pro-Communist TNI elements did indeed try to decapitate the military leadership and take power temporarily, probably believing that the latter planned to move against Sukarno. Presented with this welcome chance of grabbing power and destroying the PKI, Suharto assumed control and did not relinquish it for almost thirty-three years. See John Roosa, *Pretext for Mass Murder: The September 30th Movement and Suharto's Coup d'État in Indonesia* (Madison: University of Wisconsin Press, 2006).

17. Not coincidentally, one of the most serious challenges from within the military against Suharto's leadership was launched in 1978—at the time when the president was leaving active military service. The fact that he survived the crisis proved that he was willing (and able) to build a power base outside of his military circles.

18. Edward Aspinall, *Opposing Suharto: Compromise, Resistance, and Regime Change in Indonesia* (Stanford, Calif.: Stanford University Press, 2005).

19. David R. Mares, *Civil–Military Relations: Building Democracy and Regional Security in Latin America, Southern Asia, and Central Europe* (Boulder, Colo.: Westview Press, 1998), 7.

20. It was widely believed that Suharto had intended to appoint Habibie as vice president in 1993, but the military preempted this move by publicly nominating Try Sutrisno, its commander. Ignoring the military's nomination would have exposed splits within the regime, so Suharto decided to accept Try as his deputy. However, he also retaliated by isolating Try from government business and reducing the military's representation in Parliament.

21. Anders Uhlin, *Indonesia and the "Third Wave of Democratization": The Indonesian Pro-democracy Movement in a Changing World* (Richmond, U.K.: Curzon, 1997), 58.

22. One week before his resignation, Suharto had announced his plan to reestablish a notoriously repressive security agency that had dealt effectively with regime opposition in the 1970s. But Wiranto, commander of the armed forces, objected to the initiative, and Suharto subsequently aborted it. See Takashi Shiraishi, "The Indonesian Military in Politics," in Adam Schwarz and Jonathan Paris, eds., *The Politics of Post-Suharto Indonesia*, 73–86 (New York: Council on Foreign Relations Press, 1999), and Tatik Hafidz, *Fading Away? The Political Role of the Army in Indonesia's Transition to Democracy, 1998–2001* (Singapore: Institute of Defence and Strategic Studies, 2006).

23. Mietzner, *Military Politics, Islam, and the State in Indonesia*, 122–138.

24. David Bourchier, "Skeletons, Vigilantes, and the Armed Forces' Fall from Grace," in Arief Budiman, Barbara Hatley, and Damien Kingsbury, eds., *Reformasi: Crisis and Change in Indonesia*, 149–172 (Clayton, Australia: Monash Asia Institute, 1999).

25. Adam Schwarz, *A Nation in Waiting: Indonesia's Search for Stability*, 3rd printing (Singapore: Talisman, 2004).

26. The only group pushing for a more "revolutionary" solution to the crisis were the students, but even they began to disband after it became clear that most Indonesians were satisfied with Suharto's removal and were prepared to give Habibie a chance. Most oppositional figures rejected the idea of a transitional government in which they all would be represented because the distrust among them was so deep that cooperation seemed impossible.

27. "Reformasi ABRI batasi masa jabatan presiden" (ABRI Reform Limits Presidential Term), *Republika*, May 26, 1998.

28. Marco Bünte, "Indonesia's Protracted Decentralization: Contested Reforms and Their Unintended Consequences," in Marco Bünte and Andreas Ufen, eds., *Democratization in Post-Suharto Indonesia*, 102–123 (New York: Routledge, 2009).

29. The military reform agenda was formulated at an internal military seminar in September 1998; Habibie apparently did not provide policy directives for this event.

30. Jun Honna, "From Dwifungsi to NKRI: Regime Change and Political Activism of the Indonesian Miliarty," in Bünte and Ufen, eds., *Democratization in Post-Suharto Indonesia*, 226–248.

31. Mietzner, *Military Politics, Islam, and the State*, 207.

32. One scenario developed within TNI was the division of East Timor into a western and eastern part, with the West remaining in the Indonesian Republic. See Douglas Kammen, "The Trouble with Normal: The Indonesian Military, Paramilitaries, and the Final Solution to East Timor," in Benedict R. O'G. Anderson,

ed., *Violence and the State in Suharto's Indonesia*, 156–188 (Ithaca, N.Y.: Southeast Asia Program, Cornell University, 2001).

33. Angel Rabasa and John Haseman, *The Military and Democracy in Indonesia: Challenges, Politics, and Power* (Santa Monica, Calif.: RAND, 2003), 115.

34. The number of TNI representatives was reduced from seventy-five in the 1997 Parliament to thirty-eight in the legislature elected in 1999. Representatives of political parties initially wanted to grant TNI only "two or three" unelected members, but Yudhoyono, who negotiated the electoral laws with Parliament, criticized this offer as "cruel." Author's interview with Zarkasih Nur, senior member of Parliament, Jakarta, February 10, 1999.

35. Harold Crouch, *Political Reform in Indonesia After Suharto* (Singapore: Institute of Southeast Asian Studies, 2010).

36. The military had a very strained relationship with Wahid. That was not unusual, however—virtually every other political party or group was in permanent conflict with the president. Wahid was impeached almost unanimously.

37. Blair King, "Empowering the Presidency: Interests and Perceptions in Indonesia's Constitutional Reforms, 1999–2002," Ph.D. diss., Ohio State University, 2004.

38. Honna, "From Dwifungsi to NKRI."

39. Author's interview with Lieutenant-General (ret.) Agus Widjojo, Jakarta, August 15, 2007.

40. The People's Consultative Assembly had in 1999 still elected the president, and TNI's thirty-eight delegates were a small but significant voting block in the seven-hundred-member body. After 2004, however, the assembly lost its authority to elect the head of state and thus much of its relevance.

41. Edward Aspinall, *Islam and Nation: Separatist Rebellion in Aceh, Indonesia* (Stanford, Calif.: Stanford University Press, 2009).

42. Michael Morfit, The Road to Helsinki: The Aceh Agreement and Indonesia's Democratic Development," *Internation Negotiation 12* (1): 111–143.

43. Author's interview with General (ret.) Endriartono Sutarto, Jakarta, June 11, 2007.

44. Author's interview with Minister of Defense Juwono Sudarsono, Jakarta, May 1, 2007.

45. Interview with General Sutarto, June 11, 2007.

46. Mietzner, *Military Politics, Islam, and the State*, 360–382.

47. According to a USAID-sponsored opinion survey, support for democracy stood at 48 percent in 2008, with only 7 percent of respondents endorsing nondemocratic forms of government. See Democracy International, Inc., *Indonesia Annual Public Opinion Surveys—2008 Report* (Bethesda, Md.: Democracy International, November 11, 2008).

48. Andreas Ufen, *Political Parties in Post-Suharto Indonesia: Between* Politik Aliran *and* "Philippinisation," Paper no. 37 (Hamburg: German Institute of Global and Area Studies, 2006).

49. Jaap Hoogenboexem, "Civil Society and Control of the Military," paper presented at the ERGOMAS Ninth Biennal Conference, École Militaire, Paris, December 9–11, 2004.

50. Generals who were rivals for key military positions during their active service often become bitter political opponents after their retirement as well. Many national and local elections have been contested by a number of deeply antagonistic military candidates.

51. "Prajurit malu, prajurit tumbang di pilkada" (Officers Embarrassed About Failure in Local Elections), *Jawa Pos*, April 26, 2008.

52. "RUU peradilan militer belum tuntas" (Military Justice Bill Not Yet Completed), *Kompas*, July 29, 2008; author's interviews with Andreas Pereira, chairman of the parliamentary committee in charge of deliberating the bill on the military justice system, Jakarta, May 7, 2007, and November 14, 2008.

53. Marcus Mietzner, "Soldiers, Parties, and Bureaucrats: Illicit Fund-Raising in Contemporary Indonesia," *South East Asian Research* 16 (2) (2008): 225–254.

54. Human Rights Watch, *Out of Sight: Endemic Abuse and Impunity in Papua's Central Highlands* (New York: Human Rights Watch, July 4, 2007).

55. Samuel Finer, *The Man on Horesback: The Role of the Military in Politics* (London: Transaction, 2002).

56. See, for instance, Mainwaring, *Transitions to Democracy and Democratic Consolidation*.

57. The Freedom House data for 2009 are available at http://www.freedomhouse.org/uploads/fiw09/FIW09_Tables&GraphsForWeb.pdf, accessed March 21, 2009.

58. See Larry Diamond and Leonardo Morlino, "The Quality of Democracy: An Overview," *Journal of Democracy* 15 (2) (2004): 20–31.

6. Indonesian Government Approaches to Radical Islam Since 1998

1. Kevin O'Rourke, *Reformasi: The Struggle for Power in Post-Suharto Indonesia* (Sydney: Allen and Unwin, 2002), 186–88.

2. International Crisis Group (ICG), *Indonesia Backgrounder: Jihad in Central Sulawesi*, Asia Report no. 74 (Brussels: ICG, February 2004). Abu Bakar Ba'asyir and Adung went back in October 1998 to test the waters. They had no problem coming into the country and so returned to Malaysia with the message that it was safe to go home. ICG recorded interview with Adung, April 24, 2006. KOMPAK stands for "Komite Aksi Penanggulangan Akibat Krisis" (Crisis Management/Prevention Committee), but the group is known simply as Mujahidin KOMPAK.

3. Ali Imron, *Ali Imron: Sang pengebom* (Ali Imron: The Bomber) (Jakarta: Republika Jakarta, November 2007). The more radical members of JI saw the Ambon conflict as a local manifestation of the larger conflict involving an international "Crusader–Zionist alliance" led by the United States against Islam. Fighting local Christians was thus a way of taking on an international enemy. Whether Ambon was a legitimate jihad or not, however, was a matter of fierce debate within JI. See ICG, *Indonesia Backgrounder*.

4. Wakalah Jawa Wustho, "Laporan perkembangan Da'wah Wal Irsyad" (Report of Religious Outreach Developments), June 1999, unpublished, copy in author's files.

5. Coming to Habibie's support were many of the militant Muslim groups such as the Komite Indonesia untuk Solidaritas Dunia Islam (Indonesian Committee for Solidarity with World Islam) that had been drawn into Jakarta power politics in the late 1990s by Prabowo Subianto, Suharto's son-in-law. Wiranto, who cast his lot with Habibie and whose power depended on staying with him, saw Prabowo as his major rival and succeeded in ousting him. One of his priorities, then, became to co-opt Prabowo supporters, especially those, like some of the Muslim organizations, that had a mass base. Personal communication from Jeremy Wagstaff, author and political analyst, March 26, 2009.

6. Institut Studi Arus Informasi, *Premanisme politik* (Political Thuggery) (Jakarta: Institut Studi Arus Informasi, March 2000), 90–102; O'Rourke, *Reformasi*, 180–181.

7. Noorhaidi Hasan, *Laskar Jihad: Islam, Militancy, and the Quest for Identity in Post–New Order Indonesia* (Ithaca, N.Y.: Cornell Southeast Asia Program, 2006), 100. It is doubtful whether anyone in the government had any consciousness of the Salafis' strong ties to ulama in Saudi Arabia and Yemen or whether this knowledge would have made any difference if they had.

8. Imron, *Ali Imron*, 55.

9. KOMPAK was created in 1998 under the auspices of Dewan Dakwah Islam Indonesia, the Indonesian Islamic Propagation Council. Its head in Solo was JI member Aris Munandar, who became the main conduit for funding the Ambon operation.

10. In the Ambon conflict, as in Poso, Muslims and Christians were equally perpetrators and victims. The Christian side, because of its international network, including through diaspora Christian Moluccan groups in the Netherlands, succeeded in convincing many in the international community that they were overwhelmingly the victims. Within Indonesia, Muslim networks portrayed Christians as the aggressors. The balance did shift in favor of the Muslims after a Muslim militia called Laskar Jihad (Jihad Militia), supported by the Tentara Nasional Indonesia (TNI, Indonesian National Military), arrived in Ambon in April 2000.

11. Author's interview with Indonesian investigator, Jakarta, June 2008.

12. The TNI at the time claimed and continues to claim that the major instigator of violence had been elements of the Republic of the South Moluccas, a movement that the army had defeated in the 1950s but that retained a small band of supporters in Maluku. "Christian separatists" and their foreign backers, in many conservative Muslims' view, were also responsible for the independence movement in East Timor.

13. "Gus Dur sampaikan surat prihatin" (Gus Dur Conveys a Letter of Concern), *Pontianak Post*, August 2, 2000.

14. The officials blamed were Prabowo Subianto, the former army strategic reserve commander whom Wiranto had sacked, and Hartono, an official close to the Suharto family. See "Prabowo bantah tudingan Gus Dur" (Prabowo Denies Gus Dur's Accusation), January 16, 2002. BIN may have exploited one of those bombings (Medan); but for purposes of blaming the Acehnese rebel movement, GAM, rather than to destabilize the government.

15. One of the eleven cities where bombs went off was Medan, North Sumatra; a member of GAM was arrested for involvement, as was a man with longstanding ties to the military. JI members were clearly involved as well, but the bombing was blamed on GAM.

16. ICG, *Indonesia: The Implications of the Timor Trials*, Asia Briefing no. 16 (Brussels: ICG, May 2002).

17. Interrogation of Imam Samudra, November 28, 2002, in Abu Bakar Ba'asyir case dossier, Central Jakarta District Court, 2003. At another point in his interrogation, Imam Samudra gave a longer list of reasons: "(a) to fight the brutality of the Crusader Army of the United States and its allies—Britain, Australia, Germany, France, Japan, Russian Orthodox, and so on; (b) as the duty of all Muslims to retaliate for the two hundred thousand innocent men, women, and infants who fell under thousands of tons of bombs in September 2001 in Afghanistan; (c) because Australia intervened to separate East Timor from Indonesia as part of the international Crusader conspiracy; (d) because of the intervention of Crusader forces who worked with infidel Hindus in India to annihilate Muslims in Kashmir; (e) as a response to the brutality and involvement of Crusader forces to the ethnic cleansing in Ambon, Poso, Halmahera, and elsewhere; (f) to defend Bosnian Muslims who were being exterminated by Crusader forces; (g) to undertake Muslims' individual obligation to wage a global war on Jews and Christians in all Muslim countries; (h) as an expression of the Muslim community, unfettered by geographic boundaries; (i) to execute Allah's order in Surat An-Nisa on everyone's duty to defend innocent men, women, and children who become the targets of the inhumane American terrorists and their allies; (j) as a warning to Christians and Jews against the effort led by America and its allies to colonize the two most holy places of Islam; (k) so that American terrorists and their allies understand that the price of Muslims' blood comes high and cannot be exploited; (l) so that American terrorists understand the pain and bitterness of losing mothers, husbands, children, and wives because they have caused the deaths of Muslims around the world; (m) to show to Allah that we will do our utmost to defend vulnerable Muslims and will fight to oppose imperialists and American terrorists and their allies (may Allah curse and destroy them)." Author's translation of the original transcript.

18. Quoted in Aly Gufron bin Nurhasyim, *Jihad bom Bali: Sebuah pembelaan* (The Bali Bombings Jihad: A Defense), handwritten copy obtained by the author, no pagination, author's translation.

19. Author's interview with senior prosecutor, Jakarta, April 2008.

20. Hasan, *Laskar Jihad*, 198–199.

21. See, for example, "Noordin M Top penyusup Malaysia yang takut kemajuan Indonesia?" (Was Noordin Top Smuggled Here from Malaysia, Which Fears Indonesia's Rise?), September 25, 2009, at http://www.infospesial.com, accessed September 30, 2009.

22. Quoted in "Fugitive Militant Slain in Indonesia," *Washington Post*, September 18, 2009.

23. "Proyek Bali" (The Bali Project), document found on Dr. Azhari's computer, November 2005, my translation.

24. One of the reasons the central government had largely ignored Poso may have been that it did not want to imply that the Malino Accords had failed. See ICG, *Indonesia: Poso on the Edge*, Asia Report no. 127 (Brussels: ICG, January 24, 2007).

25. The new *pesantren* is a branch of Gontor, the school that produced some of Indonesia's best-known moderate intellectuals but also produced Abu Bakar Ba'asyir.

26. "Pengambilan sidik jari menghina pesantren" (Taking Fingerprints Is a Slight to Pesantrens), December 7, 2005, at http://www.mail-archive.com/keluarga-is-lam@yahoogroups.com/msg02186.html, accessed January 10, 2010.

27. Quoted in ICG, *Indonesia: Implications of the Ahmadiyah Decree*, Asia Briefing no. 78 (Brussels: ICG, July 7, 2008), 14.

28. Author's interview with Brigadier General (Police) Dr. Badrodin Haiti, Central Sulawesi chief of police, Palu, Central Sualwesi Indonesia, November 30, 2006. A little more knowledge of the local rifts would have shown that there was no point in trying to use Rizieq as a counterweight to Arsal because the local FPI head was Arsal's bitterest rival—there was no way that Arsal supporters were going to be attracted to FPI.

29. Laskar Jihad disbanded a day after the Bali attack, but the reasons were internal, and the process had begun long before Bali. See Hasan, *Laskar Jihad*, and ICG, *Indonesia: Why Salafism and Terrorism Mostly Don't Mix*, Asia Report no. 83 (Brussels: ICG, September 1, 2004).

30. See World Bank, "Aceh Conflict Monitoring Update," December 8–February 9, 2009, at http://www.internal-displacement.org/8025708F004CE90B/(httpDocuments)/22DD335ED31ABF04C125758400532081/$file/Aceh+Conflict+Monitoring+Update+December+08+-+February+09.pdf, accessed October 30, 2012; "Membela saudara seiman kita" (Defending Those Who Share Our Faith), *Modus Aceh*, February 5, 2009. The GAM-led government in Aceh is widely seen as having to slow down or even roll back the application of Islamic law in the province.

31. Imron, *Ali Imron*.

32. ICG, *Indonesia: Deradicalisation and Indonesian Prisons*, Asia Report no. 142 (Brussels: ICG, November 19, 2007). What the government called a "deradicalization program" was a series of ad hoc efforts to provide prisoners detained or convicted on terrorism charges with additional food and sometimes financial assistance for their families in exchange for cooperation and providing information. There was no systematic effort at religious counseling to move them away from jihadi tenets. After some twenty former prisoners were found in 2010 to be involved directly or indirectly in setting up a military training camp in Aceh, officials realized a more systematic approach was needed.

33. ICG, *Indonesia: Jihadi Surprise in Aceh*, Asia Report no. 189 (Brussels: ICG, April 20, 2010).

34. See Muhammad Ismail Yusanto, "Selamatkan Indonesia dengan syariah" (Saving Indonesia with Islamic Law), paper presented at the National Seminar on Implementation of Syariat Values in Society and State, November 25, 2007, location unknown.

35. The fatwa is reproduced in "Tanggapan Hizbut Tahrir Indonesia terhadap fatwa MUI tentang golput" (Hizbut Tahrir Indonesia's View of the Indonesian Ulama Council's Fatwa on Abstaining from Voting), January 28, 2009, Document no. 152/PU/E/01/09, Jakarta, at http://ppiuk.org/node/537, accessed February 2, 2010.

36. "Fatwa MUI: Golput wajib! Golput haram!" (The Indonesia Ulama Council Fatwa: Abstention Is Obligatory! Abstention Is Forbidden!), February 11, 2009, my translation, at http://fpionline.multiply.com/journal/item/70, accessed October 30, 2012.

37. "Tanggapan Hizbut Tahrir Indonesia terhadap fatwa."

38. "Pilih Islam atau Democrazy" (Choose Islam or "Democrazy"), flyer handed out February 15, 2009, as-Salaam Mosque, Citerueup, Bogor, author's translation.

39. JAT remains committed to jihad (here its teachings are virtually identical to JI's), and in 2010 police found it had a secret wing for military training. There was little evidence that it was interested in mounting operations in Indonesia, but after more than a dozen jihadis linked to the Aceh training camp were killed by police, one JAT cell carried out execution-style murders of three police officers. It was not clear as of late 2010 that these killings were sanctioned by the JAT leadership. But JAT was already showing signs of disarray when one of the most militant ulama on the executive council of the new body, Oman Rochman (a.k.a. Aman Abdurrahman), pulled out—or was pushed out—for taking too hard a line and effectively demanding that all Indonesian officials and politicians who do not fully support Islamic law be declared *kafir* (unbelievers). Oman was responsible for a bomb-making class that led to an explosion in Cimanggis in March 2004. He was imprisoned, released in July 2008, and rearrested in March 2010 for his role in recruiting participants for the Aceh camp. He is recognized as the most influential scholar within the radical community and is the main translator of al-Maqdisi's work from Arabic into Indonesian.

40. For a good background paper on HTI, see Greg Fealy, "Hizbut Tahrir in Indonesia: Seeking a 'Total' Islamic Identity," in Shahram Akbarzadeh and Fethi Mansouri, eds., *Islam and Political Violence: Muslim Diaspora and Radicalism in the West*, 151–164 (London: Tauris Academic Studies, 2007). It is worth noting, however, that although Indonesia routinely imprisons Papuans and Moluccans for flying the flags of their respective independence movements, it has never questioned the use of HTI's flag, which in its own way is calling for an alternative government.

7. How Indonesia Survived: Comparative Perspectives on State Disintegration and Democratic Integration

1. Most Indonesia specialists in fact argued that state breakup was unlikely. See, for example, Robert Cribb, "Not the Next Yugoslavia: Prospects for the Disintegration of Indonesia," *Australian Journal of International Affairs* 53 (2) (1999): 169–178; Donald Emmerson, "Will Indonesia Survive?" *Foreign Affairs*

79 (3) (May–June 2000): 95–106 ; Sylvia Tiwon, "From East Timor to Aceh: The Disintegration of Indonesia?" *Bulletin of Concerned Asian Scholars* 32 (1–2) (2000): 97–104; Edward Aspinall and Mark T. Berger, "The Breakup of Indonesia? Nationalisms After Decolonisation and the Contradictions of Modernity in Post–Cold War Southeast Asia," *Third World Quarterly* 22 (6) (2001): 1003–1024.

2. The figures are derived from Gerry van Klinken, *Communal Violence and Democratization in Indonesia: Small Town Wars* (London: Routledge, 2007), 4. Van Klinken in turn draws on Ashutosh Varshney, Rizal Panggabean, and Mohammad Zulfan Tadjoeddin, *Patterns of Collective Violence in Indonesia (1990–2003)* (Jakarta: United Nations Support, 2004) and my own estimate of deaths in Aceh. The figures are likely to be a serious underestimate: the United Nations report is based on a survey of newspaper reports, and my own estimate of 7,200 deaths in Aceh is based on official and newspaper tallies.

3. Mark R. Beissinger, *Nationalist Mobilization and the Collapse of the Soviet State* (Cambridge: Cambridge University Press, 2002), 3.

4. See, for example, Ann Booth, "Can Indonesia Survive as a Unitary State?" *Indonesia and the Malay World* 20 (58) (1992): 32–47.

5. Ted Robert Gurr, "Ethnic Warfare on the Wane," *Foreign Affairs* (May–June 2000): 52–64.

6. See, for example, Pranab Bardhan, "Decentralization of Governance and Development," *Journal of Economic Perspectives* 16 (4) (2002): 185–205.

7. "Observations on Indonesia's Fiscal Decentralization from a Panel of International Experts," January 2002, at http://siteresources.worldbank.org/INTINDONESIA/Resources/Decentralization/Panel_thoughts_on_IndonesiaII.pdf, accessed January 23, 2010.

8. Beissinger, *Nationalist Mobilization*, 448.

9. I analyze this mobilizational cycle in Edward Aspinall, *Opposing Suharto: Compromise, Resistance, and Regime Change in Indonesia* (Stanford, Calif.: Stanford University Press, 2005), 202–238.

10. "Dua tokoh proklamasikan Riau merdeka" (Two Leaders Proclaim Free Riau), *Jawa Pos*, March 8, 1999.

11. "People's Congress Votes for Riau Independence," *Jakarta Post*, February 2, 2000; "Gerakan Riau Merdeka latih 20.000 tentara di Malaysia" (Free Riau Movement Trains 20,000 Fighters in Malaysia), *Detik.com*, July 2, 2000.

12. Adrian Vickers, "Bali Merdeka? Migration, Tourism, and Hindu Revivalism," in Minako Sakai, ed., *Beyond Jakarta: Regional Autonomy and Local Societies in Indonesia* (Adelaide: Crawford House, 2002), 81.

13. "Mahasiswa Makassar tuntut Sulawesi merdeka" (Makassar Students Demand Free Sulawesi), *Republika*, October 23, 1999. Even more bizarrely, some supporters of Habibie's successor, Abdurrahman Wahid, threatened they would establish a "State of East Java" if he were removed from office: "FKB sepakat penugasan Mega lewat tap MPR" (National Awakening Fraction Agrees to Appointment of Mega Via an MPR Decree), *Bernas*, May 8, 2001.

14. Examples include a law on the national education system, specifically its provisions regarding religious education, and an antipornography bill, which some Hindus, Christians, and other minorities viewed as an expression of Islamist aspirations: "Education Bill Continues to Divide Indonesians," *Jakarta Post*, May 12, 2003; "Huge Turnout as Balinese Decry Porn Bill," *Jakarta Post*, March 4, 2006.

15. See, for example, Freek Colombijn, "Where There Is Nothing to Imagine: Nationalism in Riau," in Peter J. M. Nas, Gerard A. Persoon, and Rivke Jaffe, eds., *Framing Indonesian Realities: Essays in Symbolic Anthropology in Honour of Reimar Schefold*, 333–370 (Leiden: KITLV Press, 2003).

16. See, for example, van Klinken, *Communal Violence and Democratization in Indonesia*, and Jamie S. Davidson, *From Rebellion to Riots: Collective Violence on Indonesian Borneo* (Madison: University of Wisconsin Press, 2008).

17. Tim Johnston, "Indonesia Takes Final Steps Towards Devolved Democracy," *Financial Times* (London), June 3, 2005.

18. Juan J. Linz and Alfred Stepan, *Problems of Democratic Transition and Consolidation: Southern Europe, South America, and Post-Communist Europe* (Baltimore: Johns Hopkins University Press, 1996), 101.

19. The regulation at the time of writing is that political parties must have branches in at least 60 percent of the provinces, in 50 percent of the districts in those provinces, and in 25 percent of the subdistricts in those districts (Art. 3.2.d. of Law No. 2 of 2008 on Political Parties).

20. Dawn Brancati, "Decentralization: Fueling the Fire or Dampening the Flames of Ethnic Conflict and Secessionism?" *International Organization* 60 (2006), 656.

21. M. Ryaas Rasyid, "Regional Autonomy and Local Politics in Indonesia," in Edward Aspinall and Greg Fealy, eds., *Democratisation and Decentralisation in Indonesia: Local Power and Politics* (Singapore: Institute of Southeast Asian Studies, 2003), 63.

22. Sidney Tarrow, *Power in Movement: Social Movements and Contentious Politics*, 2nd ed. (Cambridge: Cambridge University Press, 1998), 74.

23. Quoted in Richard Chauvel, *Constructing Papuan Nationalism: History, Ethnicity, and Adaptation* (Washington, D.C.: East West Center, 2005), 9.

24. *Human Security Report 2005: War and Peace in the 21st Century* (New York: Oxford University Press, 2005), 149.

25. Leon Aron, "The 'Mystery' of the Soviet 'Collapse,'" *Journal of Democracy* 17 (2) (2006), 29.

26. The most widely cited exception is in Lithuania, where Soviet troops were mobilized in response to Lithuania's March 1991 declaration of independence, leading to the deaths of fourteen civilians.

27. Beissinger cites official statistics that suggest that 1,314 persons died in interethnic conflicts in the former Soviet Union between January 1988 and May 1991 (*Nationalist Mobilization*, 276) (this figure, of course, does not count the many persons who perished in the various conflicts that followed the dissolution of the Soviet state).

28. Address by H. E. Megawati Sukarnoputri, president of the Republic of Indonesia, at the United States–Indonesia Society Gala Dinner, Washington, D.C., September 19, 2001, copy sent to the author by email.

29. For one example, see Rizal Mallarangeng, "Aceh, ujian pertama dan terakhir" (Aceh, the First and Final Test), *Kompas*, November 20, 1999.

30. Human Rights Watch, *Aceh Under Martial Law: Inside the Secret War* (New York: Human Rights Watch, 2003), at http://hrw.org/reports/2003/indonesia1203/indonesia1203.pdf, accessed December 10, 2003; Amnesty International, *New Military Operations, Old Patterns of Human Rights Abuses in Aceh* (New York: Amnesty International, 2004), at http://web.amnesty.org/library/pdf/ASA210332004ENGLISH/$File/ASA2103304.pdf, accessed June 1, 2004.

31. Jennifer Robinson, "Freedom of Expression: Whether Papuans Support Autonomy or Independence, They Should Be Allowed to Speak Freely," *Inside Indonesia* 94 (2008), at http://www.insideindonesia.org/feature-editions/freedom-of-expression, accessed October 28, 2008.

32. "Empat anggota Gerakan Negara Sunda jadi tersangka" (Four Members of the Sunda State Movement Named Suspects), *Koran Tempo*, May 24, 2006; "300 anggota FKM masih buron" (300 FKM Members Still Fugitives), *Tempo Interaktif*, July 4, 2004.

33. Edward Aspinall, *The Helsinki Agreement: A More Promising Basis for Peace in Aceh?* (Washington, D.C.: East West Center, 2005), 7–14.

34. Anthony D. Smith, "State-Making and Nation-Building," in John A. Hall, ed., *States in History* (Oxford: Basil Blackwell, 1989), 261–262. I am grateful to Mark T. Berger for drawing my attention to this quotation.

35. Valerie Bunce, *Subversive Institutions: The Design and the Destruction of Socialism and the State* (Cambridge: Cambridge University Press, 1999), 136.

36. Peter Radan, *The Break-Up of Yugoslavia and International Law* (London: Routledge, 2002).

37. Valerie Bunce, *Minority Politics in Ethnofederal States: Cooperation, Autonomy, or Secession?* Working Paper Series no. 8-07 (Ithaca, N.Y.: Mario Einaudi Center for International Studies, Cornell University, 2007), 7.

38. Rogers Brubaker, *Nationalism Reframed: Nationhood and the National Question in the New Europe* (Cambridge: Cambridge University Press, 1996), 23.

39. Ronald Grigor Suny, "Learning from Empire: Russia and the Soviet Union," in Craig Calhoun, Frederick Cooper, and Kevin W. Moore, eds., *Lessons of Empire: Imperial Histories and American Power* (New York: New Press, 2005), 88.

40. Bunce, *Subversive Institutions*, 137.

41. Robert Cribb, "The Historical Roots of Indonesia's New Order: Beyond the Colonial Comparison," in Edward Aspinall and Greg Fealy, eds., *Indonesia: Soeharto's New Order and Its Legacy* (Canberra: Australian National University E-Press, 2010), 70.

42. Michael S. Malley, " New Rules, Old Structures, and the Limits of Democratic Decentralization," in Aspinall and Fealy, eds., *Democratisation and Decentralisation in Indonesia*, 107.

43. Cribb, "Not the Next Yugoslavia," 175.

44. This argument is developed in Edward Aspinall, *Islam and Nation: Separatist Rebellion in Aceh, Indonesia* (Stanford, Calif.: Stanford University Press, 2009), 18–48.

45. Robert Cribb, "Independence for Java? New National Projects for an Old Empire," in Grayson Lloyd and Shannon L. Smith, eds., *Indonesia Today: Challenges of History*, 298–307 (Singapore: Institute of Southeast Asian Studies, 2001).

46. Edward Aspinall, "Democratization and Ethnic Politics in Indonesia: Nine Theses," *Journal of East Asian Studies* 11 (2) (2011): 289–319.

47. Linz and Stepan, *Problems of Democratic Transition and Consolidation*, 16, 29.

48. Alfred Stepan, Juan J. Linz, and Yogendra Yadav, *Crafting State-Nations: India and Other Multinational Democracies* (Baltimore: Johns Hopkins University Press, 2011), 5. These authors also insist that the maintenance of strong state functions at the center was imperative to the survival of these states, unlike Yugoslavia, and what emerges are not polarized nation-only identities as in Serbia and Croatia, but nonpolarized multiple and complementary identities equally proud of being Catalan and Spanish or equally proud of being Tamil and Indian.

8. Contours of Sharia in Indonesia

1. For estimates of the numbers of such regulations and more generally for an overall argument about incentives for such regulations that provides a macrolevel complement to this chapter, see Michael Buehler, "The Rise of Shari'a By-laws in Indonesian Districts: An Indication for Changing Patterns of Power Accumulation and Political Corruption," *South East Asia Research* 16 (2): 255–285.

2. On the historical aspects of what follows in this chapter, see Daniel S. Lev, *Islamic Courts in Indonesia: A Study in the Political Bases of Legal Institutions* (Berkeley: University of California Press, 1972); Mark E. Cammack, "The Indonesian Islamic Judiciary," in R. Michael Feener and Mark E. Cammack, eds., *Islamic Law in Contemporary Indonesia: Ideas and Institutions*, 146–169 (Cambridge, Mass.: Harvard University Press, 2007).

3. For Aceh and North Sumatra, see Anthony Reid, *The Blood of the People: Revolution and the End of Traditional Rule in Northern Sumatra* (Kuala Lumpur: Oxford University Press, 1979).

4. John R. Bowen, "Normative Pluralism in Indonesia: Regions, Religions, and Ethnicities," in Will Kymlicka and Boagang He, eds., *Multiculturalism in Asia: Theoretical Perspectives*, 152–169 (Oxford: Oxford University Press, 2005).

5. For the history of the Compilation, see Cammack, "The Indonesian Islamic Judiciary."

6. Mark E. Cammack, Helen Donovan, and Tim B. Heaton, "Islamic Divorce Law and Practice in Indonesia," in Feener and Cammack, eds., *Islamic Law in Contemporary Indonesia*, 99–127; John R. Bowen, *Islam, Law, and Equality in Indonesia: An Anthropology of Public Reasoning* (Cambridge: Cambridge University Press, 2003), esp. 173–199.

7. "Pemerintah cabut 530 perda terkait pajak dan retribusi daerah" (The Government Overturns 530 Regional Regulations Concerning Taxes and Regional Revenues), *Hukumonline*, March 29, 2006.

8. Peraturan Daerah Kabupaten Indramayu (Regional Regulation in Indramayu Region), July 1999); Peraturan Daerah Kota Palembang (Regional Regulation in Palembang City, February 2004); Peraturan Daerah Kota Tangerang (Regional Regulation in Tangerang City, August 2005); Peraturan Daerah Propinsi Sulawesi Utara (Regional Regulation in North Sulawesi Province, January 2004). The Tangerang regulation was upheld by the Supreme Court in 2007.

9. In a 2008 publication, Robin Bush counted seventy-eight regional regulations having to do with morality or religion, but she did not include circulars or directives. She considers about half to be of the morals sort and half to deal with Islam. See Robin Bush, "Regional Sharia Regulations in Indonesia: Anomaly or Symptom?" in Greg Fealy and Sally White, eds., *Expressing Islam: Religious Life and Politics in Indonesia*, 174–191 (Singapore: Institute of Southeast Asian Studies, 2008).

10. *Surat ederan bupati Cianjur No. 451/2717/ASSDA.1* (Circular No. 451/2717/ASSDA.1 from Cianjur Regional Head), author's collection.

11. *Rencana strategis kabupaten Tasikmalaya tahun 2001–2005* (Strategic Plan for Tasikmalaya Region 2001–2005) (Tasikmalaya: Regional Government, 2003), author's collection. On the relationship between Islamic character building and productivity strategies in Indonesia, see Daromir Rudnyckyj, *Spiritual Economies: Islam and the Afterlife of Development* (Ithaca, N.Y.: Cornell University Press, 2010).

12. *Peraturan daerah Kota Tasikmalaya* (Regional Regulation in Tasikmalaya City) (December 2009), at http://dishubkominfo.tasikmalayakota.go.id/regulasi/Perda-12–2009.PDF, accessed on November 24, 2009.

13. Bush, "Regional Sharia Regulations in Indonesia," 14.

14. See chapter 9 in this volume by Tim Lindsey and Simon Butt for a comprehensive analysis of problems of judicial review in the context of decentralization.

15. *Jakarta Post*, September 19, 2008.

16. Quoted in "Anti-perda syariat: Ahistoris dan perpanjangan tangan colonial" (Opposition to Sharia Regional Regulations: Ahistorical and an Extension of Colonial Interference), *Media Dakwah*, no. 368 (July 2006), 49.

17. This account is drawn from Moh Yasir Alimi, "Inculcating Islam: The Public Sphere and the Islamic Traditions of South Sulawesi," Ph.D. diss., Australian National University, Canberra, 2009.

18. M. B. Hooker, *Indonesian Syariah: Defining a National School of Islamic Law* (Singapore: Institute of Southeast Asian Studies, 2008), 259–264.

19. Alimi, "Inculcating Islam," 29.

20. Ibid., 148.

21. Ibid., 186.

22. On the complex motives and statements of GAM leaders on this question, see Edward Aspinall, *Islam and Nation: Separatist Rebellion in Aceh, Indonesia* (Stanford, Calif.: Stanford University Press, 2009), 193–219.

23. The WH must refer cases to local prosecutors for enforcement, who can carry out public canings but have no authority to jail offenders. The first officially sanctioned caning took place in North Aceh in mid-2005 and involved persons arrested for gambling during the previous months. Although enforcement rose thereafter, it has been sporadic in some places; indeed, in 2008 no cases were brought to trial in Banda Aceh because suspects were never put into jail by the police and simply walked away (*Serambi Indonesia,* January 17, 2009).

24. A much-needed media study would consider the considerably softer international reactions to the much more physically damaging canings carried out for many years in Singapore and the role that fears of sharia have played in directing and shaping international human rights complaints.

25. M. B. Hooker argues that through its fatwas the MPU has fashioned an Islamic rhetoric specific to Aceh, relying neither on the Compilation nor on Shafii *fiqh*, but on direct citations of Qur'an and hadith. The *teungku dayah* remain thoroughly Shafii in orientation, however. See Hooker, *Indonesian Syariah*, 246–249.

26. Author's interview with Muslim Ibrahim, chair, MPU, Banda Aceh, January 14, 2008.

27. Arskal Salim, *Politics and Islamisation in Aceh: An Update*, Occasional Seminar paper (Melbourne: Asian Law Centre, 2009).

28. Quoted in "Aceh Stoning Law May Be Revised," *Jakarta Globe*, October 20, 2009, at http://www.thejakartaglobe.com/home/aceh-stoning-law-may-be-revised/336676, accessed October 25, 2012.

29. Interviewed on Radio Australia, December 23, 2009, at http://radioaustralia.net, accessed October 25, 2012.

30. Another likely conflict will be between the Aceh draft law on rape, which explicitly excludes the possibility of a husband raping his wife, and the 2004 national law on domestic violence.

31. This section is based on my field notes at the conference, Banda Aceh, February 25, 2007.

32. Author's interview with Hamid Sarong, Banda Aceh, January 15, 2008.

9. Unfinished Business: Law Reform, Governance, and the Courts in Post-Suharto Indonesia

1. Sri Muniggar Sarasati, "Now Indonesia's Judicial Mafia Fight Gets Serious," *Jakarta Globe*, January 6, 2009.

2. Daniel S. Lev, "Judicial Authority and the Struggle for an Indonesian Rechsstaat," *Law and Society Review* 13 (1978), 37.

3. For these accounts, see Daniel S. Lev, "Between State and Society: Professional Lawyers and Law Reform in Indonesia," in Timothy Lindsey, ed., *Indonesia: Law and Society*, 2nd ed., 48–67 (Annandale, Australia: Federation Press, 2008); Sebastiaan Pompe, *The Indonesian Supreme Court: A Study of Institutional Collapse* (Ithaca, N.Y.: Southeast Asia Program, Cornell University, 2005); Timothy Lind-

sey and Dick Howard, *Corruption in Asia: Rethinking the Governance Paradigm* (Annandale, Australia: Federation Press, 2002); Timothy Lindsey, "The Criminal State: Premanisme and the New Indonesia," in Shannon Smith and Grayson Lloyd, ed., *Indonesia Today: Challenges of History*, 283–294 (Singapore: Institution of Southeast Asian Studies, 2001); Timothy Lindsey, "Black Letter, Black Market, and Bad Faith: Corruption and the Failure of Law Reform," in Chris Manning and Peter Van Diermen, eds., *Indonesia in Transition: Social Aspects of Reformasi and Crisis*, 278–292 (London: Zed Books, 2000).

4. On impunity for human rights abuses, see Jeff Herbert, "The Legal Framework of Human Rights in Indonesia," in Lindsey, ed., *Indonesia*, 2nd ed. 456–483.

5. Daniel S. Lev, "Comments on the Judicial Reform Program in Indonesia," paper presented at the Seminar on Current Developments in Monetary and Financial Law, International Monetary Fund, Washington, D.C., June 3, 2004, n.p., copy on file with the authors.

6. On the meaning of these terms, see Todung Mulya Lubis, *In Search of Human Rights: Legal Political Dilemmas of Indonesia's New Order, 1966–1990* (Jakarta: Gramedia Pustaka Utama, 1993); Timothy Lindsey, *Corruption in Asia: Rethinking the Governance Paradigm* (Annandale, Australia: Federation Press, 2003); David Linnan, "Indonesian Law Reform, or Once More Unto the Breach," in Lindsey, ed., *Indonesia*, 2nd ed., 68–93; and David Bourchier, "Positivism and Romanticism in Indonesian Legal Thought," in Timothy Lindsey, ed., *Indonesia: Law and Society*, 1st ed., 186–196 (Annandale, Australia: Federation Press, 1999).

7. Article 1(3) provides that "[t]he Indonesian State is a law state."

8. See, for example, the People's Consultative Council's Five-Year Development Plan of 1969–1970, cited in John Ball, *Indonesian Law: Commentary and Teaching Materials*, 2nd ed. (Sydney: University of Sydney, 1995), 365; Seno Adji, "An Indonesian Perspective on the American Constitutional Influence," in Lawrence Beer, ed., *Constitutionalism in Asia: Asian Views of the American Influence* (Berkeley: University of California Press, 1979), 107; Sudargo Gautama and Robert N. Hornick, *An Introduction to Indonesian Law: Unity in Diversity* (Bandung, Indonesia: Penerbit Alumni, 1983), 191; Lubis, *In Search of Human Rights,* 88; *Angin baru dari Simposium UI* (A New Breeze from the University of Indonesia Symposium) (Bandung, Indonesia: Penerbit Angkasa, 1966); and Justice Siahaan (dissenting) in Constitutional Court Decision No. 006/2003, reviewing Law No. 30 of 2002 on the Corruption Eradication Commission, p. III.

9. Simon Butt, "Judicial Review in Indonesia: Between Civil Law and Accountability? A Study of Constitutional Court Decisions 2003–2005," Ph.D. diss., Law Faculty, Melbourne University, 2007.

10. See Articles 28A–28J (Chapter XA) of the amended Constitution of 1945. A raft of statutes and other regulations has now been passed to implement Chapter XA. They include Presidential Decree No. 181 of 1998, regulating the Komnas Perempuan (National Commission for the Rights of Women); Law 39/1999, Human Rights Law, regulating the Komnas HAM (Komisi Nasional Hak Asasi Manusia, National Commission for Human Rights); Law 26/2000, establishing the

Pengadilan HAM (Pengadilan Hak Asasi Manusia, Human Rights Courts); Law 23/2002 on Child Protection; Presidential Decree 77/2003, establishing the Komisi Perlindungan Anak Indonesia (Commission for the Protection of Indonesian Children); Law 27/2004 on the Komisi Kebenaran dan Rekonsiliasi (Truth and Reconciliation Commission); and Law 23/2004 on the Elimination of Violence in Households. In addition, Indonesia has also signed a range of human rights conventions. These conventions include the Convention on the Elimination of All Forms of Discrimination Against Women, acceded to in 1984; the Convention on the Rights of the Child, ratified in 1990; the Convention Against Torture and Other Cruel, Inhumane, or Degrading Treatments or Punishments, acceded to in 1998; the Convention on the Elimination of All Forms of Racial Discrimination, acceded to in July 1999; the International Convention of Civil and Political Rights, acceded to in 2006; and the International Covenant on Economic, Social, and Cultural Rights, acceded to in 2006. See Timothy Lindsey, "Indonesian Constitutional Reform: Muddling Towards Democracy," *Singapore Journal of International and Comparative Law* 6 (1) (2002): 244–301.

11. Simon Butt and Timothy Lindsey, "Economic Reform When the Constitution Matters: Indonesia's Constitutional Court and Article 33," *Bulletin of Indonesian Economic Studies* 44 (2) (2008): 239–262.

12. As mentioned, these rights appear to include rights to legal aid, legal certainty, access to justice, a fair trial, and due process. Butt, "Judicial Review in Indonesia."

13. See Law No. 14 of 1970.

14. To give just one example, although the Supreme Court, under the oversight of the Ministry of Justice, had responsibility for conducting "technical juridical oversight" of the Religious Courts, it was the Department of Religious Affairs that "handled organizational, administrative, and financial aspects" of the Religious Court. In practice, it was often impossible to disentangle these two overlapping areas of ministerial authority, with the result that the Religious Courts were victims of institutional and budgetary rivalry between their two masters, neither of whom felt fully responsible for them.

15. Lev, "Judicial Authority."

16. Article 24(1) (pre-amendment): "The judicial power is exercised by a Supreme Court and other such courts of law as are provided for by law." Article 24(2): "The composition and powers of these legal bodies shall be regulated by law."

17. These regulations include Law No. 5 of 2004 on the Supreme Court, amending Law No. 14 of 1985; Presidential Decree 21 of 2004 on Transferring Responsibility to the Supreme Court; and Presidential Regulation 13 of 2005 on the Secretariat of the Supreme Court. These instruments implemented Law No. 35 of 1999 (the One-Roof Law), introduced before the amendments to Article 24 as part of a rolling series of judicial system reforms between 1999 and 2005, of which the amendments to Article 24 and the creation of the Constitutional Court were part.

18. Lev, "Judicial Authority."

19. For more information on the Blueprint, see Rifqi Assegaf, "Judicial Reform in Indonesia, 1986–2006," in Naoyuki Sakumoto and Hikmahanto Juwana, eds.,

Reforming Laws and Institutions in Indonesia: An Assessment, no. 74 (Ciba, Japan: Institute of Developing Economies, Japan External Trade Organisation, and Joint Studies on Economic Development Policies in ASEAN and Neighbouring Countries, 2007), at http://www.ide.go.jp/English/Publish/Download/Asedp/074 .html, accessed March 9, 2009; and IMF/Netherlands Program, *IMF/Netherlands Program: Legal and Judicial Reform in Indonesia 2000–2004, External Evaluation. Final Report* (2005), at http://sitesources.worldbank.org/INTLAWJUSTINST/ Resources/imfexternalnetherlandsind.pdf, accessed March 9, 2009.

20. Lubis, *In Search of Human Rights*; Pompe, *The Indonesian Supreme Court*.

21. Pompe, *The Indonesian Supreme Court*; Lev, "Between State and Society."

22. William Neilson, "Reforming Commercial Laws in Asia: Strategies and Realities for Donor Agencies," in Timothy Lindsey, ed., *Indonesia: Bankruptcy & the Commercial Court*, 15–27 (Armadale, Australia: Desert Pea Press, 2000).

23. The exceptions are the Constitutional Court (Butt, "Judicial Review in Indonesia"), the Anti-corruption Court (Stewart Fenwick, "Measuring Up? Indonesia's Anti-corruption Commission and the New Corruption Agenda," in Lindsey, ed., *Indonesia*, 2nd ed., 406–429), and (albeit to a lesser extent) the Religious Court (Cate Sumner, *Justice for the Justice Seeker: Access to Justice Survey Report: 2007–2009* [Jakarta: Mahkamah Agung/AusAID, 2010]).

24. Vito Tanzi, *Fiscal Federalism and Decentralization: A Review of Some Efficiency and Macroeconomic Aspects* (Washington, D.C.: World Bank, 1995).

25. See, for example, Freedom House's assessment of Indonesia at http://www .freedomhouse.org.

26. Douglas Ramage, "Indonesia: Democracy First, Good Governance Later," in Daljit Singh and Lorraine C. Salazar, eds., *Southeast Asian Affairs* (Singapore: Institute of Southeast Asian Studies, 2007), 136.

27. Nicholas Parsons and Marcus Mietzner, "Sharia By-laws in Indonesia: A Legal and Political Analysis," *Australian Journal of Asian Laws* 11, no. 2 (2010): 190–217.

28. See, for example, Transparency International's Global Corruption Barometer (at http://www.transparency.org/research/gcb/overview, accessed October 21, 2012), which ranks Indonesia as the seventh most corrupt country; identifies the judiciary as the second most corrupt branch of government after the legislature in Indonesia; and in which 48 percent of surveyed households in Indonesia classified the judiciary as "extremely corrupt." See also the Heritage Foundation's Index of Economic Freedom, at http://www.heritage.org/Index/Country/Indonesia, accessed October 21, 2012; *World Economic Forum Global Competitiveness Report 2012–2013*, at http://www.weforum.org/reports, accessed October 21, 2012. All these sources are cited in http://www.business-anti-corruption.com/country-profiles/east-asia-the-pacific/indonesia/corruption-levels/judicial-system, accessed October 21, 2012.

29. See Wasingatu Zakiyah, Danang W, Iva Kasuma, and Ragil YE, *Menyingkap tabir mafia peradilan* (Opening the Curtain on the Judicial Mafia) (Jakarta: Indonesian Corruption Watch , 2002).

30. World Bank, *Combating Corruption in Indonesia: Enhancing Accountability for Development* (Jakarta: World Bank Office Jakarta, 2004), 83–85; *Konsorsium* Reformasi

Hukum Nasional (KHRN) and Lembaga Kajian dan Advokasi untuk Independensi Peradilan (LeIP) Indonesia, *Menuju independensi kekuasaan kehakiman* (Toward Judicial Independence), position paper (Jakarta: Indonesian Center for Environmental Law, 1999), 62; Maria Dakolias and Kimberly L. Thachuk, "Attacking Corruption in the Judiciary: A Critical Process in Judicial Reform," *Wisconsin International Law Journal* 18 (2000), 398; "ICW: Makin besar gaji hakim, makin 'gila-gilaan' korupsinya" (ICW: The Higher the Judicial Salary, the More Out of Control the Corruption), *Hukumonline*, July 23, 2002.

31. For a serious attempt to provide such data, see ICW, *Menyingkap tabir mafia peradilan.*

32. In our experience, judicial corruption or impropriety in particular cases is often presumed by the media and public based solely on the outcome of the case—the acquittal of a defendant, for instance. Yet this approach ignores other significant factors that might explain the outcome. For example, prosecutors may have put forward a weak case; evidence might not withstand in-court examination; or the presiding judges might have lacked sufficient competence to adjudicate the case effectively. See Simon Butt and Timothy Lindsey, "Judicial Mafia: The Courts and State Illegality in Indonesia," in Edward Aspinall and Gerry van Klinken, eds., *The State and Illegality in Indonesia*, 189–216 (Leiden: KITLV Press, 2011).

33. Appeal to the Supreme Court takes the form of cassation, or *kasasi*, with the option in most cases of a final rung of appeal, the Peninjauan Kembali (PK, Reconsideration), by means of an internal review of the *kasasi* decision by a different panel of judges within the Supreme Court. Decisions of the Human Rights Court, the Tipikor Court, the Fisheries Court, and the various military courts can be appealed to their respective high courts before being heard on cassation by the Supreme Court. There are, however, no appeals from the Commercial Court (established under Law No. 4 of 1998) and the Labor Court (established under Law No. 2 of 2004) to a high court; they are heard directly by the Supreme Court. Although the decisions of the new Tax Court cannot be heard on cassation, they can be heard by the Supreme Court as a PK. The Constitutional Court has first and final authority in the matters it decides (Art. 24C of the Constitution and Law No. 24 of 2003).

34. Both Sebastiaan Pompe and Daniel Lev have described the historical development of this institutional culture. See Pompe, *The Indonesian Supreme Court*; Lev, "Between State and Society."

35. The Supreme Court has, for example, entered into an agreement with AsianLII (www.asianlii.org/asianlii/) to publish selected judgments on a free public-access Internet database.

36. Nuno Garoupa and Tom Ginsburg, "Guarding the Guardians: Judicial Councils and Judicial Independence," *American Journal of Comparative Law* 57 (2009): 103–134.

37. Decision No. 005/PUU-IV/2006. For a detailed analysis of this controversy and the Constitutional Court's decision, see Simon Butt, "Between Judicial Independence and Accountability," in Andrew MacIntyre and Ross H. McLeod, eds., *Democracy and the Promise of Good Governance*, 178–199 (Singapore: Institute of Southeast Asian Studies, 2007).

38. We consider the topic of judicial corruption in detail in Butt and Lindsey, "Judicial Mafia."

39. The majority of complaints lodged with Indonesia's Ombudsman Republik Indonesia (Indonesian Ombudsman) relate solely to the judiciary. The commission has, however, had very little success in resolving such complaints to the public's satisfaction. See Melissa Crouch, "Indonesia's National and Local Ombudsman Reforms: Salvaging a Failed Experiment?" in Lindsey, ed., *Indonesia*, 2nd ed., 382–405, esp. 386.

40. Case No. 560.K/Pdt/1997, copy on file with the authors.

41. See Butt and Lindsey, "Judicial Mafia," where we discuss the Endin case in detail. See also the Endin defamation case, Central Jakarta District Court Decision No. 427/PID.B/2001/PN.JKT.PST, copy on file with the authors.

42. Dakolias and Thachuk, "Attacking Corruption in the Judiciary," 365, 398; World Bank, *Combatting Corruption in Indonesia*, vii.

43. This section draws on Simon Butt, "Regional Autonomy and the Proliferation of *Perda* in Indonesia: An Assessment of Bureaucratic and Judicial Review Mechanisms," *Sydney Law Review* 32 (2) (2010): 177–191.

44. Hans Thoolen, *Indonesia and the Rule of Law: Twenty Years of "New Order" Government: A Study* (London: F. Pinter, 1987).

45. Articles 18(1), 18(5), and 18(6) of the Constitution. Under Article 10(3) of Law No. 32 of 2004 on Regional Government, the central government retains exclusive jurisdiction over foreign affairs, defense, security, judicial affairs, national monetary and fiscal matters, and religion. The central government can, however, delegate its jurisdiction to regulate these matters to local governments (Article 10[4], Law No. 32).

46. For information about these regions, see http://www.depdagri.go.id.

47. Articles 18(3) and 18(4) of the Constitution.

48. "Hingga September 2006, ada 66 ranperda ditolak" (Up to September 2006, 66 Draft *Perda* Rejected), *Hukumonline*, October 13, 2006.

49. World Bank Independent Evaluation Group, *Decentralization in Client Countries: An Evaluation of the World Bank Support, 1990–2007* (Washington, D.C.: World Bank, 2008); International Monetary Fund and World Bank, *Local Government Discretion and Accountability: A Local Governance Framework* (Washington, D.C.: International Monetary Fund and World Bank, 2007); Pranab Bardhan and Dilip Mookherjee, "Decentralization, Corruption, and Government Accountability: An Overview," in Susan Rose-Ackerman, ed., *International Handbook on the Economics of Corruption*, 161–188 (Northampton, Mass.: Edward Elgar, 2005); James Manor, *The Political Economy of Democratic Decentralization* (Washington, D.C.: World Bank, 1999), 88–89; Paul Smoke and Rolland White, "East Asia Decentralizes," in *East Asia Decentralizes: Making Local Government Work* (Washington, D.C.: World Bank, 2005), 3; Jose Edgardo Campos and Joel Hellman, "Governance Gone Local: Does Decentralization Improve Accountability?" in *East Asia Decentralizes*, 237.

50. World Bank, *Factsheet: Perda Program*, Justice for the Poor—Decentralization Support Facility (Washington, D.C.: World Bank, 2007).

51. David Ray, "Decentralization, Regulatory Reform, and the Business Climate," in *Decentralization, Regulatory Reform, and the Business Climate*, 1–27 (Jakarta: Partnership for Economic Growth, 2003).

52. For a detailed discussion, see Parsons and Mietzner, "Sharia By-laws in Indonesia."

53. Ray, "Decentralization, Regulatory Reform, and the Business Climate."

54. Tjip Ismail, "Kebijakan pengawasan atas perda pajak daerah dan retribusi daerah" (Policy of Supervising Regional Tax and User-Charge *Perda*), in *Decentralization, Regulatory Reform, and the Business Climate*, 87–88.

55. Article 145(2) of the 2004 Autonomy Law.

56. See Ministry of Home Affairs Regulation No. 53 of 2007. Different procedures apply for the review of *perda* that set local government budgets, impose regional taxes or user charges, or relate to spatial planning (2004 Autonomy Law, Art. 185–189). These types of *perda* need prior central government approval.

57. Eko Susi Rosdianasari, Novi Anggriani, and Basri Mulyani, *Dinamika penyusunan, substansi dan implementasi perda pelayanan publik* (Dynamics of the Drafting, Substance, and Implementation of Public-Service *Perda*) (Jakarta: World Bank Justice for the Poor Project, 2009), ix; United Nations Development Program (UNDP), *Enhancing Communications, Advocacy, and Public Participation Capacity for Legal Reforms (CAPPLER) PHASE II* (Paris: UNDP, 2008), 7.

58. Ray, "Decentralization, Regulatory Reform, and the Business Climate," 18; Ismail, "Kebijakan pengawaan," 89.

59. Article 145(3) and (7) of the 2004 Autonomy Law.

60. Blane D. Lewis, "Tax and Charge Creation by Regional Governments Under Fiscal Decentralization: Estimates and Explanations," *Bulletin of Indonesian Economic Studies* 39 (2) (2003), 178; Ray "Decentralization, Regulatory Reform, and the Business Climate," 18.

61. Ray, "Decentralization, Regulatory Reform, and the Business Climate," 19.

62. Article 145(5) of the 2004 Autonomy Law.

63. The Supreme Court has jurisdiction to consider review petitions lodged by citizens using its general powers of judicial review. Under national judiciary laws, the Court can ensure that executive legal instruments—including local government laws—do not contradict the higher-order laws, including government regulations, presidential regulations, or statutes enacted by Indonesia's national Parliament (Art. 24A[1] of the Constitution; Art. 11[2][b] of the Judicial Power Law [Law No. 4 of 2004]; Art. 31[2] of the Supreme Court Law [Law No. 5 of 2004]). "Berangkat dari pembatalan perda privatisasi rumah sakit: Problem hukum pengujian perda (1)" (From the Invalidation of the *Perda* on Hospital Privatization: Legal Problems with *Perda* Review [1]), *Hukumonline*, June 22, 2006.

64. We obtained these decisions from http://www.putusan.net.

65. See, for example, MA Decision Nos. 14 P/HUM/2004, 20 P/HUM/2007, and 03 P/HUM/2009.

66. Article 2(4) of MA Regulation No. 1 of 2004; Article 5(4) of MA Regulation No. 1 of 1999. In 2011, after this chapter was written, the Supreme Court abolished the

180-day restriction, although it remains to be seen if this decision will result in any increase in the number of *perda* it invalidates.

67. Gregory Churchill, "Access to Legal Information in Indonesia: Recent Progress, Current Problems, and Future Prospects," paper presented at the Seminar on Access to Legal Information: Language, Dictionaries, Databases, "State of the Art" session, Jakarta, August 20–22, 2000.

68. See, for example, MA Decision Nos. 03 G/HUM/2002, P/HUM/2002, 06 P/HUM/2003, and 06 P/HUM/2006.

69. Tangerang City Perda No. 8 of 2005 on Prostitution.

70. "Makeup Led to Woman's Branding as Prostitute," *Jakarta Post*, May 4, 2007; Karuni Rompies, "Moral Crusaders Focus on Females," *The Age*, March 11, 2006; "Islamic Hard-liners Chip Away at Indonesia's Secular Traditions," *International Herald Tribune*, March 2, 2007; Jane Perlez, "Spread of Islamic Law in Indonesia Takes Toll on Women," *New York Times*, June 27, 2006; "MA tolak uji materiil perda anti pelacuran" (MA Refuses to Review the Anti-prostitution *Perda*), *Jawa Pos*, April 14, 2007; Mark Forbes and Karuni Rompies, "Islamic Moral Drive Spreads Fear in Indonesia," *Sydney Morning Herald*, March 11, 2006.

71. "MA tolak permohonan uji materiil perda pelacuran Tangerang" (MA Refuses to Review the Tangerang Anti-prostitution *Perda*), *Hukumonline*, April 16, 2007; "Perda pelacuran Tangerang tak bertentangan dengan UU" (Tangerang Prostitution *Perda* Does Not Breach Statute), *Gatra*, April 13, 2007; "MA: Perda pelarangan pelacuran tak bertentangan dengan undangundang" (MA: Perda Prohibiting Prostitution Does Not Breach Statute), *Republika*, April 13, 2007.

72. Law No. 22 of 1999 on Regional Government.

73. See, for example, Pratikno, "Exercising Freedom: Local Autonomy and Democracy in Indonesia, 1999–2001," in Priyambudi Sulistiyanto, Maribeth Erb, and Caroline Faucher, eds., *Regionalism in Post-Suharto Indonesia* (New York: RoutledgeCurzon, 2005), 25; Ismet Fanany, "The First Year of Local Autonomy: The Case of West Sumatra," in Damien Kinsbury and Harry Aveling, eds., *Autonomy and Disintegration in Indonesia* (New York: RoutledgeCurzon, 2002), 177.

74. Gary F. Bell, "The New Indonesian Laws Relating to Regional Autonomy: Good Intentions, Confusing Laws," *Asian-Pacific Law and Policy Journal* 2 (1) (2001), 29.

75. Article 7(1) of Law No. 10 of 2004 on Lawmaking.

76. See Parsons and Mietzner, "Sharia By-laws."

77. Lindsey, "Indonesian Constitutional Reform"; Tim Lindsey, "Indonesia: Devaluing Asian Values, Rewriting Rule of Law," in R. P. Peerenboom, ed., *Asian Discourses of Rule of Law*, 286–323 (London: RoutledgeCurzon, 2004).

78. Herbert, "The Legal Framework of Human Rights in Indonesia."

79. For example, a judicial watchdog or anticorruption court to handle corruption cases more effectively might be established. See Fenwick, "Measuring Up?"; or with regard to upholding important socioeconomic human rights of the majority of the population in the face of the competing human rights of a minority of citizens, see Butt, "Between Judicial Independence and Accountability."

Alimi, Moh Yasir. "Inculcating Islam: The Public Sphere and the Islamic Traditions of South Sulawesi." Ph.D. diss., Australian National University, Canberra, 2009.

Aspinall, Edward. *Islam and Nation: Separatist Rebellion in Aceh, Indonesia*. Stanford, Calif.: Stanford University Press, 2009.

——. *Opposing Suharto: Compromise, Resistance, and Regime Change in Indonesia*. Stanford, Calif.: Stanford University Press, 2005.

Aspinall, Edward and Mark T. Berger. "The Breakup of Indonesia? Nationalisms After Decolonization and the Contradictions of Modernity in Post–Cold War Southeast Asia." *Third World Quarterly* 22 (6) (2001): 1003–1024.

Barron, Patrick, Kai Kaiser, and Menno Pradhan. "Understanding Variations in Local Conflict: Evidence and Implications from Indonesia." *World Development* 37 (2009): 698–713.

Bell, Gary F. "The New Indonesian Laws Relating to Regional Autonomy: Good Intentions, Confusing Laws." *Asian-Pacific Law & Policy Journal* 2 (1) (2001): 1–45.

Benda, Harry. *The Crescent and the Rising Sun*. The Hague: Van Hoeve Ltd., 1958.

Benda, Harry and Ruth T. McVey, eds. *Communist Uprisings of 1926–1927 in Indonesia: Key Documents*. Ithaca, N.Y.: Cornell University Press, 1960.

Bertelsmann Stiftung. *Bertelsmann Transformation Index 2010—Indonesia Country Report*. Gütersloh, Germany: Bertelsmann Stiftung, 2010.

Bertrand, Jacques. *Nationalism and Ethnic Conflict in Indonesia*. Cambridge: Cambridge University Press, 2004.

Bjornlund, Eric, R. William Liddle, and Blair King. *Indonesia: Democracy and Governance Assessment: Final Report*. Bethesda, Md.: Democracy International, 2008.

Bourchier, David. "Positivism and Romanticism in Indonesian Legal Thought." In Timothy Lindsey, ed., *Indonesia: Law and Society*, 1st ed., 186–196. Annandale, Australia: Federation Press, 1999.

——. "Skeletons, Vigilantes, and the Armed Forces' Fall from Grace." In Arief Budiman, Barbara Hatley, and Damien Kingsbury, eds., *Reformasi: Crisis and Change in Indonesia*, 149–172. Clayton, Australia: Monash Asia Institute, 1999.

Bowen, John R. *Islam, Law, and Equality in Indonesia: An Anthropology of Public Reasoning*. Cambridge: Cambridge University Press, 2003.

——. "Normative Pluralism in Indonesia: Regions, Religions, and Ethnicities." In Will Kymlicka and Boagang He, eds., *Multiculturalism in Asia: Theoretical Perspectives*, 152–169. Oxford: Oxford University Press, 2005.

Bünte, Marco. "Indonesia's Protracted Decentralization: Contested Reforms and Their Unintended Consequences." In Marco Bünte and Andreas Ufen, eds., *Democratization in Post-Suharto Indonesia*, 102–123. New York: Routledge, 2009.

Bush, Robin. *Nahdlatul Ulama and the Struggle for Power Within Islam and Politics in Indonesia*. Singapore: Institute of Southeast Asian Studies, 2009.

Butt, Simon. "Judicial Review in Indonesia: Between Civil Law and Accountability? A Study of Constitutional Court Decisions 2003–2005." Ph.D. diss., Law Faculty, Melbourne University, 2007.

——. "Regional Autonomy and the Proliferation of *Perda* in Indonesia: An Assessment of Bureaucratic and Judicial Review Mechanisms." *Sydney Law Review* 32 (2) (2010): 177–191.

Butt, Simon and Timothy Lindsey. "Judicial Mafia: The Courts and State Illegality in Indonesia." In Edward Aspinall and Gerry van Klinken, eds., *The State and Illegality in Indonesia*, 189–216. Leiden: KITLV Press, 2011.

Cammack, Mark E. "The Indonesian Islamic Judiciary." In R. Michael Feener and Mark E. Cammack, eds., *Islamic Law in Contemporary Indonesia: Ideas and Institutions*, 146–169. Cambridge, Mass.: Harvard University Press, 2007.

Cammack, Mark E., Helen Donovan, and Tim B. Heaton. "Islamic Divorce Law and Practice in Indonesia." In R. Michael Feener and Mark E. Cammack, eds., *Islamic Law in Contemporary Indonesia: Ideas and Institutions*, 99–127. Cambridge, Mass.: Harvard University Press, 2007.

Campos, Jose Edgardo and Joel S. Hellman. "Governance Gone Local: Does Decentralization Improve Accountability?" In *East Asia Decentralizes: Making Local Government Work*, 237–252. Washington, D.C.: World Bank, 2005.

Chauvel, Richard. *Constructing Papuan Nationalism: History, Ethnicity, and Adaptation*. Washington, D.C.: East West Center, 2005.

Cribb, Robert. "The Historical Roots of Indonesia's New Order: Beyond the Colonial Comparison." In Edward Aspinall and Greg Fealy, eds., *Indonesia: Soeharto's New Order and Its Legacy*, 67–80. Canberra: Australian National University E-Press, 2010.

——. "Not the Next Yugoslavia: Prospects for the Disintegration of Indonesia." *Australian Journal of International Affairs* 53 (2) (1999): 169–178.

Crouch, Harold. *The Army and Politics in Indonesia*. Ithaca, N.Y.: Cornell University Press, 1978.

——. *Political Reform in Indonesia After Suharto*. Singapore: Institute of Southeast Asian Studies, 2010.

Davidson, Jamie S. *From Rebellion to Riots: Collective Violence on Indonesian Borneo*. Madison: University of Wisconsin Press, 2008.

Emmerson, Donald. "What Is Indonesia?" In John Bersnan, ed., *Indonesia: The Great Transition*, 7–74. Lanham, Md.: Rowman and Littlefield, 2005.

——. "Will Indonesia Survive?" *Foreign Affairs* 79 (3) (May–June 2000): 95–106.

Erb, Meredith and Priyambudi Sulistiyanto. *Deepening Democracy in Indonesia? Direct Elections for Local Leaders (Pilkada)*. Singapore: Institute of Southeast Asian Studies, 2009.

Fanany, Ismet. "The First Year of Local Autonomy: The Case of West Sumatra." In Damien Kingsbury and Harry Aveling, eds., *Autonomy and Disintegration in Indonesia*, 177–188. London: RoutledgeCurzon, 2002.

Feith, Herbert. *The Decline of Constitutional Democracy in Indonesia*. Ithaca, N.Y.: Cornell University Press, 1967.

——. *Indonesian Political Thinking 1945–1965*. Ithaca, N.Y.: Cornell University Press, 1970.

Fenwick, Stewart. "Measuring Up? Indonesia's Anti-corruption Commission and the New Corruption Agenda." In Timothy Lindsey, ed., *Indonesia: Law and Society*, 2nd ed., 406–429. Annandale, Australia: Federation Press, 2008.

Garoupa, Nuno and Tom Ginsburg. "Guarding the Guardians: Judicial Councils and Judicial Independence." *American Journal of Comparative Law* 57 (2009): 103–134.

Gunther, Richard. "Opening a Dialogue on Institutional Choice in Indonesia: Presidential, Parliamentary, and Semipresidential Systems." In R. William Liddle, ed., *Crafting Indonesian Democracy*, 149–178. Bandung, Indonesia: Mizan, 2001.

Hafidz, Tatik S. *Fading Away? The Political Role of the Army in Indonesia's Transition to Democracy, 1998–2001*. Singapore: Institute of Defence and Strategic Studies, 2006.

Hasan, Noorhaidi. *Laskar Jihad: Islam, Militancy, and the Quest for Identity in Post–New Order Indonesia*. Ithaca, N.Y.: Cornell Southeast Asia Program, 2006.

Herbert, Jeff. "The Legal Framework of Human Rights in Indonesia." In Timothy Lindsey, eds., *Indonesia: Law and Society*, 2nd ed., 456–483. Annandale, Australia: Federation Press, 2008.

Honna, Jun. "From Dwifungsi to NKRI: Regime Change and Political Activism of the Indonesian Military." In Marco Bünte and Andreas Ufen, eds., *Democratization in Post-Suharto Indonesia*, 226–248. London: Routledge, 2009.

Hooker, M. B. *Indonesian Syariah: Defining a National School of Islamic Law*. Singapore: Institute of Southeast Asian Studies, 2008.

Human Rights Watch. *Out of Sight: Endemic Abuse and Impunity in Papua's Central Highlands*. New York: Human Rights Watch, July 4, 2007.

——. *Unkept Promise: Failure to End Military Business Activity in Indonesia*. New York: Human Rights Watch, 2010.

Human Security Report 2005: War and Peace in the 21st Century. New York: Oxford University Press, 2005.

International Crisis Group (ICG). *Indonesia Backgrounder: Jihad in Central Sulawesi.* Asia Report no. 74. Brussels: ICG, February 2004.

——. *Indonesia: Deradicalisation and Indonesian Prisons.* Asia Report no. 142. Brussels: ICG, November 19, 2007.

——. *Indonesia: Implications of the Ahmadiyah Decree.* Asia Briefing no. 78. Brussels: ICG, July 7, 2008.

——. *Indonesia: The Implications of the Timor Trials.* Asia Briefing no. 16. Brussels: ICG, May 2002.

——. *Indonesia: Jihadi Surprise in Aceh.* Asia Report no. 189. Brussels: ICG, April 20, 2010.

——. *Indonesia: Poso on the Edge.* Asia Report no. 127. Brussels: ICG, January 24, 2007.

——. *Indonesia: Why Salafism and Terrorism Mostly Don't Mix.* Asia Report no. 83. Brussels: ICG, September 1, 2004.

Ismail, Tjip. "Kebijakan pengawasan atas perda pajak daerah dan retribusi daerah" (Policy of Supervising Regional Tax and User Charge *Perda*). In *Decentralization, Regulatory Reform, and the Business Climate*, page nos. not available. Jakarta: Partnership for Economic Growth, 2003.

Kahin, George McTurnan. *Nationalism and Revolution in Indonesia.* Ithaca, N.Y.: Cornell University Press, 1952.

Kammen, Douglas. "The Trouble with Normal: The Indonesian Military, Paramilitaries, and the Final Solution in East Timor." In Benedict R. O'G. Anderson, ed., *Violence and the State in Suharto's Indonesia*, 156–188. Ithaca, N.Y.: Southeast Asia Program, Cornell University, 2001.

Kaufmann, Daniel, Aart Kraay, and Massimo Mastruzzi. *Governance Matters VIII: Aggregate and Individual Governance Indicators, 1996–2008.* World Bank Policy Research Working Paper no. 4978. Washington, D.C.: World Bank, June 29, 2009. At http://ssrn.com/abstract=1424591.

Lembaga Survei Indonesia. *Prospek kepemimpinan nasional: Evaluasi publik tiga tahun presiden* (The Prospect for National Leadership: Public Evaluation of the President's Three Years). Jakarta: Lembaga Survei Indonesia, 2007.

Lev, Daniel S. "Between State and Society: Professional Lawyers and Law Reform in Indonesia." In Timothy Lindsey, ed., *Indonesia: Law and Society*, 2nd ed., 48–67. Annandale, Australia: Federation Press, 2008.

——. *Islamic Courts in Indonesia: A Study in the Political Bases of Legal Institutions.* Berkeley: University of California Press, 1972.

——. "Judicial Authority and the Struggle for an Indonesian Rechtstaat." *Law and Society Review* 13 (1978): 37–72.

——. *Legal Evolution and Political Authority in Indonesia: Selected Essays.* Berlin: Springer, 2000.

——. *The Transition to Guided Democracy: Indonesian Politics, 1957–1959.* Ithaca, N.Y.: Cornell University Press, 1966.

Lewis, Blane D. "Tax and Charge Creation by Regional Government Under Fiscal Decentralization: Estimates and Explanations." *Bulletin of Indonesian Economic Studies* 39 (2) (2003): 177–192.

Liddle, R. William. "Indonesia's Democratic Transition: Playing by the Rules." In Andrew Reynolds, ed., *The Architecture of Democracy*, 373–399. Oxford: Oxford University Press, 2002.

Liddle, R. William and Saiful Mujani. "Indonesia in 2005: A New Multiparty Presidential Democracy." *Asian Survey* 46 (2006): 132–139.

Lindsey, Timothy. "Black Letter, Black Market, and Bad Faith: Corruption and the Failure of Law Reform." In Chris Manning and Peter Van Diermen, eds., *Indonesia in Transition: Social Aspects of Reformasi and Crisis*, 278–292. London: Zed Books, 2000.

——, ed. 2008. *Indonesia: Law and Society.* 2nd ed. Annandale, Australia: Federation Press.

——. "Indonesian Constitutional Reform: Muddling Towards Democracy." *Singapore Journal of International and Comparative Law* 6 (1) (2002): 244–301.

Lindsey, Timothy and Dick Howard, eds. *Corruption in Asia: Rethinking the Governance Paradigm*. Annandale, Australia: Federation Press, 2002.

Linnan, David. "Indonesian Law Reform, or Once More Unto the Breach." In Timothy Lindsey, ed., *Indonesia: Law and Society*, 2nd ed., 68–93. Annandale, Australia: Federation Press, 2008.

Linz, Juan J. and Alfred Stepan. *Problems of Democratic Transition and Consolidation: Southern Europe, South America, and Post-Communist Europe.* Baltimore: Johns Hopkins University Press, 1996.

Lubis, Todung Mulya. *In Search of Human Rights: Legal Political Dilemmas of Indonesia's New Order, 1966–1990.* Jakarta: PT Gramedia Pustaka Utama, 1993.

Magnis-Suseno, Franz. *Javanese Ethics and World-View: The Javanese Idea of the Good Life.* Jakarta: KDT, 1997.

Malley, Michael S. "New Rules, Old Structures, and the Limits of Democratic Decentralization." In Edward Aspinall and Greg Fealy, eds., *Democratisation and Decentralisation in Indonesia: Local Power and Politics*, 102–118. Singapore: Institute of Southeast Asian Studies, 2003.

McFarling, Ian. *The Dual Function of the Indonesian Armed Forces: Military Politics in Indonesia.* Canberra: Australian Defence Studies Centre, 1996.

McVey, Ruth T. *The Rise of Indonesian Communism.* Ithaca, N.Y.: Cornell University Press, 1965.

Mietzner, Marcus. *Military Politics, Islam, and the State in Indonesia: From Turbulent Transition to Democratic Consolidation.* Singapore: Institute of Southeast Asian Studies, 2009.

——. "Soldiers, Parties, and Bureaucrats: Illicit Fund-Raising in Contemporary Indonesia." *South East Asian Research* 16 (2) (2008): 225–254.

Mujani, Saiful. *Masalah konsolidasi demokrasi dan pemilu 2009* (The Problem of the Consolidation of Democracy and the 2009 Elections). Jakarta: Lembaga Survei Indonesia, 2009.

——. "The State of Indonesian Democratic Governance: A Popular Assessment." Unpublished manuscript, 2008.

Nisa, Nurun, Gamal Ferdhi, and Nurul Huda. "Bersama menolak perda diskriminatif" (Collectively Reject Discriminatory Regulations). *Nawala: The Wahid Institute*, no. 2, II (March–June 2007): page nos. unavailable.

O'Rourke, Kevin. *Reformasi: The Struggle for Power in Post-Suharto Indonesia*. Sydney, Australia: Allen and Unwin, 2002.

Parsons, Nicholas and Marcus Mietzner. "Sharia By-laws in Indonesia: A Legal and Political Analysis." *Australian Journal of Asian Laws* 11, no. 2 (2010): 190–217.

Pompe, Sebastiaan. *The Indonesian Supreme Court: A Study of Institutional Collapse*. Ithaca, N.Y.: Southeast Asia Program, Cornell University, 2005.

Pratikno. "Exercising Freedom: Local Autonomy and Democracy in Indonesia, 1999–2001." In Priyambudi Sulistiyanto, Maribeth Erb, and Caroline Faucher, eds., *Regionalism in Post-Suharto Indonesia*, 21–35. New York: RoutledgeCurzon, 2005.

Rabasa, Angel and John Haseman. *The Military and Democracy in Indonesia: Challenges, Politics, and Power*. Santa Monica, Calif.: RAND, 2003.

Ramage, Douglas. "Indonesia: Democracy First, Good Governance Later." In Daljit Singh and Lorraine C. Salazar, eds., *Southeast Asian Affairs*, 135–157. Singapore: Institute of Southeast Asian Studies, 2007.

Rasyid, M. Ryaas. "Regional Autonomy and Local Politics in Indonesia." In Edward Aspinall and Greg Fealy, eds., *Democratisation and Decentralisation in Indonesia: Local Power and Politics*, 63–71. Singapore: Institute of Southeast Asian Studies, 2003.

Ray, David. "Decentralization, Regulatory Reform, and the Business Climate." In *Decentralization, Regulatory Reform, and the Business Climate*, 1–27. Jakarta: Partnership for Economic Growth, 2003.

Reid, Anthony. *The Blood of the People: Revolution and the End of Traditional Rule in Northern Sumatra*. Kuala Lumpur: Oxford University Press, 1979.

Ricklefs, Merle. *A History of Modern Indonesia Since c. 1200*. Stanford, Calif.: Stanford University Press, 2001.

Robinson, Jennifer. "Freedom of Expression: Whether Papuans Support Autonomy or Independence, They Should Be Allowed to Speak Freely." *Inside Indonesia* 94 (2008): n.p.

Robinson, Richard and Vedi Hadiz. *Reorganising Power in Indonesia: The Politics of Oligarchy in an Age of Markets*. London: RoutledgeCurzon, 2004.

Roosa, John. *Pretext for Mass Murder: The September 30th Movement and Suharto's Coup d'État in Indonesia*. Madison: University of Wisconsin Press, 2006.

Rosdianasari, Eko Susi, Novi Anggriani, and Basri Mulyani. *Dinamika penyusunan, substansi dan implementasi perda pelayanan publik* (Dynamics of the Drafting, Substance, and Implementation of Public-Service *Perda*). Jakarta: World Bank Justice for the Poor Project, 2009.

Rudnyckyj, Daromir. *Spiritual Economies: Islam and the Afterlife of Development*. Ithaca, N.Y.: Cornell University Press, 2010.

Said, Salim. *Genesis of Power: General Sudirman and the Indonesian Military in Politics, 1945–49*. Jakarta: Pustaka Sinar Harapan; Singapore: Institute of Southeast Asian Studies, 1992.

——. *Legitimizing Military Rule: Indonesia Armed Forces, 1958–2000*. Jakarta: Sinar Harapan, 2006.

Salim, Arskal. *Politics and Islamisation in Aceh: An Update*. Occasional Seminar paper. Melbourne: Asian Law Centre, 2009.

Schwarz, Adam. *A Nation in Waiting: Indonesia's Search for Stability*. 3rd printing. Singapore: Talisman, 2004.

Sherlock, Stephen. *The Indonesian Parliament After Two Elections: What Has Really Changed?* Centre for Democratic Institutions Policy Papers on Political Governance. Canberra: Centre for Democratic Institutions, Australian National University, 2007.

Shiraishi, Takashi. "The Indonesian Military in Politics." In Adam Schwarz and Jonathan Paris, eds., *The Politics of Post-Suharto Indonesia*, 73–86. New York: Council on Foreign Relations Press, 1999.

Smith, Anthony D. "State-Making and Nation-Building." In John A. Hall, ed., *States in History*, 228–263. Oxford: Basil Blackwell, 1989.

Smoke, Paul and Rolland White. "East Asia Decentralizes." In *East Asia Decentralizes: Making Local Government Work*, 1–24. Washington, D.C.: World Bank, 2005.

Stepan, Alfred, Juan J. Linz, and Yogendra Yaday. *Crafting State-Nations: India and Other Multinational Democracies*. Baltimore: Johns Hopkins University Press, 2011.

Sumner, Cate. *Justice for the Justice Seeker: Access to Justice Survey Report: 2007–2009*. Jakarta: Mahkamah Agung/AusAID, 2010.

Sundhaussen, Ulf. *The Road to Power: Indonesian Military Politics, 1945–1967*. Kuala Lumpur: Oxford University Press, 1982.

Tadjoeddin, Mohammed Zulfan. *Anatomy of Social Violence in the Context of Transition: The Case of Indonesia 1990–2001*. Jakarta: United Nations Support Facility for Indonesian Recovery, 2002.

Thoolen, Hans. *Indonesia and the Rule of Law: Twenty Years of "New Order" Government: A Study*. London: F. Pinter, 1987.

Tiwon, Sylvia. "From East Timor to Aceh: The Disintegration of Indonesia?" *Bulletin of Concerned Asian Scholars* 32 (1–2) (2000): 97–104.

Uhlin, Anders. *Indonesia and the "Third Wave of Democratization": The Indonesian Pro-democracy Movement in a Changing World*. Richmond, U.K.: Curzon, 1997.

Van Klinken, Gerry. *Communal Violence and Democratization in Indonesia: Small Town Wars*. London: Routledge, 2007.

Varshney, Ashutosh. "Analyzing Collective Violence in Indonesia: An Overview." *Journal of East Asian Studies* 8 (2008): 341–359.

Edward Aspinall is a senior fellow in the Department of Political and Social Change and the School of International, Political, and Strategic Studies at the Australian National University. Prior to assuming his current position, he was a lecturer in Southeast Asian studies at the University of Sydney and a lecturer in Indonesian studies at the University of New South Wales. He is the coordinating editor of the journal *Inside Indonesia*. In 2010, Aspinall was awarded the Asian Studies Association of Australia's Mid-Career Researcher Prize for Excellence in Asian Studies for his book *Islam and Nation: Separatist Rebellion in Aceh* (2009). His other publications include *Opposing Suharto: Compromise, Resistance, and Regime Change in Indonesia* (2005) and *Problems of Democratisation in Indonesia: Elections, Institutions, and Society* (coedited with Marcus Mietzner, 2010).

John R. Bowen is the Dunbar–Van Cleve Professor in Arts and Sciences at Washington University in St. Louis. Bowen won the Herbert Jacobs Prize from the Law Society Association for his book *Islam, Law, and Equality in Indonesia: An Anthropology of Public Reasoning* (2003). His other noted publications are *Can Islam Be French? Pluralism and Pragmatism in a Secularist State* (2009) and *Why the French Don't Like Headscarves: Islam, the State, and*

Public Space (2008). He is former president of the Association for Political and Legal Anthropology (2004–2007) and associate editor of *American Anthropologist*. In 2010, he received a National Science Foundation research grant for the article "Shariah Without Courts: A Study of Islamic Judicial Practices in England."

Simon Butt is a current ARC Australian Postdoctoral Research Fellow and Associate Director (Indonesia) for the Centre for Asian and Pacific Law at The University of Sydney where he teaches Indonesian law. He has written widely on aspects of Indonesian law, including two recent books: *Corruption and Law in Indonesia* (2012) and *The Constitution of Indonesia: A Contextual Analysis* with Tim Lindsey (2012).

Sidney Jones is a senior adviser to the Asia Program of the International Crisis Group (ICG) and the primary author of all ICG reports on Southeast Asia. Jones has examined the separatist conflicts of Aceh, Papua, and Mindanao; the communal conflicts of Poso and Maluccas; and the ethnic conflict of Kalimantan. Her analyses have been included in the *New York Times*, the *Financial Times*, the *Jakarta Post*, and *The Australian* as well as on CNN, BBC, ABC, NBC, and NHK. Before joining the ICG in 2002, Jones worked for the Ford Foundation in Jakarta and New York (1977–1984); Amnesty International in London as the Indonesia–Philippines researcher (1985–1988); and Human Rights Watch in New York as the Asia director (1989–2001). She holds a B.A. and an M.A. from the University of Pennsylvania and conducted doctoral research in Kediri, East Java, on Nahdlatul Ulama. She lived in Shiraz, Iran, for one year as a university student (1971–1972) and studied Arabic in Cairo and Tunisia. Jones received an honorary doctorate in 2006 from the New School in New York.

Mirjam Künkler is an assistant professor in the Department for Near Eastern Studies at Princeton University. She received her Ph.D. in political science from Columbia University. Künkler is currently working on a book that analyzes the impact of contemporary Islamic thought and social movement activism on the transformation of authoritarian rule in Iran (1989–2005) and Indonesia (1974–1998). Apart from contributions to political science journals and edited volumes, Künkler's work appears in the recent book *Zur Rolle von Religion in Demokratisierungspro-zessen* (On the Role of Religious Actors in Democratization Processes), which she coedited with Julia Leininger

(2009). Mirjam Künkler is coprincipal investigator of Princeton's Luce Grant on Religion and International Affairs, coprincipal investigator on a British Academy Grant on Female Religious Authority in Islam, and lead principal investigator on the Social Science Research Council–sponsored Iran Social Science Data Portal.

R. William Liddle is a professor of political science at the Ohio State University. He served as the chair of the Indonesia Committee and Southeast Asia Council of the Association for Asian Studies and has been named Distinguished Visiting Lecturer by the National Democratic Institute. His recent publications include *Leadership and Culture in Indonesian Politics* (1996), "Indonesia's Approaching Elections: Politics, Islam, and Public Opinion," in *Asian Survey* (January 2004); "Leadership, Party, and Religion: Explaining Voting Behavior in Indonesia," coauthored with Saiful Mujani, in *Comparative Political Studies* (2007); and "Personalities, Parties, and Voters," also coauthored with Saiful Mujani, in *Journal of Democracy* (April 2010).

Tim Lindsey is Malcolm Smith Professor of Asian Law and Director of the Centre for Indonesian Law, Islam, and Society in the Law School at the University of Melbourne. He is also a founding editor of the *Australian Journal of Asian Law* and a former Australian Research Council Federation Fellow. His publications include a three-volume series *Islam, Law and the State in Southeast Asia* (2012), as well as *The Constitution of Indonesia: A Contextual Analysis* with Simon Butt (2012) and *Indonesia: Law and Society* (2nd ed., 2008).

Franz Magnis-Suseno SJ, a Jesuit priest, is professor at the Driyarkara School of Philosophy and at Universitas Indonesia in Jakarta. Born in 1936 in Germany, Magnis-Suseno has lived in Indonesia since 1961 and has long been an Indonesian citizen. He studied philosophy, theology, and political science in Pullach, Yogyakarta, and München Munich and got a doctorate in philosophy from the University of München Munich. He has extensively published in the fields of ethics, political philosophy, and Javanese spirituality, including *Javanese Ethics and World-View: The Javanese Idea of the Good Life* (1997).

Marcus Mietzner is a lecturer in the School of Culture, History, and Language at the Australian National University. His research focuses on the political role of the military in Indonesia, political campaign financing issues, and comparative electoral politics in Southeast Asia. Noted publications include his 2009 book *Military Politics, Islam, and the State in Indonesia: From Turbulent Transition to Democratic Consolidation*, the 2009 article "Indonesia: Democratic Consolidation in Soeharto's Shadow" in *Southeast Asian Affairs*(2009), and the 2010 collected volume *Problems of Democratisation in Indonesia: Elections, Institutions, and Society* (coedited with Edward Aspinall, 2010).

Saiful Mujani is Associate Professor in the Department of Political Science at the Universitas Islam Negeri Syarif Hidayatullah, Jakarta, and founder of the Lembaga Survei Indonesia (Indonesian Survey Institute). His published works include *Kuasa Rakyat* (People Power) (2012) with R. William Liddle and Kuskridha Ambardi; *Muslim Demokrat* (Democratic Muslims) (2007); and articles in *Comparative Political Studies, American Journal of Political Science, Journal of Democracy,* and *Asian Survey.* He also serves as a member of the Advisory Board of the Varieties of Democracy Project (V-Dem) at the Kellogg Institute, Notre Dame University.

Alfred Stepan is the Wallace Sayre Professor of Government; director of the Center for the Study of Democracy, Toleration, and Religion; and codirector of the Institute for Religion, Culture, and Public Life at Columbia University. He is the author of *Arguing Comparative Politics* (2001) as well as the coauthor of *Problems of Democratic Transition and Consolidation: Southern Europe, South America, and Post-Communist Europe* (with Juan J. Linz, 1996) and *Crafting State Nations: India and Other Multinational Democracies* (with Juan J. Linz and Yogendra Yadav, 2011). He is a member of the American Academy of Arts and Sciences and a fellow of the British Academy.